[THE SOURCEBOOKS SHAKESPEARE]

Richard III

TEXT EDITOR
WILLIAM PROCTOR WILLIAMS

ADVISORY EDITORS
DAVID BEVINGTON AND PETER HOLLAND

SERIES EDITORS
MARIE MACAISA AND DOMINIQUE RACCAH

William Shakespeare

sourcebooks
mediaFusion

An Imprint of Sourcebooks Inc.®
Naperville, Illinois

Published by Sourcebooks MediaFusion, an imprint of Sourcebooks, Inc.
P.O. Box 4410, Naperville, Illinois 60567-4410
(630) 961-3900
Fax: (630) 961-2168
www.sourcebooks.com
www.sourcebooksshakespeare.com
For more information on The Sourcebooks Shakespeare, email us at shakespeare@sourcebooks.com

Library of Congress Cataloging-in-Publication Data

Shakespeare, William, 1564-1616.
  Richard III / text editor, William Proctor Williams ; advisory editors, David Bevington
and Peter Holland.
    p. cm. -- (The Sourcebooks Shakespeare)
  ISBN 978-1-4022-0778-5 (trade pbk.)
 1. Richard III, King of England, 1452-1485--Drama. 2. Great
Britain--History--Richard III, 1483-1485--Drama. I. Williams, William
Proctor, 1939- II. Bevington, David M. III. Holland, Peter, 1951- IV. Title.

PR2821.A2W55 2007
822.3'3--dc22

2007020249

Printed and bound in the United States of America.
LB 10 9 8 7 6 5 4 3 2 1

To students, teachers, and lovers of Shakespeare

Contents

ABOUT SOURCEBOOKS MEDIAFUSION

Launched with the 1998 *New York Times* bestseller
We Interrupt This Broadcast and formally founded in 2000,
Sourcebooks MediaFusion is the nation's leading publisher
of mixed-media books. This revolutionary imprint is dedicated
to creating original content—be it audio, video, CD-ROM,
or Web—that is fully integrated with the books we create.
The result, we hope, is a new, richer, eye-opening,
thrilling experience with books for our readers.
Our experiential books have become both bestsellers
and classics in their subjects, including poetry (*Poetry Speaks*),
children's books (*Poetry Speaks to Children*),
history (*We Shall Overcome*), sports (*And The Crowd Goes Wild*),
the plays of William Shakespeare, and more.
See what's new from us at www.sourcebooks.com.

About the Text

Richard III, the second-longest play in the Shakespeare canon (only *Hamlet* is longer), was probably written in 1592 or 1593 as the fourth of the First Tetralogy of English history plays (*Henry VI, Parts 1-3* being the other three). The play was first published as a quarto edition (Q1) in 1597. The source of the copy used to print this edition has been much debated, but it seems to have been a theatrical document at some remove from Shakespeare's original manuscript of the play. The influence of performance on the text can be seen, for instance, in the combining of the roles of the Keeper and Brakenbury in 1.4, something regularly done in modern performances, though it seems not to have been Shakespeare's original conception of the scene. There were five more quarto editions, each one set from the preceding quarto (Q2, 1598; Q3, 1602; Q4, 1605; Q5, 1612; Q6, 1622), before the play was published in the First Folio (F1) of Shakespeare's plays in 1623. There were two further quarto editions (Q7, 1629 and Q8, 1634) after F1 but they are of no textual significance.

Textual evidence demonstrates that parts of F1 were printed from a copy of Q3 and other parts from a copy of Q6, but also that both quartos were heavily corrected from an early authoritative manuscript, although probably not in Shakespeare's hand. Furthermore, the printer's copy of F1 was probably some kind of composite document made up of leaves from the two quartos with the manuscript additions from that earlier document. From compelling evidence, I believe that the text of F1 is, in general, actually earlier and more authoritative, though printed twenty-six years after Q1. This can be seen in countless instances, but a striking one is at 2.4.1-2 where Q1 erroneously "corrects" F1's accurate reading (see note to those lines). The sort of truncation of the language which occurred during the transmission of the copy used to print Q1, as opposed to the more fully formed language of the earlier and less removed document used to print F1, can be seen is this passage from 1.2.14-16:

Q1
Curst be the hand that made these fatall holes
Curst be the heart that had the heart to doe it.

F1

O cursed be the hand that made these holes:
Cursed the Heart, that had the heart to do it:
Cursed the Blood, that let this blood from hence:

Consequently, the copy-text for the present edition is F1 except in two instances, 3.1.1-166 and 5.3.49 to end of play, where the copy for F1 was clearly not corrected and here the present edition follows Q1 as the next best version of the text. F1 has act and scene divisions I generally follow; the quartos do not. However, even F1's scene divisions are not wholly satisfactory and I have noted where I have added to or subtracted from F1's divisions.

On May 26, 1606, the "Act to Restrain the Abuses of Players" was promulgated, and although its primary function was to regulate conduct on the stage, in most printings of plays after that, oaths were removed either because the document used for printing the play had had them removed or because printers and publishers did not wish to run the risk of publishing them. Hence, even though the text of F1 is an earlier form of the play than that of Q1, the oaths have been removed from it. For example, at 3.7.218-19, F1 reads, "Come Citizens, we will entreat no more.", but Q1 contains the oath that produces an additional humorous line for Richard not found in F1: "Come Citizens, zounds Ile intreat no more. / *Glo.* O do not sweare my Lord of Buckingham". In the present edition, the oaths have been restored along with responses to them, all noted.

Lineation in Shakespeare's texts always presents some difficulties. Specifically, early printings almost always begin a new verse line at the left margin, whether the line is a full line or a partial line, making it difficult for editors to tell which of the part lines are to be read as a single line shared with another character and which are to be single short lines. Also, since some lines are clearly too long, should they be broken up into appropriate verse units? 1.1.42-47 provides an illustration of the problem. In F1 this reads:

Brother, good day: What meanes this armed guard
That waites upon your Grace?
Cla. His Majesty tendring my persons safety,
Hath appointed this Conduct to convey me to th' Tower.
Rich. Upon what cause?
Cla. Because my name is *George*.
Rich. Alacke my Lord, that fault is none of yours:

In this edition, and in many modern editions, this becomes:
Brother, good day. What means this armèd guard
That waits upon your Grace?

CLARENCE

His Majesty   43
Tendering my person's safety, hath appointed
This conduct to convey me to th' Tower.

RICHARD
Upon what cause?

CLARENCE

Because my name is George.   46

RICHARD
Alack, my lord, that fault is none of yours.

Here 43 and 46 are shared part lines. Over the last three hundred years, various editors have dealt with this matter in a number of ways. In this edition, I have treated part lines as shared when it seems that one character is responding to or completing the thought of another character and have treated others as single, unshared lines when this does not appear to be the case. These sorts of editorial decisions are what account for the variation in line numbers from modern edition to modern edition.

To provide a fixed and unvarying point of reference, Through-Line-Numbering [TLN] is supplied at the foot of every left-hand, or notes, page indicating the TLNs to be found in this portion of text. TLN was a system devised by Charlton Hinman for *The Norton Facsimile: The First Folio of Shakespeare* (1968) and this system numbers every line of type in F1, thereby providing a fixed system of reference. Since critics, scholars, and editors increasingly use TLNs in their references, sometimes in conjunction with conventional act-scene-line references and sometimes without, the inclusion of them in this edition may assist users of this edition in working their way through secondary materials.

Although the F1 text, and the Q1 text in the two sections indicted, has been silently modernized, any significant variations in wording are recorded in the notes, and speech prefixes have been regularized, usually without notation. Although I have attempted to follow the punctuation in F1 and Q1 so far as that is possible, I have silently emended where I think a modern reader might be misled by the early punctuation. Material, particularly stage directions, that has been editorially added is enclosed in [square brackets]. The line numbering of each scene numbers every spoken line but not lines containing act and scene divisions or only stage directions.

William Proctor Williams

On the CD

1. Introduction to the Sourcebooks Shakespeare *Richard III*
   Sir Derek Jacobi

ACT 1, SCENE 1, LINES 1-41
2. Narration: Sir Derek Jacobi
3. Laurence Olivier as Richard
   Granada International • 1955
4. Peter Finch as Richard
   Living Shakespeare • 1963

ACT 1, SCENE 2, LINES 140-207
5. Narration: Sir Derek Jacobi
6. Saskia Wickham as Lady Anne and David Troughton as Richard
   The Complete Arkangel Shakespeare • 2003
7. Estelle Kohler as Lady Anne and Bill Homewood as Richard
   Naxos AudioBooks—Shakespeare's Lovers • 1994

ACT 1, SCENE 2, LINES 229-265
8. Narration: Sir Derek Jacobi
9. Kenneth Branagh as Richard
   Naxos AudioBooks • 1999
10. Antony Sher as Richard
    Royal Shakespeare Company • 1984-85

ACT 1, SCENE 4, LINES 9-75
11. Narration: Sir Derek Jacobi
12. Tenniel Evans as Clarence
    Living Shakespeare • 1963
13. Clifford Rose as Clarence
    Naxos AudioBooks—Great Speeches and Soliloquies • 1994

ACT 3, SCENE 7, LINES 94-154

14. Narration: Sir Derek Jacobi
15. Peter Yapp as Lord Mayor, Nicholas Farrell as Buckingham,
    and Kenneth Branagh as Richard
    Naxos AudioBooks • 1999

ACT 4, SCENE 3, LINES 1-27

16. Narration: Sir Derek Jacobi
17. Brian Spink as Tyrrel and Peter Finch as Richard III
    Living Shakespeare • 1963
18. Steve Hodson as Tyrrel and David Troughton as Richard III
    The Complete Arkangel Shakespeare • 2003

ACT 4, SCENE 4, LINES 34-77

19. Narration: Sir Derek Jacobi
20. Celia Imrie as Queen Elizabeth, Geraldine McEwan as
    Queen Margaret, and Auriol Smith as Duchess of York
    Naxos AudioBooks • 1999
21. Sonia Ritter as Queen Elizabeth, Margaret Robertson as
    Queen Margaret, and Mary Wimbush as Duchess of York
    The Complete Arkangel Shakespeare • 2003

ACT 5, SCENE 1, LINES 1-29

22. Narration: Sir Derek Jacobi
23. Philip Voss as Duke of Buckingham
    The Complete Arkangel Shakespeare • 2003
24. Nicholas Farrell as Duke of Buckingham
    Naxos AudioBooks • 1999

ACT 5, SCENE 3, LINES 178-207

25. Narration: Sir Derek Jacobi
26. Kenneth Branagh as Richard III
    Naxos AudioBooks • 1999
27. David Troughton as Richard III
    The Complete Arkangel Shakespeare • 2003

ACT 5, SCENE 3, LINES 228-271

28. Narration: Sir Derek Jacobi
29. Charles Simpson as Earl of Richmond
    The Complete Arkangel Shakespeare • 2003
30. Jamie Glover as Earl of Richmond
    Naxos AudioBooks • 1999

ACT 5, SCENE 4, LINES 1-13

31. Narration: Sir Derek Jacobi
32. Jonathan Keeble as Catesby and Kenneth Branagh as Richard III
    Naxos AudioBooks • 1999
33. Richard Gale as Catesby and Peter Finch as Richard III
    Living Shakespeare • 1963

34. Introduction to Speaking Shakespeare: Sir Derek Jacobi
35. Speaking Shakespeare: Andrew Wade with Nathaniel Shaw

36. Conclusion of the Sourcebooks Shakespeare *Richard III*
    Sir Derek Jacobi

Featured Audio Productions

NAXOS AudioBooks (1999)

Richard, Duke of Gloucester, later King Richard III	Kenneth Branagh
Clarence	Michael Maloney
Lord Hastings	John Shrapnel
Lady Anne	Stella Gonet
Queen Elizabeth	Celia Imrie
Duke of Buckingham	Nicholas Farrell
Lord Stanley, Earl of Derby	John Woodvine
Queen Margaret	Geraldine McEwan
King Edward IV	Bruce Alexander
Duchess of York	Auriol Smith
Prince/Clarence's Boy	Raphael Clarkson
Clarence's Girl	Louise Alder
Duke of York – Boy	Dominic Kraemer
Earl of Richmond	Jamie Glover
Director	David Timson
Engineer	Simon Weir
Producer	Nicolas Soame

THE COMPLETE ARKANGEL SHAKESPEARE (2003)

King Richard III	David Troughton
Duke of Buckingham	Philip Voss
Lady Anne	Saskia Wickham
Queen Margaret	Margaret Robertson
Queen Elizabeth	Sonia Ritter
King Edward IV	Stephen Boxer
Duke of Clarence	John McAndrew
Lord Stanley	David Yelland
Duchess of York	Mary Wimbush
Lord Hastings	Christian Rodska
Earl of Richmond	Charles Simpson
Earl Rivers	Gavin Muir
Marquess of Dorset	Jamie Glover
Sir William Catesby	Nicholas Murchie
Sir James Tyrrel	Steve Hodson
Sir James Blunt	Trevor Martin
Sir Robert Brakenbury	Arthur Cox
Sir Richard Ratcliffe	Ben Martin
First Murderer	John Hollis
Edward, Prince of Wales	Jay Barrimore
Richard, Duke of York	George Miller

Other parts played by: Peter Marinker, Cameron Powie, Helena Rice, Colin Salmon and David Tennant

LIVING SHAKESPEARE (1963)

Richard	Peter Finch
George, Duke of Clarence	Tenniel Evans
Sir Robert Brackenbury	Peter Ellis
Narrator	Dennis Vance
Lady Ann	Ingrid Hafner
Queen Margaret	Fay Compton
Duke of Buckingham	Dennis Compton Shaw
Sir William Catesby	Richard Gale
Queen Elizabeth	Margaret Whiting
Earl Rivers	Brian Spink
1st Murderer	Paul Curran
2nd Murderer	George Yeatman
King Edward IV	Charles West
Duchess of York	Nancy Nevinson
Edward, Prince of Wales	John Coxall
Lord Mayor of London	Peter Ellis
Lord Hastings	George Yeatman
Richard, Duke of York	Kit Williams
Lord Stanley, Earl of Derby	Paul Curran
Sir James Tyrrel	Brian Spink
Sir Richard Ratcliff	Tenniel Evans
Henry, Earl of Richmond	Richard Gale

Naxos AudioBooks— Shakespeare's Lovers (1994)
Estelle Kohler as Lady Anne and Bill Homewood as Richard

Naxos AudioBooks—Great Speeches and Soliloquies (1994)
Clifford Rose as Clarence

Note from the Series Editors

For many of us, our first and only encounter with Shakespeare was in school. We may recall that experience as a struggle, working through dense texts filled with unfamiliar words. However, those of us who were fortunate enough to have seen a play performed have altogether different memories. It may be of an interesting scene or an unusual character, but it is most likely a speech. Often, just hearing part of one instantly transports us to that time and place. "Friends, Romans, countrymen, lend me your ears", "But, soft! What light through yonder window breaks?", "To sleep, perchance to dream", "Tomorrow, and tomorrow, and tomorrow".

The Sourcebooks Shakespeare series is our attempt to use the power of performance to help you experience the play. In it, you will see photographs from various productions, on film and on stage, historical and contemporary, known worldwide or in your community. You may even recognize some actors you don't think of as Shakespearean performers. You will see set drawings, costume designs, and scene edits, all reproduced from original notes. Finally, on the enclosed audio CD, you will hear scenes from the play as performed by some of the most accomplished Shakespeareans of our times. Often, we include multiple interpretations of the same scene, showing you the remarkable richness of the text. Hear Laurence Olivier deliver Richard's famous opening soliloquy, and compare that to the rendition by Peter Finch in a 1963 audio recording from Living Shakespeare. The actors create different worlds, different characters, different meanings.

As you read the text of the play, you can consult explanatory notes for definitions of unfamiliar words and phrases or words whose meanings have changed. These notes appear on the left pages, next to the text of the play. The audio, photographs, and other production artifacts augment the notes and they too are indexed to the appropriate lines. You can use the pictures to see how others have staged a particular scene and get ideas on costumes, scenery, blocking, etc. As for the audio, each track represents a particular interpretation of a scene. Sometimes, a passage that's difficult to comprehend opens up when you hear it out loud. Furthermore, when you hear more than one version, you gain a keener understanding of the characters. Is

Richard a cunning villain or a tragic hero? Do we sympathize with him or loathe him? Do our feelings for him change as the play progresses? The actors made their choices and so can you. You may even come up with your own interpretation.

The text of the play, the definitions, the production notes, the audio–all of these work together, and they are included for your enjoyment. Because the audio consists of performance excerpts, it is meant to entertain. When you see a passage with an associated clip, you can read along as you hear the actors perform the scene for you. Or, you can sit back, close your eyes, and listen, and then go back and reread the text with a new perspective. Finally, since the text is a script, you may find yourself reciting the lines out loud and doing your own performance!

You will undoubtedly notice that some of the audio does not match the text exactly. Also, there are photographs and facsimiles of scenes that are not in your edition. There are many reasons for this, but foremost among them is the fact that Shakespeare scholarship continues to move forward and the prescribed ways of dealing with and interpreting text is always changing. Thus, a play that was edited and published in the 1900s will be different from one published in 2007. Finally, artists have their own inter- pretation of the play and they, too, cut and change the lines and scenes according to their vision.

The ways in which *Richard III* has been presented have varied consider- ably through the years, so we have included essays in the book to give you glimpses into the range of the productions, showing you how other artists have approached the play and providing examples of just what changes were made and how. In "As Performed", Lois Potter discusses the film and stage productions starring Ian McKellen (directed in the film by Richard Loncraine and on stage at the National Theatre by Richard Eyre). She iden- tifies the challenges of making this history play appeal to contemporary audiences and considers the obstacles actors face when trying to portray Richard's villainy and vulnerability. Assessing famous productions of the play throughout history, text editor William Proctor Williams analyzes the legacy of *Richard III* in his essay, "In Production". From the long-lasting textual emendations of eighteenth century playwright Colley Cibber, to more recent productions, Williams discusses the play's history in performance and assesses its place in the Shakespeare canon. In "Determined to be a Villain", Douglas Lanier's essay on *Richard III* in popular culture, he cites a number of references to famous quotations from the play. Illustrating the play's pervasiveness as a cultural reference, Lanier describes episodes from the TV shows *Blackadder* and *The Simpsons*, book titles, a number of comedic parodies, and even advertisements for engagement rings. He also discusses a variety of film adaptations derived from the basic characters and premise of the play. Finally, for the actor in you, (and for those who want to peek behind the curtain), we have two essays that you may find especially intriguing. Andrew Wade, voice coach of the Royal Shakespeare Company for sixteen years, shares his point of view on how to understand the text and speak it. You can also listen to him working with an actor on the opening speech of the play; perhaps you too can learn the art of speaking Shakespeare. The last essay is from Sir Antony Sher. In it, he describes the process by which his widely acclaimed portrayal of Richard came to be, including the origins of those famous crutches. It is a rare glimpse into the creation of a character for the stage.

One last note: we are frequently asked why we did not include the whole play, either in audio or video. While we enjoy the plays and are avid theatergoers, we are trying to do something more with the audio (and the production notes and the essays) than just present them to you. In fact, our goal is to provide you with tools that will enable you to explore the play on your own, from many different directions. Our hope is that the different pieces of audio, the voices of the actors, and the old production photos and notes will all engage you and illuminate the play on many levels, so that you can construct your own understanding and create your own "production," a fresh interpretation unique to you.

Though the productions we referenced and the audio clips we have included are but a miniscule sample of the play's history, we hope they encourage you to delve further into the works of Shakespeare. New editions of the play come out yearly; movie adaptations are regularly being produced; there are hundreds of theater groups in the U.S. alone; and performances could be going on right in your backyard. We echo the words of noted writer and poet Robert Graves, who said, "The remarkable thing about Shakespeare is that he is really very good – in spite of all the people who say he is very good."

We welcome you now to The Sourcebooks Shakespeare edition of *Richard III*.

Dominique Raccah

Marie Macaisa

Dominique Raccah and Marie Macaisa
Series Editors

track 1

***Introduction to the Sourcebooks Shakespeare* Richard III**
Sir Derek Jacobi

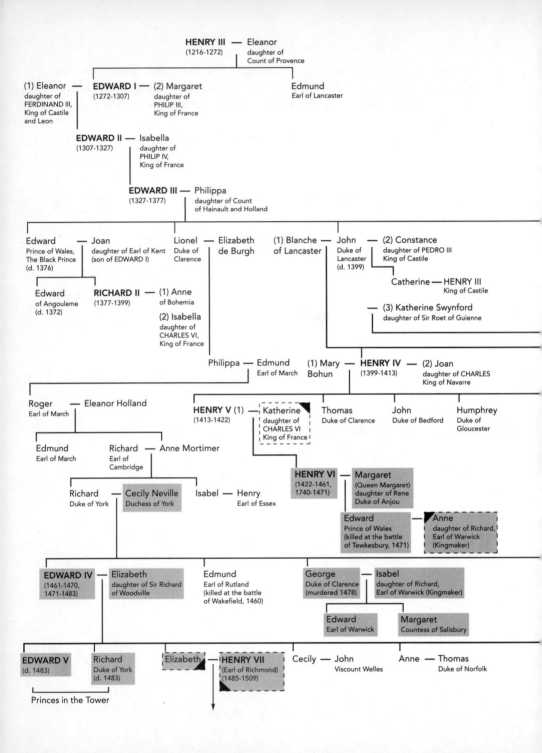

THE PLANTAGENET DYNASTIES
1216–1485

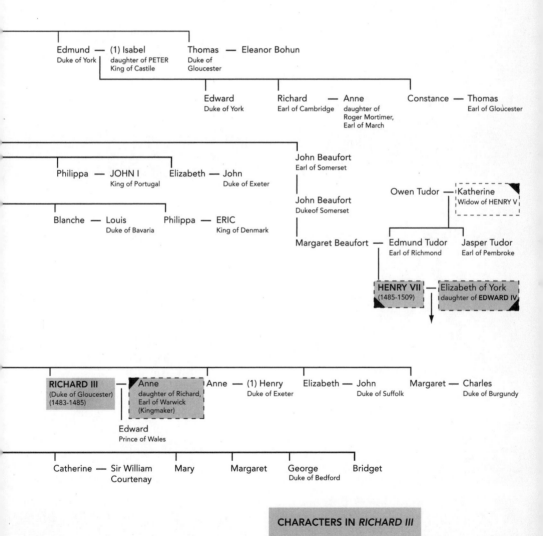

CHARACTERS IN *RICHARD III*

appears more than once

In Production

William Proctor Williams

We cannot be certain of the date of the first performance of *Richard III*, but it is probably around 1592, and with the formation of the Lord Chamberlain's Men (Shakespeare's company) in 1594, the play became part of the company's repertory. Their leading actor, Richard Burbage, so completely made the role of Richard his that in 1602, John Manningham could record in his diary:

> Upon a time when Burbage played Richard III there was a citizen grew so far in liking him that before she went from the play she appointed him to come that night unto her in the name of Richard the Third. Shakespeare, overhearing their conclusion, went before, was entertained...ere Burbage came. Then message being brought that Richard the Third was at the door, Shakespeare caused return to be made that William the Conqueror was before Richard the Third.

It is a pretty story and almost certainly a fiction, but we can still conclude that by at least 1602, the play was very well known and liked (the Q2 edition appeared in 1598, Q3 in 1602), that Burbage was equally well known in the role of Richard, and that Shakespeare was also as well known as the author (both Q2 and Q3 had Shakespeare's name on the title page), a player, and a witty man about London. The text of the play as it comes down to us cannot fail to have been influenced by Burbage and the Company's playing of it, so although the play is certainly by Shakespeare, there is probably a great deal of Burbage in it. That it was a popular play from the start is attested to by the fact that 1) it was printed in six separate quarto editions from 1597 to 1622 before it appeared in the First Folio in 1623, and 2) Burbage and his portrayal of the leading role lived on in anecdotes about the theater well into the 1660s and 1670s.

However, in 1699 a change took place that would alter the play on stage for about 200 years, though it had no effect on how the play appeared in the standard printed editions of Shakespeare's works. Colley Cibber, a successful actor (and later, Poet Laureate), produced an adaptation for Drury Lane and continued to modify the text until the end of the first decade of the century.

This version removed Edward IV, Queen Margaret, and Clarence from the script, decreased the role of Buckingham, greatly simplified the wooing of Lady Anne, removed many of the historical references and generally concentrated the play on Richard. What was already a star part in the early editions

Colley Cibber (1671-1757)
Etching by G. Vandergucht, c. 1738, after a painting by J. Vanloo

became even more so with Cibber's alterations. Although Cibber did not have much critical success himself with this adaptation, David Garrick's use of it in 1741 to launch his theatrical career assured this version a remarkably long life on the stage. Theatrical productions of this version could be seen as late as the 1930s and Olivier even gave Cibber and Garrick script credits for his 1955 film. In fact, of all the adaptations of Shakespeare that occurred after the Restoration of 1660, Cibber's *Richard III* has had the longest life.

Since the history of Richard on stage during the eighteenth and nineteenth centuries is almost entirely the history of this version, it would repay us to examine it a little more closely. First of all, Cibber wrote seven additional soliloquies for Richard and so enlarged the part that Richard now had forty percent of the lines in the play rather than the thirty-one percent he had had in the original, and he appears in fifteen of twenty scenes rather than fifteen of twenty-five. Furthermore, there was very little development in Richard's character: he was a villain from start to finish rather than a gradually diminishing character (after 4.2 in the original). Cibber expanded 3.7 by adding a meeting between Anne and Richard that concludes with Richard rather openly hinting to her that her death is imminent; this served to create a character whose only mode of existence is the doing of evil. By painting Richard as a heartless schemer, considerable emphasis was placed on his deformities and stature (it is said that Garrick chose this part because he was not tall enough for some of the more sympathetic roles in Shakespeare's plays). The result of all this was a slick melodrama which audiences loved and leading actors adored.

Garrick introduced a naturalness to the role which was a distinct departure from Cibber's more declamatory style. However, because he played the part for so long (up until 1776), many of his ways of performing became mannerisms that were almost imitations of himself. Nevertheless, audiences remained impressed, and he was even praised for the consistency of his playing. Garrick set the seal on certain aspects of the character that would last until Olivier's Stratford performances in 1944. These are of Richard as 1) the heartless schemer, 2) a man who can use his voice and body to convey something like a notion of pure evil, and 3) a character who seems to have a back story. The latter is no doubt the result of Cibber having stripped much of the historical context from the text and having

David Garrick as Richard III
From a mezzotint by John Dixon (1772)

eliminated or diminished the roles of such characters as Margaret, Clarence, and Edward IV. No matter, this was the Richard the English-speaking world got and it was, apparently, the one they wanted.

The next great Richard was Edmund Kean, who in 1814 performed Richard for the first time at Drury Lane. Kean was a small man, as were Burbage and Garrick, and he was also noted for his naturalness. If Garrick's interpretation of the part had been smooth and stylized, relying on certain turns and gestures (such as his interpretation of the stage direction at 5.3.177, "Richard III starteth up out of a dream," which was much admired and even painted by Hogarth), Kean specialized in playing each scene as almost a separate instance rather than as an overall interpretation of the character, and the production was largely concerned with stage effects. In part, this was because of what had happened to the London theaters. When the Drury Lane and Covent Garden theaters burned in 1808 and 1809, they were rebuilt on a huge scale. Drury Lane now had a capacity of 3,500, and there were many complaints that the actors could be neither seen nor heard. Hence, any subtle touches of speech and movement were out, replaced by what was described as ranting and extravagant gestures. Also, because Cibber's version so thoroughly concentrated attention on Richard, the tendency to play him as a sort of demon king became even more pronounced. Though fitting the style of Kean and other actors such as John Philip Kemble, it would have been far too melodramatic for our tastes.

A change came in 1845 when Samuel Phelps, the actor-manager of Sadler's Wells theater in London, produced a *Richard III* with the text of Cibber cast away and the text of Shakespeare almost fully restored. This, particularly the restoration of the role of Margaret, was greeted with enthusiasm, and she received as much attention from the commentators as did Richard. For the first time since 1700, the play became a collection of strong characters and not merely a vehicle for the actor playing Richard. Yet, Phelps later reverted to the Cibber text, perhaps because he could not find another actress to take the part of Margaret after Isabella Glynn left the stage. The Shakespearean text was not played again until Charles Calvert's production in Manchester in 1870, twenty-five years later.

Henry Irving (1838-1905), the first actor knighted (in 1895), performed the play in 1877 and again in 1896 at the Lyceum Theater in London. He used a Shakespearean text, not Cibber's, and it was the dominance of Irving's productions as well as his dominance as a theatrical personality that mostly banished the Cibber text from the stage (although it held on in scattered places). Again, a crucial aspect was the restoration of Margaret (in 1877 she appeared only in 1.3, but in 1896, she was fully present, being in 4.4 as well) and of Clarence and his murder scene (1.4). Also, in keeping with the general theatrical trends of the nineteenth century, Irving's staging was quite elaborate, the play being divided into fifteen scenes with complex sets, extravagant costumes and a structuring of the performance so that a "picture" was created at the end of each scene upon which the curtain would fall. For example, at the end of 3.7, citizens cheered as Irving stood triumphantly, taking in their cheers and then glancing at Buckingham over his prayer book as the curtain fell. Although Irving's text placed the emphasis upon the star, other actors continued to produce their own restorations, including Edwin Booth in New York in 1878.

However, it is hard to keep an old adaptation down, and two major twentieth-century productions once again relied heavily on Cibber's text. The first featured Laurence Olivier (another actor who, like Irving, would be knighted) as Richard at the Old Vic in 1944-45. According to Michael Billington, "in place of downright transpontine villainy Olivier offered a spellbinding mixture of the inner strategist and the outward hypocrite." Unlike even Irving, Olivier allowed us to see the gradual decay of Richard's abilities after his coronation. And with supporting actors such as Ralph

Sir Laurence Olivier as Richard III in his 1955 film
Courtesy of Douglas Lanier

Richardson (Buckingham), John Gielgud (Clarence), and Sybil Thorndike (Margaret), there was a more equitable division of thespian authority than had been case with earlier productions. Because this version was preserved on film (complete with Olivier's particular touches such as the forcing of Buckingham to kneel and kiss his ring at the end of 3.7), this is a version of Richard known throughout the world, even to those who have never entered the door of a theater.

The second twentieth century production relying heavily on Cibber opened at the National Theatre in 1990 and starred Ian McKellen (knighted that same year), co-directed with Richard Eyre. It was set in a 1930s Britain, and although the motives of Richard and the others are still dynastic, the overtones are of what might have been if the royal family had gone over to the Nazis and taken control of the nation. The set and the staging were very basic (it was called a black box) and all of the medievalism of past productions was done away with in favor of scenes called, in the prompt book, "Victoria Station" and "Downing Street." It was as far from Olivier's conception of the play as one is likely to get. McKellen reports that, "as we rehearsed Richard Eyre's production, he kept saying, 'if we were doing this as a film, here would be a close-up,'" and so it transpired. McKellen produced a screenplay based on the National Theatre production and collaborated with director Richard Loncraine to produce a film in 1995. Here Cibber creeps in again, showing Richard's murder of the Prince of Wales and Henry VI with the opening credits, the removal of Margaret, and the considerable cutting and rearrangement of the text. Perhaps the most jarring aspect is the appearance of Richmond as a member of the court circle as early as 2.4 (instead of in 5.2) and the constant references to Stanley as Richmond's uncle rather than father or, more properly, stepfather. However, it was a great success and will, like the Olivier film, influence our view of Richard for years to come. (See Lois Potter's essay on pages 11-16 for more on this production.)

After these two plays that became films, it is appropriate to say something about a television film that is nearly a play. As part of the BBC's "Shakespeare's Plays," Jane Howell directed all four plays in the First Tetralogy (*Henry VI, parts 1, 2, 3*, and *Richard III*). All four used essentially the same cast, as would have been the case at the Globe in Shakespeare's time, and the sets consisted of simple wooden structures with a bridge serving as the upper stage, a few entry doors, and little else. *Richard III* (first broadcast in January 1983) used a very full, almost uncut, text (its running time is four hours), and starred Ron Cook, another less-than-tall actor, as Richard. He is less purely evil and more wittily cunning and sardonic than many other Richards. Michael Byrne's Buckingham is more thoughtful, and perhaps more sympathetic, than many others who have taken the roles, and Julia Foster's Margaret is costumed and played more like a slightly mad bag lady than as the wrath of God, as had been typical since her restoration to the text. Although this was a television production, it preserves almost all the theatrical conventions we would expect in a stage performance. This production is also notable for its amazing non-textual conclusion, showing Margaret madly laughing and cradling Richard's pierced body atop a pile of the slain victims of the civil wars.

Of twentieth-century theatrical productions, two more require notice, and both were done by the Royal Shakespeare Company (RSC). In 1963-64, as part of the celebrations of the 400th anniversary of Shakespeare's birth, Peter Hall and John Barton mounted a three-play version of the First Tetralogy (Barton created two plays, *Henry VI* and *Edward IV* out of the three parts of *Henry VI*) with *Richard III* as the finish. This production reasserted, probably for the first time since the seventeenth century, the play's place in the whole stretch of English history of the fifteenth century. Hall saw the play as one of retribution, retribution for all those wrongs committed during the Wars of the Roses as portrayed in the other two plays. Barton's textual revisions tended to lessen the role of the female characters, making the play very much about male aggression. Peggy Ashcroft played Margaret and established again the commanding presence of this role. It seems to be the fate of the character of Margaret to keep being rediscovered by actors/directors and then forgotten again. Ian Holm (another short actor) took the part of Richard and did not play him as either a domineering satanic presence nor as the crafty con man. Where earlier actors had roared Richard's lines, Holm spoke them quietly, almost whispering them at times. One of the most noted instances of this occurred during the council scene when Richard's accusations of treason against Hastings (3.4.58-75) are treated as a jest by those present until Richard's armed thugs come in to remove Hastings. This was considerably different from Richard shouting and the others recoiling, the usual way of playing the scene. Although many were put off by the overtly political, slightly Marxist, interpretation of this production, it set a very high standard.

That standard was probably exceeded by what is, at least for those who saw it, the best theatrical *Richard III* of the twentieth century, the Royal Shakespeare Company's 1984 production starring Antony Sher as Richard. Directed by Bill Alexander, it was decided that this production and this Richard would, among other things, take Queens Margaret's and Elizabeth's descriptions of Richard as a "bottled spider" and "bunch-backed toad" (1.3.241, 4.4.80, and 1.3.245) at more or less face value. Sher not only played the role with a considerable hunchback but also played the entire show on elbow crutches. Although there had been many hunchbacked Richards, there had never been so clearly a bottled spider, a spider appearing to be hunchbacked because it was swollen with venom. The athleticism required to sustain this for the entire performance and to do it day after day for the extensive run of the play (it ran from June 19, 1984 through March, 1985 at Stratford and other venues) was much remarked upon. However, far more interesting to many was the change this production made in the portrayal of Richard. No longer was he the demon king or political force of nature as he had usually been played; here he was not a metaphoric or cosmetic deformed cripple but an actual one. Indeed, Sher's crutches became an extension of the character and, on occasion, the character's weapons. In the wooing scene (1.2) he disarms the guards around Henry VI's corpse with only his crutches, and at 3.4.75, as he says, "Off with his head!" he clapped his crutches around Hastings' neck. He is only seen without his crutches five times in the production, and the two most significant are 1) the coronation scene, where he must struggle to the throne unaided, and 2) his fight with Richmond, when his sword had to serve him as a cane. If Sher lacked the vocal range to do justice to some of the subtler rhetorical tricks of Richard, as even Sher admitted, he made up for it with frenetic business and with his portrayal of the gradual diminishing of Richard from his coronation onward. This decline, which Shakespeare's text clearly shows but which performances from Cibber to the close of the nineteenth century and after had failed to demonstrate, was made more than manifest in this production. Although the word is overworked, this was clearly a bravura performance. (Read more about Sir Antony's performance in his own words, in the essay "Actor Speaks" on pages 375-379.)

The RSC has mounted seven major productions of *Richard III* since Sher's, and there are probably a score of productions playing around the globe this year alone. It is one of the most performed plays of Shakespeare, and the deformed and evil aristocrat and his political and murderous wiles speak in various ways to each generation.

I would like to thank the following for the help and information they have provided. The Shakespeare Centre Library, Stratford-upon-Avon; Julie Hankey, *Plays in Performance: Richard III*. 2nd ed. Bristol: Bristol Classical Press, 1988; Hugh M. Richmond. *Shakespeare in Performance: Richard III*. Manchester: Manchester University Press, 1989; Gillian Day. *Shakespeare at Stratford: King Richard III*. London: Tomson–Arden Shakespeare, 2002; and Paul Prescott. *The Shakespeare Handbooks: Richard III*. Basingstoke: Palgrave, 2006. *The Year of the King: An Actor's Diary and Sketchbook*. London: Methuen, 1985; Antony Sher.

As Performed

Lois Potter

The popularity of *Richard III* in the theater might surprise anyone who knows it only from reading. It is a long play and frequently a bleak one. Many of its characters die, though all the deaths except Richard's take place off stage. They also curse. The former Queen, Margaret, who refuses to pity anyone's sufferings but her own, calls down horrible fates on the other characters and rejoices to see them come true. The imprisoned Duke of Clarence has a prophetic nightmare about the "dark monarchy" of the dead, where he will be punished for the sins he committed in what someone else appropriately calls the "dead time" of the past. Within minutes, he will be killed by hired murderers who, to make matters worse, behave like low comedians. There's something petty, too, in most of the characters: Edward IV's relatives despise his queen because she's merely a knight's widow and the former queen, Margaret, keeps insisting that everyone else's sufferings are nothing compared to *hers*. By contrast, Shakespeare offers very few positive elements: the occasional remorse and piety of the villains (always too late), the (compromised) honesty of most of the standers-by, and the final hope of young Richmond and his followers that they can restore peace to a wounded and divided nation.

So what do people like so much about this play? In a word: Richard. Ironically, this death-bringer is full of life. Bubbling over with evil plans, he confides mainly in us, the audience. He even jokes with us, often at the same time as he's fooling other characters. Making the same mistake as these other characters, we start to trust him, thinking that, however much he may betray others, he surely won't turn on *us*. But by the end of the play he has betrayed us too: he becomes less funny, less clever, and, in his confused soliloquy after he sees the ghosts of his victims in a nightmare, almost a different person. Shakespeare may have wanted to make sure that his audience did not go away with the idea that villainy was fun. His solution, which he must have liked since he did the same thing later in *Macbeth,* was to construct the play like a pyramid: energetic upward climbing followed by a gloomy descent toward defeat and death (death, moreover, without even a death speech).

Depicting the ultimate emptiness of evil may be morally right, but it can make the second half of the play boring for the audience. Colley Cibber, who in 1699 cut and rewrote the play as a star vehicle for himself, made it much more upbeat: he removed most of the scenes that show the sufferings of Richard's victims, but added a heroic fight, a defiant final speech, and even a respectful tribute from his conqueror. It was this version that made the play so popular in the next two centuries. Even when directors returned to Shakespeare's text, many of them cut the play in the same ways that Cibber did. This also happened in the two heavily cut commercial films: Laurence Olivier's in 1955 and Ian McKellen's, directed by Richard Loncraine, in 1995. Olivier even said "Richard's himself again!"—the line with which Cibber showed the character recovering from his nervousness and despair to become again the jolly villain of the beginning.

A modern production must inevitably wonder what it means for Richard to be "himself." We now tend to think that the self is the product of a society, yet Richard's late-medieval world is meaningless to most spectators, as is the late-Elizabethan world in which Shakespeare created him. Sometimes he is depicted as a grotesquely comic performer belonging entirely to the timeless world of the theatre, with no inner life at all; sometimes he is embedded in a society recognizable to his audience. Bertolt Brecht's *The Resistible Rise of Arturo Ui* (written in 1941) simultaneously parodied both the play and Hitler's rise to power in the blank-verse story of a Chicago gangster. After World War II, there were so many Richard-as-Hitler productions as to make this interpretation almost a cliché.

When Richard Eyre directed Ian McKellen as Richard at the National Theatre in London 1990, the production looked at first as if it was going to be yet another of those. In fact, it was more about British society than about Germany. In what Auden called the "low, dishonest decade" of the 1930s, some members of the British Establishment flirted with Nazism and others compromised with it in the hope of rescuing something from the chaos. "To me," Eyre said in an interview, "the play is set in a mythological landscape,

even if it draws on a precise historical period...The language of dema-
goguery in this [the twentieth] century is identical everywhere" (1). So
Richard's success is due to the corruption and indifference of his own
society. No one resists the resistible rise.

On a more personal level, the production decided (as had Antony Sher, in
conversations with his psychiatrist during preparation for an earlier production) that Richard's mother clearly hated him. The motive for Richard
himself was found in his own statement in the opening soliloquy that he has
nothing to do now that the war is over. Totally successful and emotionally
fulfilled as a professional soldier, but out of place in civilian life, he now
deploys the skills acquired in war to destroy everything that stands between
him and the throne. Hatred bred hatred in the Wars of the Roses: a key line
in *Henry VI, Part 3*, spoken to a young child who is pleading for his life, is
"Thy father killed my father, therefore die". Perhaps Richard, the child-killer,
has started by killing the child in himself.

Audiences always eagerly await the first entrance of Richard Gloucester.
How much will he stress the deformity? Ian McKellen's first entrance
seemed almost designed to tease us. As the sound effects of war died down
and we heard the bugles of the Armistice that ended World War I, he
appeared at the back of the stage, moving slowly forward through the smoke.
His long army overcoat made it hard to see the extent of his disability. It was
only at the end of the scene, as he followed Hastings off stage, that one
became aware that "Go you before, and I will follow you," was not just a
formulaic exit line but a way of avoiding a potentially awkward scrambling
to keep up with someone who in any case was not going to wait for him.

There is always an element of physical risk in performing Richard III on
stage. Like all of Shakespeare's long roles (and this is the longest after
Hamlet) it is tiring for the memory, the voice, and the body, which has to be
held in a contorted position for long periods. This was one reason why
Antony Sher, in 1985, played the part on crutches; they allowed him not only
to move rapidly across the stage but also to rest occasionally. McKellen's
Richard never attempted to move in a way that might accentuate his deformity; his risk-taking had to do with the ordinary activities that most people
are able to perform with two hands but which he carried out even better with
only one. When he offered to let Lady Anne run him through with his sword,

his deft, one-handed removal of his hat and unbuttoning of his jacket and shirt made one aware of the effort that both Richard and McKellen were taking in making the scene's effect depend on physical dexterity. When it came time to offer his ring to her, he first took it from his finger into his mouth (having used his free hand to pull off his glove), then took the slimy object back in his hand. This Lady Anne was a flapper, with the brittle sophistication of an Evelyn Waugh character barely concealing her helpless loneliness. At the end of the first court scene, which was played at a long table lit by candelabra, Richard went around, alone, extinguishing all the lights but one. Anne came in, presumably to an arranged rendezvous with him; both were almost expressionless. As he took hold of her, he blew out the one remaining light. This moment, all we ever saw of their relationship, could have been interpreted as menacing toward her, like Othello's "Put out the light, and then put out the light," or in the wider sense of the famous words attributed to Sir Edward Grey, the Foreign Secretary, just before the outbreak of World War I: "The lamps are going out all over Europe; we shall not see them lit again in our lifetime."

Set Design from the 1990 National Theatre production directed by Richard Eyre
Photo: Donald Cooper

What kept this Richard from losing momentum as the play went on was that the production's imagery took us further and further into his fantasy world. For the coronation, designer Bob Crowley created a huge image of a naked, perfect, heroic figure based on a photograph of McKellen, "the left arm wholly restored and held aloft, in the manner of the Third Reich's monumental symbols of manhood."

When the play was performed on tour in the United States, McKellen adds, the figure in the portrait was "modestly clad in a full suit of armour". The appearance of medieval costumes at the coronation, and later, the playing of the battle scenes in full armor, suggested the world in which the character had been imaginatively living. Richard's call for a horse on the battlefield, the most famous line in the play, came across as his longing for something to carry him away into a land of mythical heroes. The final example of fantasy came in the ghost scene, where Richard looked on wistfully as the characters whose lives he had ruined were restored to happiness; his murdered wife Anne not only prayed for Richmond, as in the text, but danced with him, something she could never have done with Richard.

Perhaps because it involves a physical transformation, the role seems to take over an actor's life. Antony Sher had written, even before he had officially agreed to play the role for the Royal Shakespeare Company: "I'm totally obsessed by it, like being in love – this one person dominating your every thought" (2). It is not surprising, then, that McKellen, even after an international tour of the National Theatre production, still did not feel ready to stop playing Richard III. When he recreated his performance for Richard Loncraine's film in 1995, their script further accentuated the sense of a parallel universe with its own parallel history. Lines disappeared, often wittily translated into visual effects. Close-ups of horrific killings replaced horrific Senecan descriptions. England's many relics of Victorian Gothic architecture were the backdrop for costumes suggesting the 1930s.

On the whole, film buffs preferred the film, and theater fans preferred the play. The film exploited its ability to provide realistic detail (much of it designed to be appreciated only on repeated viewings) and outrageous excess. The Wars of the Roses ended as Richard crashed through the Lancastrian camp in a tank and machine-gunned everyone there. By contrast, the most terrifying moment in the play came from the scraping of a match on a matchbox. The scrivener, apparently alone on a darkened stage, had just told us that he knew Hastings' execution was a frame-up; the men lighting their cigarettes from the match turned out to be two of Richard's thugs, who took the terrified man away to his own nightmarish fate.

On the screen, McKellen's Richard can be seen doing much more dangerous things than in the stage version, but, paradoxically, none of them seem daring. Thus, the unbuttoning episode was cut in the film; as McKellen wrote later in his notes on the screenplay, he knew that it was "an actor's trick, mine as much as Richard's" (3); on film, it would probably have been taken (like some of the stunts that Harold Lloyd used to perform himself) for trick photography. In the film, the haunting echoes of medieval myth were absent. Richard spoke "a horse, a horse, my kingdom for a horse!" from a tank whose wheels were spinning uselessly in the mud; the line sounded like a wittily apt quotation from Shakespeare. The comic Richard of the film and the mythic Richard of the theatrical vision seem destined to exist in parallel universes, with the myth, appropriately enough, lasting only in the memories of spectators.

NOTES:

(1) Richard Eyre, "On directing *Richard III*" (interview with Dominique Goy-Blanquet) in *Le Tyran: Shakespeare contre Richard III* (Amiens, France: Presses de UFR Clerc Université Picardie, 1990), 133-9.

(2) Antony Sher, *Year of the King* (London: Chatto & Windus, 1985), 82.

(3) Ian McKellen, *William Shakespeare's Richard III* (Woodstock, New York: Overlook Press, 1996)

"Determined to be a Villain"

Richard III in Popular Culture

Douglas Lanier

Richard III provides an instructive example of the changing fortunes of Shakespeare's plays with audiences. As late as the early twentieth century, it was among Shakespeare's most popular and widely performed works. It may be surprising to learn, for example, that one of America's first feature-length films was a silent version of *Richard III*, made in 1912 and starring the noted British stage star Frederick Warde, a film only recently rediscovered and restored. And when sound film first arrived in the late twenties, it was Richard Gloucester's triumphal speech over the dead Henry VI from *Henry VI, Part 3*, delivered by no less than John Barrymore, that marked Shakespeare's first appearance in the Hollywood talkies. (This vignette appears in the extravaganza *Show of Shows*, dir. John G. Adolphi, 1929.)

Richard III's long-standing popularity was sustained by several factors. Chief among them is that the title role has come to be regarded as an actor's showcase, not least because Richard is himself a consummate actor who delights in his own black wit. Richard III thereby became one of the preeminent Shakespearean roles, assayed by many famous stage actors—among them, David Garrick, Edmund Kean, Edwin Forrest, William Charles Macready, Samuel Phelps, Frank Benson, John Barrymore, Donald Wolfit, Laurence Olivier, and Antony Sher. In earlier eras, performances of Richard were familiar enough to audiences to be confidently referenced by artists. Decorative porcelains of actors playing Richard III were among the most popular Shakespearean figurines in the nineteenth century, often reproducing famous poses captured in famous paintings such as William Hogarth's portrait of Garrick as Richard III haunted by ghosts. Caricatures too testify to the public's broad familiarity with performances of Richard III. George Cruikshank's "The Theatrical Atlas" (1814), for example, pictures Edmund Kean as Richard bearing the Drury Lane Theatre on his hunchback, an allusion to how the actor's electrifying performance in the role saved the financially troubled theater. In William Heath's "The Rival Richards," also from 1814, we see Kean and his stage rival and imitator Junius Brutus Booth, both dressed as Richard III, engaged in a fierce tug-of-war, each pulling on one arm of a very alarmed Shakespeare.

By contrast, only a very few performances of Richard were familiar enough to be the stuff of modern pop parody. Though it is unlikely that many

"The Theatrical Atlas": Painting by George Cruikshank of Edmund Kean as Richard III, carrying the Drury Lane Theatre on this back, 1814
Library of Congress, Prints & Photographs Division, British Cartoon Prints Collection

caught the allusion, Kean's portrayal was briefly lampooned by Vincent Price as the murderous Shakespearean actor Edward Lionheart in the comedy horror film *Theatre of Blood* (dir. Douglas Hickox, 1973). Eight years earlier in an installment of the TV variety show *Top of the Pops*, Peter Sellers offered a sublimely off-the-wall parody of Laurence Olivier's Richard III. Dressed in full period costume and using Olivier's distinctive accent and vocal style, he recited not Shakespearean verse but the lyrics to the Beatles' "A Hard Day's Night." Later released as a comedy single, his performance reached #14 on the UK pop charts. Tellingly, both twentieth-century examples are parodies.

As Al Pacino notes in his documentary *Looking for Richard* (1996), Richard's notoriety has fallen considerably during the twentieth and twenty-first centuries. A key reason for that fall may be the play's thicket of references to the dynastic struggle between the Yorks and Lancasters, references with which most modern audiences are unfamiliar. Unlike *Henry V*, which seems less heavily allusive to the plays it follows and generally somewhat less thick with historical reference, *Richard III* depends upon an audience's close knowledge of the War of the Roses and of Shakespeare's own retelling of it in his first tetralogy of history plays. Though Pacino offers the viewer an engaging guide through *Richard III*'s maze of historical allusions, ultimately his film seeks to convince us that it isn't necessary for us to grasp all the antiquarian minutiae to enjoy the play. Mid-film, one scene in particular drives this point home. Among the authorities Pacino and co-director Frederick Kimball consult is Emrys Jones, the distinguished literary scholar. When asked about Richard's wooing of Anne, Jones admits that he doesn't know why Richard felt he needed to marry her. Momentarily the camera fastens on Kimball's furious expression, as he fumes about the inability of literary historians to answer even the most basic questions of dramatic motivation. (Of course, there are very good reasons why Richard would want to marry Anne, not least of which is his desire to legitimize a claim to the throne.) Despite its skepticism about the reliability of historical research or its value for modern performances of the play, Pacino's film is nevertheless haunted by the problem of *Richard III*'s embeddedness in history. Symptomatic of the film's struggle with that issue, the excerpted performances of *Richard III* in it oscillate between modern dress and period costume, moving decidedly in the direction of the latter in the second half.

Two passages from the play, one from its beginning and the other from its end, have taken on allusive lives of their own in popular culture. The first of these, from Richard's opening speech, "Now is the winter of our discontent / Made glorious summer by this son of York" (1.1.1-2), is habitually referenced in popular works, though the allusion rarely makes it beyond the first two lines. One indication of its familiarity in popular culture is that variations on "winter of our discontent" and "glorious summer" appear in many book titles; Guy Townsend uses a later phrase from the opening speech, *To Prove a Villain*, as the title of his 1985 novel, which posits a contemporary serial killer out to avenge the dead princes in the Tower. Another indicator of the line's currency in pop culture is that it has been referenced by one of most reliable barometers of pop literacy, Bart Simpson (in "Radioactive Man," an episode of *The Simpsons*, aired September 24, 1995). Its usefulness also extends to advertising. One example, referenced in John D. Barrows' *Book of Nothing* (2001) and so clever that it may be apocryphal, reportedly appeared in the window of a Stratford-upon-Avon camping goods shop during the post-Christmas sales: "Now is the discount of our winter tents." (This quip is also the title of a novel by Jim Mize and of Neil Tait's 2006 installation at London's White Cube gallery.) In the film *Reality Bites* (dir. Ben Stiller, 1994), the brooding slacker Troy Dyer answers his phone with the line "Hello, you've reached the winter of our discontent," a quip that at once signals Troy's intellectual nature, his resentment at his impoverished lot, and his smart-alecky cynicism. The line's connection to Shakespearean grandiloquence is manifest in "Atomic Shakespeare," an episode of *Moonlighting* which plays primarily on *The Taming of the Shrew* (aired November 25, 1986). When Petruchio seeks to make his entrance into Padua with a grand, famous speech, he keeps choosing the wrong play; one of the three speeches he cycles through is Richard's opening soliloquy (the other two are Hamlet's "To be or not to be" and Mark Antony's "Friends, Romans, countrymen").

Richard's desperate plea from the battle of Bosworth, "A horse! A horse! My kingdom for a horse!" (5.4.7), is equally familiar in popular culture, so much so that the line has been the subject of myriad riffs. Percy Stow's silent film *A Horse! A Horse!* (1913) is built around a single joke based on the line: a cleaning woman, assigned the task of finding a horse for the actor playing Richard III, instead provides him an ass. The line also makes occasional cameo appearances in popular song, surfacing in, for example, Queen's "Lily of the Valley" (from the album *Sheer Heart Attack*, 1974) and Sparklehorse's

"Homecoming Queen" (from the album *vivadixesubmarinetransmissionplot*, 1995). Oddly enough, variations on "my kingdom for a horse" appear in the titles of several books on horses, apparently without any trace of irony: Carol Streeter, *My Kingdom for a Horse: An Owner's Manual* (1980), Maia Wojciechowska, *A Kingdom in a Horse* (1986), and Betty Ann Schwartz and Alix Berenzy, *My Kingdom for a Horse: An Anthology of Poems about Horses* (2001), to name a few.

One last reference from the play underlines the unintended irony of quoting Shakespeare out of context. As if in testimony to the power of Richard's seductive rhetoric, a passage from his wooing speeches to Lady Anne appears in what is otherwise a touching scene in the comedy *Ball of Fire* (dir. Billy Wilder, 1941). To profess his love for gangster moll "Sugarpuss" O'Shea, shy Bertram Potts gives her a ring inscribed "Richard III, 1.2.204." As Potts explains, the reference is to Richard's lines (1.2.205-207),

> Look how my ring encompasseth thy finger,
> Even so thy breast encloseth my poor heart.
> Wear both of them, for both of them are thine,

Despite the fact that Potts is otherwise a meticulous professor and disarmingly sincere, he (or rather, screenwriters Charles Brackett and Billy Wilder) seems to have missed the sordid original context of this speech: in Shakespeare's play Richard speaks this as he perversely courts Lady Anne, widow of a man he himself killed. It only compounds the irony that the same lines have been referenced more recently in magazine advertisements for engagement rings.

Though close familiarity with *Richard III* as a whole has fallen away for most popular audiences, there remains a residual sense that playing the tyrant king establishes one's star quality or standing as a genuine artist on the stage. Certainly the role had that effect on the career of American actor John Barrymore, for before Barrymore played Richard (and soon after Hamlet), he had been regarded as little more than a handsome matinee idol. His status as a Shakespearean and his subsequent fall into Hollywood hackery and alcoholism are the subjects of William Luce's play *Barrymore* (1996), which features several substantial references to the play. The association of the play with theatrical artistry is equally strong in Carlyle Brown's 1994 play *The African Company Presents Richard III*, which chronicles the heroic (and finally unsuccessful) attempts of a nineteenth-century African-American theater company to establish cultural legitimacy by performing Shakespeare's play.

More often, however, this connection is played for comedy. A classic example can be found in *The Goodbye Girl* (dir. Herbert Ross, 1977), in which Elliot Garfield, an up-and-coming actor, regards his being cast as Richard in an off-Broadway production of the play as his big break. He soon

John Barrymore as Richard III
Courtesy of Douglas Lanier

learns to his dismay that the director has conceived of Richard as a prancing prince in pink whose murderousness is motivated by his homosexuality. Though the humor of the situation now looks very dubious, the comic tension between director and actor depends upon our recognition that Richard III is indeed a potentially career-making part for Elliot. Richard Dreyfuss, who played the part of Elliot, also appears as actor Jack Noah in Paul Mazursky's *Moon Over Parador* (1988); as the film begins, Noah is auditioning for the role of Richard, a role which mirrors an assignment he has just completed, that of impersonating a Latin American dictator. Versions of this motif appear periodically in popular culture. Along with Hamlet, Richard III is referenced in the Monty Python routine "Hospital for Over-Actors" (first broadcast 1970). In *Galaxy Quest* (dir. Dean Parisot, 1999), a film about has-been former stars of a science-fiction series, one of the stars—Alexander Dane, the one British member of the cast (and played with delicious irony by Alan Rickman)—complains that though he once played Richard III, he has now been reduced to appearing at fan conventions and in local commercials. When Craig Schwartz and Maxine Lund first discover the portal to John Malkovich's brain in *Being John Malkovich* (dir. Spike Jonze, 1999), they enter his mind as he is rehearsing Richard's "was ever woman in this humor wooed" speech, lines that take on added resonance given the bizarre romance that dominates the last third of the film.

Perhaps the most enduring legacy of *Richard III* in popular culture can be found not in references to specific lines or scenes but in the kind of villainy Richard practices. His insidious, charismatic quality, his cruel glee and unremorseful pursuit of power (until the final act), his status as a rejected and thus vengeful outsider, and his invitation to the audience to admire his villainy—all are qualities that mark a strain of "bad boys" in literature and popular culture stretching from Milton's Satan to Hannibal Lecter from *The Silence of the Lambs* (dir. Jonathan Demme, 1991). Shakespeare reshaped the historical king he encountered in Holinshed's *Chronicles* to fit the contours of the seductive Vice figure from English morality plays of the late Middle Ages, and he incorporated techniques for generating audience identification with a morally problematic character that he picked up from his friend and rival playwright Christopher Marlowe. Likewise, the stature of Shakespeare's Richard III as one of his most compelling villains may have partly and indirectly inspired latter-day creators of a distinctive sort of popular villain—a charismatic, ambitious, smart but dangerous sociopath whose villainy has its source in his outsider status, one whose initial chutzpah often (though not always) turns into overreaching, self-destructive tyranny by work's end.

Though there are few direct parallels between Shakespeare's play and the film *Scarface* (dir. Brian DePalma, 1983), several critics have noted striking resemblances between Shakespeare's villain and the unforgettably ruthless hero-villain Tony Montana. This link between Shakespeare's play and the sly, superficially seductive villains of "gangs in the hood" films is explicit in James Gavin Bedford's 2001 film *The Street King* (aka *Rikki the Pig*), which transfers the basic narrative of *Richard III* to the milieu of a crime-ridden Los Angeles barrio. Abandoned by his mother, Rikki Ortega, a Chicano immigrant, concocts an elaborate plan to foment mutual suspicion among Ortega family members, in order to take over their illegal drug business and in the process get revenge for his mistreatment as a child. Like the women of *Richard III*, the women of the Ortega family recognize and lament his evil nature, but not so his brothers, who, with only one exception, go to their deaths without recognizing Rikki's hand in their fates. Throughout the film, Rikki speaks directly to the viewer with beguiling if utterly heartless wit, and in the end, he is killed by Juan Valleja, a childhood friend who, now a cop, pursues him throughout the film's second half. Interestingly, unlike Richmond, Juan is not presented as a clear moral alternative to Rikki, for after killing him Juan picks up Rikki's satchel of ill-gotten cash.

This ending points to a crucial difference between Shakespeare's play and much of contemporary popular culture's handling of justice to such villains. In Shakespeare, ghostly dreams and the figure of Richmond offer a reassuring providential rebuke to Richard's ascendancy. By contrast, post-sixties popular culture has often seemed skeptical about the moral forces that engineer Richard's defeat. Tellingly, in two recent films of the play, Richard's death is handled in ways that mute or even contradict the triumphal nature of Shakespeare's version. In Richard Loncraine's *Richard III* (1995), updated to a mythical 1930s, Richard confronts Richmond atop the girders of a ruined railway station, in a sequence which evokes the final *mano a mano* of good and evil that concludes many detective films and thrillers. This moment is complicated by two touches. First, after Richmond shoots at Richard (it's not clear whether Richmond hits Richard or Richard commits suicide), he looks at the camera and gives a sly, conspiratorial smile. It is as if Richmond has taken on Richard's political cynicism rather than serving as the tyrant's virtuous alternative. Second, the shot of the film depicts Richard in slow motion free fall, laughing and waving as he gleefully plunges to his death in the fire below; to gild the blackly ironic lily, the jaunty strains of "Sittin' on Top of the World" play on the soundtrack, echoing criminal Cody Jarrett's glorious self-destruction at the end of *White Heat*, with the famous line, "Sittin' on top of the world, Ma!"

In *Looking for Richard*, by contrast, Richard's death is unremitting in its brutality. In a wordless sequence, Richard, isolated on a grassy hillside, is repeatedly shot by arrows by Richmond's men, thus portrayed like a wounded animal. The dying Richard, lying on his back, fumbles for his sword as Richmond approaches, but Richmond pins his arm underfoot. As Richmond raises his sword with grim determination to deal the death blow, we see the moment of the kill from Richard's point of view. Though this version borrows qualities from the endings of action films in which the killing of the villain is drawn out and relished for its cruelly satisfying justice, here the tone is different. Although we do get bits of Richmond's final triumphal speech, stress falls on the brutal ignobility of Richard's death. Our identification with Richard is heightened by the fact that as Richmond plunges the sword into Richard's breast, Pacino cuts away to himself clowning with co-director Frederick Kimball, exclaiming with mock joy "I'm free!" These films pointedly do not offer an unambiguous triumph of good over evil and even encourage different forms of sympathy for the devil.

Richard III's dual status as a stage villain and actual English king has prompted a number of responses from those concerned over the dramatic license Shakespeare took with the historical record. Indeed, the Richard III Society is devoted to rehabilitating Richard's reputation, done considerable damage, its members point out, by Shakespeare's fictional misrepresentation. Related to this phenomenon are perennial attempts by amateur historians to address "the mystery of the princes" and thereby to rescue Richard from the charge that he ordered them to be killed. At least three silent films were made on the murdered princes, an indication of the long-lived nature of popular fascination with Richard's involvement with their deaths; interestingly, two of them feature the boys returning as ghosts to haunt Richard. Two fine, now classic, mystery novels are built around sleuths researching the historical facts of Richard III's involvement in the murders: Elizabeth Peters, *The Murders of Richard III* (1947) and Josephine Tey's *The Daughter of Time* (1951). Tey's much-beloved novel is especially well-written and clever: Inspector Alan Grant pursues the mystery of Richard and the princes with unrelenting deductive savvy while never leaving the bed in which he is convalescing. Mary W. Schaller's play *The Final Trial of Richard III* (1986) goes one step further, laying out the evidence for Richard's criminality in the form of a one-act courtroom drama. Historical novelists have also taken up Richard's story, often with an eye toward redeeming Richard's image. Rosemary Hawley Jarman's *We Speak No Treason* (1971) offers an oblique portrait of the king through the voices of several characters who discuss their dealings with him. Sharon Kay Penman's *The Sunne in Splendour* (1989) sets her revisionary portrait of Richard within a richly detailed historical overview of the period; Paula Symonds Zabka's *Desire the Kingdom* (2002) and Meredith Whitford's *Treason* (2004) follow in a similar fantasy vein.

Several popular adaptations address the gap between the real Richard and Shakespeare's character in a much freer, less historical fashion. R. Rex Stephenson's children's play *Glorious Son of York* (1998, published 2000) stars the historical Richard III, who has returned to the present to answer the charges laid against him in Shakespeare's play. Though Maxwell Anderson's play *Richard and Anne* (1955) opens with Shakespeare's "winter of our discontent" speech, the play soon morphs into a provocatively alternate view of Richard's actions, revising, for example, the romance between Richard and Anne to resemble that of Romeo and Juliet. At one point, the ghost of the real Richard III–ironically, the person that Shakespeare's Richard has "killed" in the public's mind–appears to the character Richard III in the play. Further afield is John Ford's alternate history / fantasy novel *The Dragon Waiting: A Masque of History* (1983) which imagines that Richard was actually a benevolent king attended by evil vampires. A telling reference to the controversy surrounding Shakespeare's Richard III and history can be found in *The Bride* (dir. Frank Roddam, 1985), a retelling of *The Bride of Frankenstein* (minus the original's campy appeal). In this version, Doctor

Frankenstein not only creates a female bride Eva for his male monster, but also gives her a cultural education. When he first introduces her to polite society at a dinner party, the topic of conversation turns to Shakespeare's *Richard III*, of which one guest observes that Shakespeare distorted the historical record with his Richard; in reply Eva offers the controversial opinion that Shakespeare's fictional works were more interesting than his history plays, one of the first signs of not only her intellect but also her independence.

Inevitably, this concern with correcting Shakespeare's "distortion" of the historical record invites parody. A brilliant example can be found in the opening episode of the *Blackadder* TV series, "The Foretelling" (1983). A parody of the pieties of British heritage television, this show turns Shakespeare's portrayal of Richard III on its head. Richard, we are told in the short prologue, was in reality a kind and generous king, and Henry Tudor, his successor, was a usurping, conniving tyrant who rewrote history to serve his own interests. This account resembles, in outline but not in tone, a now venerable perspective on Shakespeare's history play-writing, first advanced by E. M. W. Tillyard in *Shakespeare's History Plays* (1944). When we first meet Richard (played by Peter Cook), he is offering a sunny version of his "now is the winter of our discontent" speech to his assembled troops:

> Now is the summer of our sweet content
> Made o'ercast winter by these Tudor clowns,
> And I that am not shaped for blackfaced war, [*protests from soldiers*]
> I that am rudely cast and want true majesty, [*more protests from soldiers*]
> Set forth to set sweet England free.
> I pray to heaven we fare well
> And all who fight us, go to hell!

Ironically, it is not Richmond who kills Richard at Bosworth Field but Edmund Blackadder, the comically craven and inept knight who accidentally beheads the king as he searches for a horse. Throughout the remainder of the episode, Blackadder struggles to cover up his mistake and at the same time take advantage of the situation, all the while being haunted by appearances of Richard's bloody corpse which parody Banquo's ghostly visitation at Macbeth's victory banquet and Richard III's guilty nightmare before his final battle.

RICHARD III [28

Richard's reputation as a despicable tyrant has long made him useful to political satirists. Productions of the play directed by Jürgen Fehling (1937) and Donald Wolfit (1942) used parallels between Hitler and Richard III to protest the rise of Nazism; Richard Loncraine's recent film *Richard III* (1995), set in the 1930s, alludes darkly to British aristocratic sympathies in the period with fascism. Richard Nixon's serendipitous sharing of a first name with Shakespeare's king perhaps made the connection between the two irresistible in three political lampoons of the early 70s, Steven Bush and Richard McKenna's *Richard Thirdtime* (1972), Charles S. Preston's *T'e Tragedy of King Rich'rd t'e T'ird: My Kingdom for a Bomb* (1972) and David Edgar's play *Dick Deterred* (1974), all of which were inspired by Barbara Garson's famous Shakespearean parody of Lyndon Johnson's administration, *Macbird* (1965).

Women figure strongly in *Richard III* as bearers of royal children and prophecy, and they also figure strongly in the tradition of popular adaptations of the play. Adaptations which make women even more central to the narrative (in the process offering actresses bigger parts) can be found as early as the Restoration with John Caryll's *The English Princess, or the Death of Richard III* (1667); Buckingham's mistress becomes the subject of her own play with Nicholas Rowe's *Jane Shore* (1714), a spinoff which perhaps reflects the morally problematic status of actresses during the early eighteenth century, when the relatively new phenomenon of women on the English stage was still regarded as sexually provocative. Contemporary writers have found the nobility and dissidence of Queen Margaret a fruitful topic for elaboration. Normand Chaurette's play *Les Reines* (1990), a Quebecois adaptation, imagines six aristocratic women from *Richard III* as they vie for supremacy while Richard rises to power. As if in answer to Pacino's documentary, Lorraine Helms's play *Looking for Margaret* (1999) addresses the relationship between the queen's prophetic status and madness.

Two screen adaptations of *Richard III* filter Shakespeare's narrative through the conventions of horror films: Rowland V. Lee's *Tower of London* (1939) and Roger Corman's remake, also titled *Tower of London* (1962). Lee's film, produced in the midst of Universal Studio's horror film cycle in the thirties, splits Shakespeare's villain into two personalities, each representative of the two genres–costume drama and horror thriller–being hybridized in this adaptation. One villain is the suave Richard, played by Basil Rathbone as a swashbuckling, barely hunch-backed villain, the kind of role Rathbone specialized in throughout the thirties. In his climb to the throne, Rathbone's Richard perversely keeps score with dollhouse figures that he tosses in the fire after he kills each character. Aided by Edward IV, who functions as the film's substitute for Shakespeare's Buckingham, Richard principally targets children, women and weak men; his main nemesis is the plucky John Wyatt who early on recognizes Richard's treacherous nature and defies him. The film's second villain is the sinister executioner Mord, played by Boris Karloff. A clubfooted Neanderthal straight out of a monster movie, Mord is pathetically worshipful of Richard and eagerly tortures or kills his enemies. Given its production date, the film invites being read in light of the rise of Nazism, with Richard as a ruthless fascist leader, Mord as his apparatus of surveillance, terror and propaganda, and John Wyatt and his allies as the resistance. Many details from *Richard III* (e.g., the wooing of Anne, the drowning of Clarence in a butt of malmsey, the murder of the princes in the Tower, Richard's being urged by Londoners to accept the crown, the battle of Bosworth Field) appear in radically altered form in *Tower of London*, though none of Shakespeare's concern with prophecy and providence remains.

However, prophecy, providence, and above all, guilt, do figure prominently in Roger Corman's remake. Essentially a variation on the free film adaptations of Edgar Allan Poe's works Corman made with Vincent Price in the 1960s, *Tower of London* blends horror film iconography—torture in dungeons, foggy battlements, secret passageways—with elements from *Richard III*, all refashioned as a tale of ambition, murder and conscience reminiscent of *Macbeth*. As the film's prologue declares, this Richard "escaped the headsman's block, but he could not escape the ghosts of his conscience." Of some interest are the script's attempts at pseudo-Elizabethan English and Shakespearean imagery, qualities particularly on display in Richard's many speeches of mannered madness. Early in this version, Richard III's partner in crime is his wife Anne who, like Lady Macbeth, shares her husband's ruthless desire for power; only later, after Richard accidentally murders her, is she replaced by Ratcliff, Richard's evil henchman. Vincent Price plays Richard III as an ambitious tyrant alternately

Basil Rathbone as Richard and Boris Karloff as Mord in the 1939 film, "Tower of London," directed by Rowland V. Lee
Courtesy of Douglas Lanier

sadistic and remorseful, increasingly driven insane by the haunting reappearances of those he has dispatched. Ghosts repeatedly tempt him to danger, and the specter of Clarence, Richard's first victim, predicts that his brother will meet his doom at Bosworth Field at the hands of a dead man. Accordingly, while fleeing the ghosts of his victims on the battlefield, Richard dies by falling from his horse onto the pike of a dead soldier, a fate which Sir Justin, ally of Stanley and Richmond, declares the working of justice. Corman's *Tower of London* testifies to the long legacy of morality drama, a genre which shapes Shakespeare's own retelling of history in *Richard III*, though Corman's version refracts Richard's rise and fall through Gothic cliché.

The future of *Richard III* in an increasingly global context is uncertain. The play's close concern with details of British history seems to have discouraged non-English-speaking authors from producing many adaptations. Though Ariane Mnouchkine produced a provocative French adaptation using elements of Kabuki and Indian theater for the Théâtre du Soleil in 1982, and Ken Phillips' *The Seduction of Lady Anne* (2001) uses elements of the traditional Indian theatrical form Kathakali in its production, there have been to date relatively few cross-cultural adaptations, particularly when compared to other Shakespearean plays of equal stature. One fascinating exception is an Arabic reworking of the play reminiscent of Sadaam Hussein's rise in Iraq. This adaptation by Sulayman Al-Bassam, a noted Shakespearean adaptor, was staged for the Royal Shakespeare Company's Complete Works Festival in 2007. Perhaps Al-Bassam's production (and the RSC's imprimatur upon it) may signal the potential for a new twenty-first century global audience for what was once among Shakespeare's most popular tragedies.

Dramatis Personae

King Edward the Fourth

Sons of the King:
    Edward, Prince of Wales, afterwards King Edward V
    Richard, Duke of York

Brothers of the King:
    George, Duke of Clarence
    Richard, Duke of Gloucester, afterwards King Richard III

Elizabeth, Queen to King Edward IV
Margaret, widow of King Henry VI
Duchess of York, mother to King Edward IV, and the Dukes of Gloucester (Richard III) and Clarence
Lady Anne, widow of Edward, Prince of Wales, son to King Henry VI; afterwards married to Richard, Duke of Gloucester and Richard III

The Young Son of Clarence (Edward Plantagenet, Earl of Warwick)
The Young Daughter of Clarence (Lady Margaret Plantagenet, later Countess of Salisbury)

Archbishop of Canterbury (Cardinal Bourchier)
Archbishop of York (Thomas Rotherham)
Bishop of Ely (John Morton)
Duke of Buckingham
Lord Hastings
Sir Thomas Vaughan

Anthony Woodville, Earl Rivers, brother of King Edward IV's Queen
Marquess of Dorset, son of King Edward IV's Queen
Lord Grey, son of King Edward IV's Queen

Richard's followers:
      Lord Lovell
      Sir Richard Ratcliff
      Sir William Catesby
      Sir James Tyrrel
      Duke of Norfolk
      Earl of Surrey, Norfolk's son

Henry Tudor, Earl of Richmond, afterwards King Henry VII

Richmond's followers:
      Lord Stanley, Earl of Derby
      Earl of Oxford
      Sir James Blunt
      Sir Walter Herbert
      Sir William Brandon
      Christopher Urswick, a priest

Sir Robert Brakenbury, Lieutenant of the Tower
Keeper in the Tower
Lord Mayor of London
Sheriff of Wiltshire
Tressel and Berkeley, gentlemen attending on Lady Anne
Ghosts of Richard's victims

Lords, Gentlemen, Attendants, a Pursuivant, Priest, Scrivener, Page,
Bishops, Aldermen, Citizens, Soldiers, Messengers, Guards, Servants,
Murderers

[Richard III

Act 1

0: Location: A tradition has grown up of saying this scene is set in a London street, though it could as easily be in a palace, at a gate to the Tower (of London), or else-where.

0: Scene: From Colley Cibber's production in 1700 until W. C. Macready's production in 1819-20, the play opened in a garden and incorporated significant materials from *Henry VI, Part 3*, including Richard's killing of Henry VI, as an "introduction" to the play. Remnants of Cibber's adaptation can be found as late as 1955 (Olivier's film) and 1995 (Loncraine/McKellen's film).

tracks 2-4

1-41:
Laurence Olivier as Richard
Peter Finch as Richard

2: **son of York:** The First Folio and Quarto spell the first word "sonne" and "Son," and the word could be correctly modernized to either "sun" or "son." The reference is to Richard's brother, Edward IV, who is both the eldest surviving son of the House of York [see chart on p. xviii] and who had as his badge three suns in splendor. The pun also fits with the seasonal reference to "winter of discontent" in the first line.
3: **loured:** also, "lowered," scowled or looked dark and threatening; **house:** i.e., the House of York
7: **stern alarums:** calls to battle by trumpet and drum; **merry meetings:** light or amorous gatherings, in contrast to the "stern alarums"
8: **dreadful marches:** marches into battle both full of dread or fear and inspiring dread on the part of the enemy; **delightful measures:** pleasant dances
10: **barbèd steeds:** warhorses with protective coverings over their breasts and flanks made of metal plates with metal spikes
11: **fright:** frighten; **fearful adversaries:** both those of whom we are afraid and/or those who are afraid of us
16: **rudely stamped:** roughly formed, deformed; **want:** lack
20: **sent before my time:** born prematurely
23: **halt:** limp
24: **piping time of peace:** marked by the music of pipes or flutes rather than the trumpet and drum of war
27: **descant on:** discourse on
32: **inductions:** initial steps, or introductions

Act 1, Scene 1]

Enter RICHARD, DUKE OF GLOUCESTER, solus

RICHARD
   Now is the winter of our discontent
   Made glorious summer by this son of York,
   And all the clouds that loured upon our house
   In the deep bosom of the ocean buried.
   Now are our brows bound with victorious wreaths,   5
   Our bruisèd arms hung up for monuments,
   Our stern alarums changed to merry meetings,
   Our dreadful marches to delightful measures.
   Grim-visaged war hath smoothed his wrinkled front;
   And now, instead of mounting barbèd steeds   10
   To fright the souls of fearful adversaries,
   He capers nimbly in a lady's chamber
   To the lascivious pleasing of a lute.
   But I, that am not shaped for sportive tricks,
   Nor made to court an amorous looking glass;   15
   I, that am rudely stamped, and want love's majesty
   To strut before a wanton ambling nymph;
   I, that am curtailed of this fair proportion,
   Cheated of feature by dissembling nature,
   Deformed, unfinished, sent before my time   20
   Into this breathing world scarce half made up,
   And that so lamely and unfashionable
   That dogs bark at me as I halt by them.
   Why I, in this weak piping time of peace,
   Have no delight to pass away the time,   25
   Unless to spy my shadow in the sun
   And descant on mine own deformity.
   And therefore, since I cannot prove a lover
   To entertain these fair well-spoken days,
   I am determinèd to prove a villain,   30
   And hate the idle pleasures of these days.
   Plots have I laid, inductions dangerous,

1-41:
Laurence Olivier as Richard
Peter Finch as Richard

tracks 2-4

33: **By:** through, or by means of
38: **mewed:** caged or confined

42-43: "What means this armèd guard / That waits upon your Grace?": Sir Laurence Olivier as Richard and Sir John Gielgud as Clarence in the 1955 film directed by Sir Laurence Olivier

Courtesy of Douglas Lanier

44: **Tendering:** regarding or respecting
48: **godfathers:** those who give the name of the child during baptism. In the *Book of Common Prayer*, in use in Shakespeare's time, the minister is instructed to take the child in his arms and to say to the godparents, "Name this Child." Richard plays with the idea of re-baptism in the lines that follow.
49: **belike:** perhaps
50: **new-christened:** Re-baptism was against the teachings of both the Roman Catholic Church and the Church of England except, in the case of the latter, when there was reasonable doubt about the validity of the original baptism, in which case "Conditional Baptism" was performed.
55: **cross-row:** the alphabet. Called the Christ-cross-row or criss-cross-row because an image of the cross preceded the alphabet in the hornbook (a leaf of paper mounted on board and covered with a translucent layer of horn, used to teach children the alphabet).

By drunken prophecies, libels and dreams,
To set my brother Clarence and the King
In deadly hate the one against the other;   35
And if King Edward be as true and just
As I am subtle, false, and treacherous,
This day should Clarence closely be mewed up,
About a prophecy, which says that G
Of Edward's heirs the murderer shall be.   40
Dive thoughts down to my soul, here Clarence comes.

Enter CLARENCE, guarded, and BRAKENBURY

Brother, good day. What means this armèd guard
That waits upon your Grace?

CLARENCE

His Majesty
Tendering my person's safety, hath appointed
This conduct to convey me to th' Tower.   45

RICHARD

Upon what cause?

CLARENCE

Because my name is George.

RICHARD

Alack, my lord, that fault is none of yours.
He should for that commit your godfathers.
O, belike his Majesty hath some intent
That you shall be new-christened in the Tower.   50
But what's the matter, Clarence? May I know?

CLARENCE

Yea, Richard, when I know; but I protest
As yet I do not. But as I can learn,
He hearkens after prophecies and dreams,
And from the cross-row plucks the letter G.   55
And says a wizard told him that by G
His issue disinherited should be.
And, for my name of George begins with G,

60: **toys:** trifles or fancies

64: **My Lady Grey his wife:** i.e., Queen Elizabeth. Here, and throughout the play, Richard, Clarence, and those of their party constantly slight Edward IV's wife, who had previously been married to Sir John Grey.

65: **tempers:** regulates, directs, or governs

66: **good man of worship:** literally, honorable man, but Richard says this ironically

67: **Anthony Woodville:** Earl Rivers

72: **night-walking heralds:** messengers, particularly secret ones

73: **Mistress Shore:** Elizabeth Shore (nicknamed Jane), wife of William Shore, a London merchant, and mistress of Edward IV. Clarence is playing with the title of "Mistress" meaning wife (now abbreviated "Mrs.") and the more salacious meaning of the word.

75: **to her for his:** from the First Quarto, the First Folio reads "was, for her"

76: **her deity:** mocking title for Jane Shore

77: **Lord Chamberlain:** i.e., Lord Hastings. The Lord Chamberlain was a senior officer of the royal household.

81: **jealous o'erworn widow:** Queen Elizabeth, Edward IV's wife, is the widow of Sir John Grey; **herself:** i.e., Jane Shore

82: **dubbed them gentlewomen:** "dubbed" is a slur on both women since only knights were dubbed; "gentlewomen" is a slightly different slur implying that only Edward IV's favor has made them members of the gentry

85: **straitly:** strictly

86-87: **no man...degree soever:** no one, no matter what his or her social rank

88- 102: Scene: **And please...betray me:** This exchange had been cut by Cibber, and when it was restored by Macready, many thought these lines to be indelicate. In the twentieth century, actors have made much of this indelicacy; for example, Sher (Alexander, 1984) had the guards snickering when he said "Naught to do with mistress Shore!" and rubbed his crutches together.

It follows in his thought that I am he.
These, as I learn, and such like toys as these   60
Have moved his Highness to commit me now.

RICHARD
Why, this it is, when men are ruled by women.
'Tis not the King that sends you to the Tower.
My Lady Grey his wife, Clarence, 'tis she
That tempers him to this extremity.   65
Was it not she and that good man of worship,
Anthony Woodville, her brother there,
That made him send Lord Hastings to the Tower,
From whence this present day he is delivered?
We are not safe, Clarence; we are not safe.   70

CLARENCE
By heaven, I think there is no man is secure
But the Queen's kindred and night-walking heralds
That trudge betwixt the King and Mistress Shore.
Heard ye not what an humble suppliant
Lord Hastings was to her for his delivery?   75

RICHARD
Humbly complaining to her deity
Got my Lord Chamberlain his liberty.
I'll tell you what; I think it is our way,
If we will keep in favor with the King,
To be her men and wear her livery.   80
The jealous o'erworn widow and herself,
Since that our brother dubbed them gentlewomen.
Are mighty gossips in this monarchy.

BRAKENBURY
I beseech your Graces both to pardon me.
His Majesty hath straitly given in charge   85
That no man shall have private conference,
Of what degree soever, with his brother.

RICHARD
Even so? And please your worship, Brakenbury,
You may partake of any thing we say.

92: **Well struck in years:** old

94: **passing:** surpassing

97, 98, 99: **naught:** the first use of the word means "nothing" and Richard then plays with its other meaning of "naughty" or "wicked"

101-102: **BRAKENBURY...betray me:** This exchange first appears in the Second Quarto, a text thought to have been a mere reprint of the First Quarto.

102: **Her husband:** In fact, Jane Shore's marriage was annulled in 1476 at her petition, on the grounds of impotence, which may be part of Richard's joke.

103: **withal:** also, or at the same time

105: **charge:** command

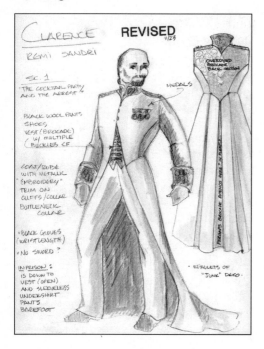

Costume rendering for Clarence by Deborah M. Dryden from the 1993 Oregon Shakespeare Festival production directed by James Edmondson

Courtesy of Oregon Shakespeare Festival

106: **abjects:** lowest servants, but Richard is punning on "subjects"

109: **King Edward's widow sister:** i.e., Edward's wife and Richard's sister-in-law, Queen Elizabeth, was a widow when Edward married her.

110: **enfranchise:** release from imprisonment

We speak no treason, man. We say the King   90
Is wise and virtuous, and his noble Queen
Well struck in years, fair, and not jealous;
We say that Shore's wife hath a pretty foot,
A cherry lip, a bonny eye, a passing pleasing tongue,
And that the Queen's kindred are made gentlefolks.   95
How say you sir? Can you deny all this?

BRAKENBURY
With this, my lord, myself have naught to do.

RICHARD
Naught to do with Mistress Shore! I tell thee, fellow,
He that doth naught with her, excepting one,
Were best he do it secretly, alone.   100

BRAKENBURY
What one, my lord?

RICHARD
Her husband, knave; wouldst thou betray me?

BRAKENBURY
I beseech your Grace to pardon me, and withal
Forbear your conference with the noble duke.

CLARENCE
We know thy charge, Brakenbury, and will obey.   105

RICHARD
We are the Queen's abjects, and must obey.
Brother, farewell. I will unto the King,
And whatsoe'er you will employ me in,
Were it to call King Edward's widow sister,
I will perform it to enfranchise you.   110
Meantime, this deep disgrace in brotherhood
Touches me deeper than you can imagine.

CLARENCE
I know it pleaseth neither of us well.

115: **lie for you:** go to prison in your place (with pun on "telling lies" to help you)

116: **perforce:** of necessity

116: Stage Direction: ***[BRAKENBURY, and GUARD]:*** not in any of the early editions. Edward Capell (1768) is the first editor to make this emendation.

117-120 and 145-162: **Go...hands** and **He cannot...my gains:** These two asides or mini-soliloquies can be, and often are, performed as extensions of Richard's opening soliloquy, for they continue explaining his plans though he is first interrupted by the entry of Clarence and then of Hastings.

Basic set rendering from the 1953 production at the Shakespeare Memorial Theatre in Stratford-upon-Avon directed by Glen Byam Shaw

Rare Book and Special Collection Library, University of Illinois at Urbana-Champaign

125: **brooked:** tolerated

133: **kites:** birds of prey; **prey:** from the First Quarto, the First Folio reads "play"

RICHARD
Well, your imprisonment shall not be long;
I will deliver you or else lie for you.   115
Meantime, have patience.

CLARENCE
I must perforce. Farewell.
Exeunt CLARENCE, [BRAKENBURY, and GUARD]

RICHARD
Go, tread the path that thou shalt ne'er return.
Simple, plain Clarence. I do love thee so,
That I will shortly send thy soul to heaven,
If heaven will take the present at our hands.   120
But who comes here?

Enter HASTINGS
The new-delivered Hastings?

HASTINGS
Good time of day unto my gracious lord.

RICHARD
As much unto my good Lord Chamberlain.
Well are you welcome to this open air.
How hath your lordship brooked imprisonment?   125

HASTINGS
With patience, noble lord, as prisoners must.
But I shall live, my lord, to give them thanks
That were the cause of my imprisonment.

RICHARD
No doubt, no doubt; and so shall Clarence too;
For they that were your enemies are his,   130
And have prevailed as much on him as you.

HASTINGS
More pity that the eagle should be mewed,
While kites and buzzards prey at liberty.

137: **fear:** fear for

138: **Saint John:** Many editors follow the First Quarto's reading of "Saint Paul" since it is one of Richard's habitual oaths, but there seems little justification for this.

139: **diet:** way of life

Stacy Keach as Richard in the 1990 Shakespeare Theatre Company production directed by Michael Kahn

Photo: Joan Marcus

146: **with post-horse:** quickly; post-horses were used for express delivery of messages

148: **steeled:** strengthened with iron

153: **Warwick's youngest daughter:** i.e., Anne Neville, daughter of the Earl of Warwick. The earl was known as "Warwick the Kingmaker" having first helped Edward IV and then Henry VI to the throne.

154: **husband:** Anne Neville was betrothed, but not married, to Prince Edward, son of Henry VI; **father:** i.e., father-in-law, Henry VI

160: **run...market:** a proverb

RICHARD
    What news abroad?

HASTINGS
    No news so bad abroad as this at home: 135
    The King is sickly, weak and melancholy,
    And his physicians fear him mightily.

RICHARD
    Now, by Saint John, this news is bad indeed.
    O, he hath kept an evil diet long,
    And overmuch consumed his royal person: 140
    'Tis very grievous to be thought upon.
    Where is he, in his bed?

HASTINGS
    He is.

RICHARD
    Go you before, and I will follow you.
                                              Exit HASTINGS
    He cannot live, I hope, and must not die   145
    Till George be packed with post-horse up to heaven.
    I'll in to urge his hatred more to Clarence,
    With lies well steeled with weighty arguments,
    And, if I fall not in my deep intent,
    Clarence hath not another day to live;   150
    Which done, God take King Edward to His mercy,
    And leave the world for me to bustle in.
    For then I'll marry Warwick's youngest daughter.
    What though I killed her husband and her father?
    The readiest way to make the wench amends   155
    Is to become her husband and her father;
    The which will I, not all so much for love
    As for another secret close intent
    By marrying her which I must reach unto.
    But yet I run before my horse to market.   160
    Clarence still breathes; Edward still lives and reigns.
    When they are gone, then must I count my gains.
                                                      Exit

0: Scene: There is no clear textual indication of setting, and there is no reason why this scene should not be continuous with the previous one. However, following the First Folio, this is marked as a new scene; the setting must be the same as that of the previous one. Cibber (1700) chose to set it in a church (St. Paul's Cathedral), and that convention continued through the eighteenth century. By the early nineteenth century, the setting had become simply a procession through an arch. However, that century also saw a tendency for increasingly elaborate shows and in 1854, Charles Kean's production at the Princess's Theatre, London, had a funeral procession of about seventy-two people with six peers in scarlet robes winding through cloisters, bearing the royal pall.

0: Stage Direction: *Halberds*: a combination of spear and battleaxe on a long shaft

2: **shrouded:** both wrapped in a shroud and also given refuge; **hearse:** the funeral pall and probably also the wooden frame supporting it over the body

4: **fall of virtuous Lancaster:** Anne is most immediately mourning the death of Henry VI, the head of the House of Lancaster, but also the fall of the whole Lancaster family.

5: **key-cold:** as cold as a metal key

8: **invocate:** call up

13: **helpless:** providing no help

17: **direful hap:** terrible fortune

22: **Prodigious:** abnormal; **untimely:** 1) premature, or 2) under an evil sign

25: **that:** i.e., the child; **unhappiness:** ill fortune

29: **Chertsey:** a great abbey on the river Thames west of London, founded in 666 and of great size and importance

30: **Paul's:** St. Paul's Cathedral, London. Henry VI died, or was put to death, in The Tower of London on May 21, 1471. The next evening the body was taken to St. Paul's where it bled on the pavement and lay overnight before it was then taken to Chertsey Abbey, where it was interred.

Act 1, Scene 2]

Enter the corpse of KING HENRY THE SIXTH [on a bier,]
with Halberds to guard it, LADY ANNE being
the mourner[, with gentlemen]

LADY ANNE
Set down, set down your honorable load,
If honor may be shrouded in a hearse,
Whilst I awhile obsequiously lament
Th' untimely fall of virtuous Lancaster.
Poor key-cold figure of a holy king,   5
Pale ashes of the House of Lancaster,
Thou bloodless remnant of that royal blood,
Be it lawful that I invocate thy ghost
To hear the lamentations of Poor Anne,
Wife to thy Edward, to thy slaughtered son,   10
Stabbed by the selfsame hand that made these wounds.
Lo, in these windows that let forth thy life
I pour the helpless balm of my poor eyes.
O, cursèd be the hand that made these holes;
Cursèd the heart that had the heart to do it;   15
Cursèd the blood that let this blood from hence.
More direful hap betide that hated wretch
That makes us wretched by the death of thee
Than I can wish to wolves, to spiders, toads,
Or any creeping venomed thing that lives.   20
If ever he have child, abortive be it,
Prodigious, and untimely brought to light,
Whose ugly and unnatural aspect
May fright the hopeful mother at the view,
And that be heir to his unhappiness   25
If ever he have wife, let her he made
More miserable by the death of him
Than I am made by my young lord and thee.
Come now towards Chertsey with your holy load,
Taken from Paul's to be interrèd there.   30

31: **still:** yet
32: **whiles:** during which time; **corse:** corpse

34-35: "What black magician conjures up this fiend, / To stop devoted charitable deeds?": Sir Laurence Olivier as Richard and Claire Bloom as Lady Anne in the 1955 film directed by Sir Laurence Olivier
Courtesy of Douglas Lanier

35: **devoted:** holy, or consecrated
39: **stand thou:** halt; from the First Quarto, the First Folio has "Stand'st thou"

39-42: Scene: **Unmannered dog...thy boldness:** Jarvis (Bogdanov, 1989) was armed with two flick knives, which he carried in the pockets of his suit jacket. Sher (Alexander, 1984) attacked and disarmed the pallbearers and guards using no other weapon than his crutches.

40: **Advance...breast:** hold your weapon upright (in a non-attacking position)
42: **spurn:** trample
46: **Avaunt:** be gone
49: **curst:** shrewish
52: **exclaims:** exclamations

And still, as you are weary of the weight,
Rest you, whiles I lament King Henry's corse.

Enter RICHARD, DUKE OF GLOUCESTER

RICHARD
Stay, you that bear the corse, and set it down.

LADY ANNE
What black magician conjures up this fiend,
To stop devoted charitable deeds?   35

RICHARD
Villains, set down the corse or, by Saint Paul,
I'll make a corse of him that disobeys.

GENTLEMAN
My lord, stand back, and let the coffin pass.

RICHARD
Unmannered dog, stand thou, when I command!
Advance thy halberd higher than my breast,   40
Or by Saint Paul I'll strike thee to my foot,
And spurn upon thee, beggar, for thy boldness.

LADY ANNE
What, do you tremble? Are you all afraid?
Alas, I blame you not, for you are mortal,
And mortal eyes cannot endure the devil.   45
Avaunt, thou dreadful minister of hell.
Thou hadst but power over his mortal body;
His soul thou canst not have. Therefore be gone.

RICHARD
Sweet saint, for charity, be not so curst.

LADY ANNE
Foul devil, for God's sake, hence, and trouble us not,   50
For thou hast made the happy earth thy hell,
Filled it with cursing cries and deep exclaims.
If thou delight to view thy heinous deeds,
Behold this pattern of thy butcheries.

55: **see dead Henry's wounds:** A number of productions, particularly of late, have had Henry's wounds bleed at this line. The volume of blood was especially impressive in Bogdanov's 1989 production.

55-56: **O...afresh:** see note 1.2.30

58: **exhales:** brings out

65: **quick:** alive

68: **charity:** one of the three Theological Virtues, the others being Faith and Hope (see St. Paul in 1 Corinthians 13)

69: **for...for:** in return for

74: "More wonderful, when angels are so angry": George C. Scott as Richard and Marcia Morris as Lady Anne in the 1957 Public Theater production directed by Stuart Vaughan

Photo: George E. Joseph

75: **Vouchsafe:** grant or permit

77: **circumstance:** detailed explanation or argument

78: **defused:** spread widely or disordered; **a man:** The First Folio omits the article; the First Quarto supplies it.

O, gentlemen, see, see dead Henry's wounds   55
Open their congealed mouths and bleed afresh.
Blush, Blush, thou lump of foul deformity,
For 'tis thy presence that exhales this blood
From cold and empty veins where no blood dwells.
Thy deeds, inhuman and unnatural,   60
Provokes this deluge most unnatural.
O God, which this blood mad'st, revenge his death!
O earth, which this blood drink'st, revenge his death!
Either heaven with lightning strike the murderer dead,
Or earth gape open wide and eat him quick,   65
As thou dost swallow up this good King's blood
Which his hell-governed arm hath butcherèd.

RICHARD
  Lady, you know no rules of charity,
  Which renders good for bad, blessings for curses.

LADY ANNE
  Villain, thou know'st no law of God nor man.   70
  No beast so fierce but knows some touch of pity.

RICHARD
  But I know none, and therefore am no beast.

LADY ANNE
  O wonderful, when devils tell the truth!

RICHARD
  More wonderful, when angels are so angry.
  Vouchsafe, divine perfection of a woman,   75
  Of these supposèd crimes to give me leave,
  By circumstance, but to acquit myself.

LADY ANNE
  Vouchsafe, defused infection of a man,
  For these known evils, but to give me leave
  By circumstance, to curse thy cursèd self.   80

82: **patient:** calm

84: **current:** authentic

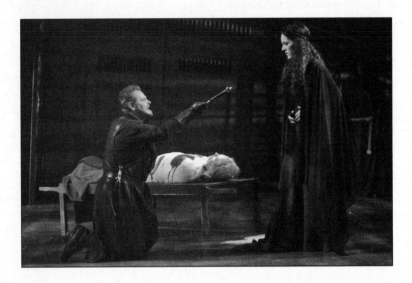

92: "I did not kill your husband": Geraint Wyn Davies as Richard and Claire Lautier as Lady Anne in the 2007 Shakespeare Theatre Company production directed by Michael Kahn
Photo: Carol Rosegg

95: **foul throat thou liest:** reference to a proverbial expression, "to give one the lie in the throat"

95-96: **Queen...blood:** in *Henry VI, Part 3* Edward IV and Richard both stab the prince

96: **falchion:** sword with a slight hook; **smoking:** steaming

97: **The which:** the same; **bend:** turn

RICHARD
      Fairer than tongue can name thee, let me have
      Some patient leisure to excuse myself.

LADY ANNE
      Fouler than heart can think thee, thou canst make
      No excuse current, but to hang thyself.

RICHARD
      By such despair, I should accuse myself.   85

LADY ANNE
      And by despairing, shalt thou stand excused,
      For doing worthy vengeance on thyself,
      That didst unworthy slaughter upon others.

RICHARD
      Say that I slew them not?

LADY ANNE
      Then say they wee not slain.   90
      But dead they are, and, devilish slave, by thee.

RICHARD
      I did not kill your husband.

LADY ANNE
      Why then, he is alive.

RICHARD
      Nay, he is dead, and slain by Edward's hands.

LADY ANNE
      In thy foul throat thou liest. Queen Margaret saw   95
      Thy murderous falchion smoking in his blood;
      The which thou once didst bend against her breast,
      But that thy brothers beat aside the point.

102: **aught:** anything
103: **grant:** agree with
104: **hedgehog:** a mocking reference to Richard's heraldic symbol of the boar
109: **holp:** helped

113: Scene: **Some...bedchamber:** In light of what has been said in the preceding 112 lines this can be either a startling or a frightening exchange. Olivier, who broke the wooing scene into two parts, had Anne (Claire Bloom) spit in Richard's face at this point, then exit with the body of Henry VI. Olivier then inserted an augmented version of his meeting with Clarence (lines 42-116), afterwards resuming the wooing scene at line 119. Thus, Anne spits on him again. Sher (Alexander, 1984) hovered over Anne from behind, with legs and crutches astride her as she knelt at the head of Henry VI's corpse. Zoe Wanamaker (Howell, 1983) looked at Richard with wide eyes, and on line 146 clapped her hands over her mouth in surprise and fright after she spat on him. Kristin Scott Thomas (Loncraine, 1995) appeared not to hear Richard.

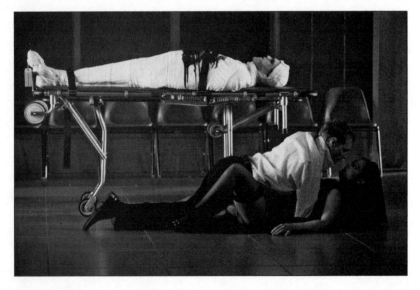

113: "Your bedchamber": Wallace Acton as Richard and Caroline Bootle as Lady Anne in the 2003 Shakespeare Theatre Company production directed by Gale Edwards
Photo: Carol Rosegg

RICHARD
I was provokèd by her sland'rous tongue,
That laid their guilt upon my guiltless shoulders.   100

LADY ANNE
Thou wast provokèd by thy bloody mind,
That never dream'st on aught but butcheries.
Didst thou not kill this king?

RICHARD
                                        I grant ye.

LADY ANNE
Dost grant me, hedgehog? Then God grant me too
Thou mayst be damnèd for that wicked deed.   105
O, he was gentle, mild, and virtuous.

RICHARD
The fitter for the King of heaven that hath him.

LADY ANNE
He is in heaven, where thou shalt never come.

RICHARD
Let him thank me, that holp to send him thither,
For he was fitter for that place than earth.   110

LADY ANNE
And thou unfit for any place, but hell.

RICHARD
Yes, one place else, if you will hear me name it.

LADY ANNE
Some dungeon.

RICHARD
                        Your bedchamber.

119: **timeless:** untimely

122: **effect:** executioner or agent, see line 121

123: **effect:** consequence or result

129: **wrack:** ruin

129-130: "These eyes could not endure that beauty's wrack. / You should not blemish it, if I stood by": Aidan McArdle as Richard and Aislin McGuckin as Lady Anne in the 2001 Royal Shakespeare Company production directed by Michael Boyd

Photo: Donald Cooper

LADY ANNE
  Ill rest betide the chamber where thou liest.

RICHARD
  So will it, madam, till I lie with you.   115

LADY ANNE
  I hope so.

RICHARD
                    I know so. But, gentle Lady Anne,
  To leave this keen encounter of our wits,
  And fall something into a slower method:
  Is not the causer of the timeless deaths
  Of these Plantagenets, Henry and Edward,   120
  As blameful as the executioner?

LADY ANNE
  Thou wast the cause, and most accursed effect.

RICHARD
  Your beauty was the cause of that effect;
  Your beauty, that did haunt me in my sleep,
  To undertake the death of all the world,   125
  So I might live one hour in your sweet bosom.

LADY ANNE
  If I thought that, I tell thee homicide,
  These nails should rend that beauty from my cheeks.

RICHARD
  These eyes could not endure that beauty's wrack.
  You should not blemish it, if I stood by.   130
  As all the world is cheerèd by the sun,
  So I by that. It is my day, my life.

LADY ANNE
  Black night o'ershade thy day, and death thy life.

Denzel Washington as Richard and Sharon Washington as Lady Anne in the 1990
Public Theater production directed by Robin Phillips

Photo: George E. Joseph

136: **quarrel:** argument

138: **quarrel:** cause or reason

145: **nature:** character

RICHARD
Curse not thyself, fair creature, thou art both.

LADY ANNE
I would I were, to be revenged on thee.   135

RICHARD
It is a quarrel most unnatural
To be revenged on him that loveth thee.

LADY ANNE
It is a quarrel just and reasonable
To be revenged on him that killed my husband.

RICHARD
He that bereft thee, lady, of thy husband,   140
Did it to help thee to a better husband.

LADY ANNE
His better doth not breathe upon the earth.

RICHARD
He lives that loves thee better than he could.

LADY ANNE
Name him.

RICHARD
                    Plantagenet.

LADY ANNE
                              Why, that was he.

RICHARD
The selfsame name, but one of better nature.   145

LADY ANNE
Where is he?

tracks 5-7

140-207:
Saskia Wickham as Lady Anne and David Troughton as Richard
Estelle Kohler as Lady Anne and Bill Homewood as Richard

146: Scene: **Where...me:** On the early stages the spit might only be a sound and motion involving no liquid ejection, hence Richard's "Why dost thou spit at me?" Cibber and all productions in the eighteenth and nineteenth centuries cut the spitting, usually replacing it with contemptuous looks on the part of Anne. Once the spitting was restored in the twentieth century, lighting and realism seemed to require that a considerable volume of liquid should be projected, and many a Richard uttered his part-line with spittle dripping from his face, no doubt in response to Anne's "Never hung poison on a fouler toad" (line 149). Sher (Alexander, 1984) wiped the spittle from his face and transferred it to Anne's, continuing the motion down between her breasts.

147: **mortal:** deadly
149: **toad:** toads were considered to be poisonous
152: **basilisks:** mythical reptiles able to kill with their look
153: **at once:** once and for all

153-172: Scene: **I would...speak:** Cibber, following the First Quarto, cut the historical references, as did many productions well into the nineteenth century. Some Richards have heavily emphasized his weeping, notably Branagh (Naxos Audio, 2001).

158-160: **No...at him:** Edmund (Earl of Rutland, son of Richard, Duke of York and brother to Edward IV, Clarence, and Richard) was killed by Lord Clifford (Young Clifford) in *Henry VI, Part 3*, 1.3 after the Battle of Wakefield, 30 December 1460.
161: **warlike father:** Anne's father was Richard Neville, Earl of Warwick, known as The Kingmaker (see note 1.1.153).
162: **father's death:** According to Shakespeare in *Henry VI, Part 3* (1.4), Richard, Duke of York, was also killed after the Battle of Wakefield by Queen Margaret and Clifford, who put a paper crown on him and taunted him. Historical records show he was indeed killed at that time, his head struck off and displayed on the walls of the city of York.
167: **exhale:** draw forth
169: **sued:** appealed

RICHARD

        Here.

[She] spits at him

        Why dost thou spit at me?

LADY ANNE
Would it were mortal poison for thy sake.

RICHARD
Never came poison from so sweet a place.

LADY ANNE
Never hung poison on a fouler toad.
Out of my sight, thou dost infect mine eyes.   150

RICHARD
Thine eyes, sweet lady, have infected mine.

LADY ANNE
Would they were basilisks, to strike thee dead.

RICHARD
I would they were, that I might die at once;
For now they kill me with a living death.
Those eyes of thine from mine have drawn salt tears,   155
Shamed their aspect with store of childish drops.
These eyes which never shed remorseful tear,
No, when my father York and Edward wept,
To hear the piteous moan that Rutland made
When black-faced Clifford shook his sword at him.   160
Nor when thy warlike father, like a child,
Told the sad story of my father's death,
And twenty times made pause to sob and weep,
That all the standers-by had wet their cheeks
Like trees bedashed with rain. In that sad time   165
My manly eyes did scorn an humble tear;
And what these sorrows could not thence exhale,
Thy beauty hath, and made them blind with weeping.
I never sued to friend nor enemy;

tracks 5-7

140-207:
Saskia Wickham as Lady Anne and David Troughton as Richard
Estelle Kohler as Lady Anne and Bill Homewood as Richard

170: **smoothing:** flattering
171: **fee:** i.e., fee for pleading his case
172: **sues:** pleads
179: **lay it naked:** lay his chest bare, or unarmed

180: Stage Direction: *He lays his breast open: she offers at [it] with his sword*: Only the First Folio provides this direction (the First Quarto has none) with no indication that she offers to stab him more than once, even though lines 181 and 183 might indicate two or three attempts. Cibber added four more lines of dialogue during which the sword could be raised and lowered four times in all. This tradition of multiple sword lifts persisted well into the nineteenth century.

180: Stage Direction: *He lays his breast open*: Kevin Kline as Richard and Madeleine Potter as Lady Anne in the 1983 Public Theater production directed by Jane Howell
Photo: George E. Joseph

183: **dispatch:** make haste
188: Scene: **Then...do it:** Although the early editions provide no direction here, most productions have Richard take up the weapon Anne has dropped and direct it against himself.

My tongue could never learn sweet smoothing word,   170
But now thy beauty is proposed my fee,
My proud heart sues, and prompts my tongue to speak.
                                        She looks scornfully at him
Teach not thy lip such scorn, for it was made
For kissing, lady, not for such contempt.
If thy revengeful heart cannot forgive,   175
Lo, here I lend thee this sharp-pointed sword,
Which if thou please to hide in this true breast
And let the soul forth that adoreth thee,
I lay it naked to the deadly stroke,
And humbly beg the death upon my knee.   180
                                        He lays his breast open:
                                she offers at [it] with his sword.
Nay, do not pause, for I did kill King Henry,
But 'twas thy beauty that provokèd me.
Nay, now dispatch; 'twas I that stabbed young Edward,
But 'twas thy heavenly face that set me on.
                                        She [lets] fall the sword
Take up the sword again, or take up me.   185

LADY ANNE
    Arise, dissembler: though I wish thy death,
    I will not be the executioner.

RICHARD
    Then bid me kill myself, and I will do it.

LADY ANNE
    I have already.

RICHARD
                        That was in thy rage.
    Speak it again, and, even with the word,   190
    This hand, which, for thy love did kill thy love,
    Shall for thy love kill a far truer love.
    To both their deaths thou shalt be accessory.

LADY ANNE
    I would I knew thy heart.

140-207:
Saskia Wickham as Lady Anne and David Troughton as Richard
Estelle Kohler as Lady Anne and Bill Homewood as Richard

195: **figured:** described
197: **was man:** from the First Quarto, the First Folio reads, "Man was"
198: **put up:** put away, sheathe
203: Speech Prefix: **RICHARD:** the speech prefix is omitted in the First Folio
203: Scene: **Vouchsafe to wear this ring:** McKellen (Eyre, 1990) removed his ring by using his teeth and sucking so that the ring, when presented to Anne, was covered in his saliva.
203-204: **RICHARD Vouchsafe...give:** from the First Quarto, the line is not in the First Folio

205: "Look how my ring encompasseth thy finger": Sir Laurence Olivier as Richard and Claire Bloom as Lady Anne in the 1955 film directed by Sir Laurence Olivier
Courtesy of Douglas Lanier

RICHARD
  'Tis figured in my tongue.   195

LADY ANNE
  I fear me both are false.

RICHARD
  Then never was man true.

LADY ANNE
  Well, well, put up your sword.

RICHARD
  Say then my peace is made.

LADY ANNE
  That shalt you know hereafter.   200

RICHARD
  But shall I live in hope?

LADY ANNE
  All men I hope live so.

RICHARD
  Vouchsafe to wear this ring.

LADY ANNE
  To take is not to give.

RICHARD
  Look how my ring encompasseth thy finger,   205
  Even so thy breast encloseth my poor heart.
  Wear both of them, for both of them are thine,
  And if thy poor devoted servant may
  But beg one favor at thy gracious hand,
  Thou dost confirm his happiness forever.   210

LADY ANNE
  What is it?

214: **presently:** at once; **Crosby House:** once Richard's London residence on the Thames in what is now Chelsea, often called Crosby Place; owned later (1532) by Sir Thomas More

Kenneth Branagh as Richard and Claire Price as Lady Anne in the 2002 Sheffield Crucible production directed by Michael Grandage

Photo: Donald Cooper

226: Stage Direction: *[Exeunt LADY] ANNE, with [TRESSEL and BERKELEY]:* The First Folio's direction is *"Exit two with Anne."* and the First Quarto's is merely *"Exit."* Since Tressel and Berkeley are her attendants, they are the likely pair to escort her.

227: **RICHARD...the corse:** from the First Quarto, the line is not in the First Folio. It would appear that the question in the second half of this line must be in response to a previous command.

228: **Whitefriars:** a Carmelite monastery on Fleet Street in London. Since it was not lesser in dignity than Chertsey, we must assume Richard chooses it because it is closer.

229: **humor:** style or spirit

229–265:
Kenneth Branagh as Richard
Antony Sher as Richard

tracks 8-10

RICHARD
    That it would please thee leave these sad designs
    To him that hath more cause to be a mourner,
    And presently repair to Crosby House,
    Where, after I have solemnly interred   215
    At Chertsey monastery this noble King,
    And wet his grave with my repentant tears,
    I will with all expedient duty see you.
    For divers unknown reasons, I beseech you,
    Grant me this boon.   220

LADY ANNE
    With all my heart, and much it joys me too,
    To see you are become so penitent.
    Tressel and Berkeley, go along with me.

RICHARD
    Bid me farewell.

LADY ANNE
                    'Tis more than you deserve;
    But since you teach me how to flatter you,   225
    Imagine I have said farewell already.
                    [Exeunt LADY] ANNE with [TRESSEL and BERKELEY]

RICHARD
    Sirs, take up the corse.

GENTLEMEN
                    Towards Chertsey, noble lord?

RICHARD
    No, to Whitefriars. There attend my coming.
                    [Exeunt GENTLEMEN with] corpse
    Was ever woman in this humor wooed?
                    [Manet RICHARD]
    Was ever woman in this humor won?   230
    I'll have her, but I will not keep her long.
    What? I, that killed her husband and his father,

Stacy Keach as Richard in the 1990 Shakespeare Theatre Company production directed by Michael Kahn

Photo: Joan Marcus

tracks 8-10

229–265:
Kenneth Branagh as Richard
Antony Sher as Richard

237: **withal:** as well

239: **All the world to nothing:** against vast odds, proverbial

243: **Tewkesbury:** battle at which Edward IV defeated the forces of Henry VI (1471); Shakespeare portrays this battle in *Henry VI, Part 3*

245: **Framed...nature:** extremely well formed

246: **right:** very

247: **afford:** produce

248: **abase:** make base, cast down

251: **moiety:** half

252: **halts:** limps

253: **My dukedom...denier:** A denier was a small copper coin of little value; Richard is saying either that he has misjudged his worth (his dukedom) or that he would bet his dukedom against a denier.

257: **be at charges:** pay for

258: **entertain:** employ

264: **glass:** mirror

To take her in her heart's extremest hate,
With curses in her mouth, tears in her eyes,
The bleeding witness of her hatred by,   235
Having God, her conscience, and these bars against me,
And I no friends to back my suit withal,
But the plain devil, and dissembling looks,
And yet to win her? All the world to nothing.
Ha!   240
Hath she forgot already that brave prince,
Edward, her lord, whom I some three months since
Stabbed in my angry mood at Tewkesbury?
A sweeter and a lovelier gentleman,
Framed in the prodigality of nature,   245
Young, valiant, wise, and, no doubt, right royal,
The spacious world cannot again afford.
And will she yet abase her eyes on me,
That cropped the golden prime of this sweet prince,
And made her widow to a woeful bed?   250
On me, whose all not equals Edward's moiety?
On me, that halts and am misshapen thus?
My dukedom to a beggarly denier,
I do mistake my person all this while!
Upon my life, she finds, although I cannot,   255
Myself to be a marv'lous proper man.
I'll be at charges for a looking glass,
And entertain some score or two of tailors,
To study fashions to adorn my body.
Since I am crept in favor with myself,   260
I will maintain it with some little cost.
But first I'll turn yon fellow in his grave,
And then return lamenting to my love.
Shine out fair sun, till I have bought a glass,
That I may see my shadow as I pass.   265

Exit

0: Scene: This was omitted by Cibber and other productions well into the nineteenth century. Olivier (1955) heavily cut it, eliminating Margaret's character entirely. Loncraine (1995) abbreviated the scene considerably and introduced Edward IV toward the end of it; Richard did not appear in it. Without Margaret this scene loses a good deal of its fun. Loncraine assigned some of Margaret's worst epithets for Richard to Queen Elizabeth.

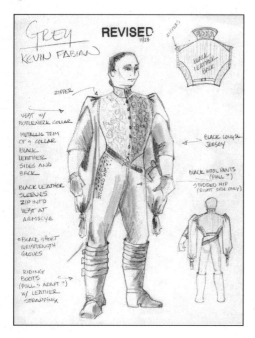

Costume rendering for Lord Grey by Deborah M. Dryden from the 1993 Oregon Shakespeare Festival production directed by James Edmondson

Courtesy of Oregon Shakespeare Festival

3: **In that:** because; **brook it:** take it
4: **entertain:** accept
5: **quick:** lively
6: **If...me:** In the First Folio this line is printed twice without variation. However, there is no reason for Queen Elizabeth to speak the line twice, so the repetition is deleted; **betide on:** become of
11: **minority:** period when he is too young to govern alone
15: **concluded:** officially determined and decreed
16: **miscarry:** die

Act 1, Scene 3]

Enter QUEEN [ELIZABETH], LORD RIVERS, and LORD GREY

RIVERS
    Have patience, madam: there's no doubt his Majesty
    Will soon recover his accustomed health.

GREY
    In that you brook it ill, it makes him worse.
    Therefore, for God's sake, entertain good comfort,
    And cheer his Grace with quick and merry eyes.   5

QUEEN ELIZABETH
    If he were dead, what would betide on me?

RIVERS
    No other harm but loss of such a lord.

QUEEN ELIZABETH
    The loss of such a lord includes all harms.

GREY
    The heavens have blessed you with a goodly son,
    To be your comforter when he is gone.   10

QUEEN ELIZABETH
    Ah, he is young, and his minority
    Is put unto the trust of Richard Gloucester,
    A man that loves not me, nor none of you.

RIVERS
    Is it concluded he shall be Protector?

QUEEN ELIZABETH
    It is determined, not concluded yet.   15
    But so it must be, if the King miscarry.
        Enter BUCKINGHAM and [LORD STANLEY, EARL OF] DERBY

20: **Countess Richmond:** i.e., Margaret Beaufort, now Stanley's wife. She was first married to Edmund Tudor, Earl of Richmond, by whom she had Henry, the Earl of Richmond of this play.

26: **envious:** malicious

29: **wayward sickness:** an illness not readily responding to treatment; **grounded:** firmly established

31: **But now:** just now

33: **amendment:** recovery

GREY
  Here come the Lords of Buckingham and Derby.

BUCKINGHAM
  Good time of day unto your royal Grace.

STANLEY
  God make your Majesty joyful as you have been.

QUEEN ELIZABETH
  The Countess Richmond, good my Lord of Derby,   20
  To your good prayers will scarcely say amen.
  Yet, Derby, notwithstanding she's your wife,
  And loves not me, be you, good lord, assured
  I hate not you for her proud arrogance.

STANLEY
  I do beseech you, either not believe   25
  The envious slanders of her false accusers;
  Or if she be accused on true report,
  Bear with her weakness which, I think, proceeds
  From wayward sickness, and no grounded malice.

QUEEN ELIZABETH
  Saw you the King today, my Lord of Derby?   30

STANLEY
  But now the Duke of Buckingham and I
  Are come from visiting his Majesty.

QUEEN ELIZABETH
  What likelihood of his amendment, lords?

BUCKINGHAM
  Madam, good hope; his Grace speaks cheerfully.

QUEEN ELIZABETH
  God grant him health. Did you confer with him?   35

36: **atonement:** reconciliation

37: **brothers:** Only one of Queen Elizabeth's brothers, Anthony Woodville, whose titles were Earl Rivers and Lord Scales, has a part in this play. Shakespeare has Richard split them into three separate persons at 2.1.67 and 2.1.69.

39: **warn:** summon

42-53: Scene: **They...Jacks:** This is an abrupt and verbally violent entry, typical of Richard's dealing with those around him, be they friend or enemy. Richard's usual entrance is to burst onto the stage. Olivier (1955), using the medium of film, showed Richard joking with his associates outside the door before bursting in with indignation. Here, as in most other cases in the first half of the play, Richard is almost always acting.

45: **holy Paul:** i.e., St. Paul

48: **smooth:** flatter; **cog:** cheat

49: **Duck:** bow, in the affected French manner

53: **With:** by; **silken, sly:** smooth and deceitful; **Jacks:** low class worthless fellows, with perhaps a play on the French name "Jacques"

55: "To thee, that hast nor honesty nor grace": Shane McRae as Lord Grey, Mercedes Herrero as Queen Elizabeth, Peter Dinklage as Richard and James Yaegashi as Marquess of Dorset in the 2004 Public Theater production directed by Peter DuBois
Photo: Michal Daniel

60: **a breathing while:** the time it takes to draw a breath

61: **lewd:** wicked

62: **Brother:** i.e., brother-in-law

63: **disposition:** inclination

BUCKINGHAM
  Ay, madam, he desires to make atonement
  Between the Duke of Gloucester and your brothers,
  And between them and my Lord Chamberlain,
  And sent to warn them to his royal presence.

QUEEN ELIZABETH
  Would all were well, but that will never be,   40
  I fear our happiness is at the height.
                    Enter RICHARD, [HASTINGS, and DORSET]

RICHARD
  They do me wrong, and I will not endure it.
  Who is it that complains unto the King,
  That I, forsooth, am stern, and love them not?
  By holy Paul, they love his Grace but lightly   45
  That fill his ears with such dissentious rumors.
  Because I cannot flatter and look fair,
  Smile in men's faces, smooth, deceive and cog,
  Duck with French nods, and apish courtesy,
  I must be held a rancorous enemy.   50
  Cannot a plain man live, and think no harm,
  But thus his simple truth must be abused
  With silken, sly, insinuating Jacks?

GREY
  To whom in all this presence speaks your Grace?

RICHARD
  To thee, that hast nor honesty nor grace.   55
  When have I injured thee? When done thee wrong?
  Or thee? or thee? or any of your faction?
  A plague upon you all. His royal Grace,
  Whom God preserve better than you would wish,
  Cannot be quiet scarce a breathing while,   60
  But you must trouble him with lewd complaints.

QUEEN ELIZABETH
  Brother of Gloucester, you mistake the matter.
  The King, of his own royal disposition,

65: **Aiming, belike, at:** probably looking at

68: **send:** send for; **ground:** basis

71: **Jack became a gentleman:** proverbial expression, "Jack would be a gentleman," for "Jack" see line 1.3.53

72: **gentle person:** those with the right to bear a coat of arms; a gentleman or higher rank

76: **we:** from the First Quarto, the First Folio reads "I". Richard means himself and his family (see the following lines) and may, even at this early stage, be employing the royal "we".

81: **scarce:** scarcely; **noble:** 1) gold coin worth a third of a pound, and 2) nobleman

82: **careful height:** exalted position full of care

83: **hap:** fortune or chance

88: **in:** into; **suspects:** suspicions

89: **mean:** instrument, agency, or method employed to bring about a result

And not provoked by any suitor else,
Aiming, belike, at your interior hatred,   65
That in your outward action shows itself
Against my children, brothers, and myself,
Makes him to send, that thereby he may learn the ground.

RICHARD
I cannot tell. The world is grown so bad
That wrens make prey where eagles dare not perch.   70
Since every Jack became a gentleman
There's many a gentle person made a Jack.

QUEEN ELIZABETH
Come, come, we know your meaning, brother Gloucester.
You envy my advancement and my friends'.
God grant we never may have need of you.   75

RICHARD
Meantime, God grants that we have need of you.
Our brother is imprisoned by your means,
Myself disgraced, and the nobility
Held in contempt; whilst many fair promotions
Are daily given to ennoble those   80
That scarce some two days since were worth a noble.

QUEEN ELIZABETH
By Him that raised me to this careful height
From that contented hap which I enjoyed,
I never did incense his Majesty
Against the Duke of Clarence, but have been   85
An earnest advocate to plead for him.
My lord, you do me shameful injury,
Falsely to draw me in these vile suspects.

RICHARD
You may deny that you were not the mean
Of my Lord Hastings' late imprisonment.

                                                              90
RIVERS
She may, my lord, for—

96: **desert:** merits, deserts
97: **marry:** indeed
101: **Iwis:** certainly

102: Scene: **My Lord of Gloucester:** In the BBC production (Howell, 1983), Margaret (Julia Foster) entered on this line and crouched at the back of the chair or throne upon which Queen Elizabeth sat. Her asides were delivered directly to the camera.

105: **gross:** flagrant
108: **baited:** harassed, tormented, as in bull or bear baiting

108: Stage Direction: ***QUEEN MARGARET:*** i.e., Margaret of Anjou, the widow of Henry VI. Her role in this play is extra-historical since she lived in France from January 22, 1476 until her death in 1482. She was, therefore, neither in England nor alive during the time being here portrayed; ***[behind]:*** Edward Capell (1768) is the first editor to emend this direction to indicate that Queen Margaret does not enter among the others at this point. This is further supported by what she says at 1.3.156-158.

110: Scene: ***[Aside]:*** Margaret's asides have always presented a problem for both actors and directors. As portrayed, she is an embittered former queen, and she runs the risk of being something of a bore. In addition, although her asides are comments on what is being said by the others, they are also interruptions to the free flow of the argument between the court factions. Henry Irving in his 1877 production simply cut them; Olivier (1955) cut the entire character; Loncraine (1995) changed the scene by merging Margaret and the Duchess of York into a single character (Maggie Smith). Bill Alexander (1984) handled the asides in an interesting fashion, having the other actors freeze when Margaret was talking, and, in at least the first one, darkening the stage save for a light on Margaret.

111: **state:** high rank or greatness; **seat:** throne
112: **threat:** threaten
113: **Tell...said:** (found only in the quarto editions)
114: **avouch:** acknowledge
115: **adventure:** risk
116: **pains:** efforts, on Edward's behalf

RICHARD
    She may, Lord Rivers, why, who knows not so?
    She may do more, sir, than denying that.
    She may help you to many fair preferments,
    And then deny her aiding hand therein,   95
    And lay those honors on your high desert.
    What may she not, she may, ay, marry may she—

RIVERS
    What marry may she?

RICHARD
    What, marry, may she? Marry with a king,
    A bachelor, a handsome stripling too,   100
    Iwis your grandam had a worser match.

QUEEN ELIZABETH
    My Lord of Gloucester, I have too long borne
    Your blunt upbraidings, and your bitter scoffs.
    By heaven, I will acquaint his Majesty
    Of those gross taunts I often have endured.   105
    I had rather be a country servant maid
    Than a great Queen, with this condition,
    To be thus baited, scorned, and stormèd at.
                 Enter old QUEEN MARGARET, [behind]
    Small joy have I in being England's Queen.

QUEEN MARGARET
    [Aside] And lessened be that small, God, I beseech Him,   110
    Thy honor, state, and seat is due to me.

RICHARD
    What? threat you me with telling of the King?
    Tell him, and spare not. Look, what I have said,
    I will avouch in presence of the King.
    I dare adventure to be sent to the Tower.   115
    'Tis time to speak, my pains are quite forgot.

121: **packhorse:** beast of burden or drudgery

124: **spent:** 1) spilt or 2) lost

127: **factious for:** of the faction supporting

128: **husband:** i.e., Sir John Grey, Queen Elizabeth's first husband

129: **battle:** battalion; **Saint Albans:** Second Battle of St. Albans, February 17, 1461

132: **Withal:** at the same time

134: **father:** i.e., father-in-law

135: **forswore:** perjured

138: **meed:** reward; **mewed:** caged or imprisoned

QUEEN MARGARET
> [*Aside*] Out, devil, I remember them too well.
> Thou killed'st my husband Henry in the Tower,
> And Edward, my poor son, at Tewkesbury.

RICHARD
> Ere you were Queen, ay, or your husband King,   120
> I was a packhorse in his great affairs,
> A weeder-out of his proud adversaries,
> A liberal rewarder of his friends,
> To royalize his blood, I spent mine own.

QUEEN MARGARET
> [*Aside*] Ay, and much better blood than his or thine.   125

RICHARD
> In all which time you and your husband Grey
> Were factious for the House of Lancaster;
> And, Rivers, so were you. Was not your husband
> In Margaret's battle at Saint Albans slain?
> Let me put in your minds, if you forget,   130
> What you have been ere now, and what you are;
> Withal, what I have been, and what I am.

QUEEN MARGARET
> [*Aside*] A murd'rous villain, and so still thou art.

RICHARD
> Poor Clarence did forsake his father Warwick,
> Ay, and forswore himself, which Jesu pardon!—   135

QUEEN MARGARET
> [*Aside*] Which God revenge!

RICHARD
> —To fight on Edward's party for the crown.
> And for his meed, poor lord, he is mewed up.
> I would to God my heart were flint, like Edward's,
> Or Edward's soft and pitiful, like mine.   140
> I am too childish-foolish for this world.

142: **Hie:** go quickly

143: **cacodemon:** evil spirit

154: **As:** all early editions read "A" and this reading has been much debated. Benjamin Heath (1765) proposed "As" which has been widely adopted, but R. G. White (1865) emended to "And", Antony Hammond (1987) emended to "Ay,", David Bevington (1988) and Peter Holland (2000) emended to "Ah,". Some editors, such as G. Blakemore Evans (1969 and 1974) retain the early editions' reading of "A". Here, it is emended to "As" since it is a parallel grammatical construction with Queen Elizabeth's preceding speech.

157: **fall out:** quarrel

158: **pilled:** pillaged

163: **what mak'st thou:** what are you doing

163: "Foul, wrinkled witch, what mak'st thou in my sight?": Alan Howard as Richard and Barbara Leigh-Hunt in the 1980 Royal Shakespeare Company production directed by Terry Hands

Photo: Donald Cooper

QUEEN MARGARET
[*Aside*] Hie thee to hell for shame, and leave the world,
Thou cacodemon, there thy kingdom is.

RIVERS
My Lord of Gloucester, in those busy days
Which here you urge to prove us enemies,   145
We followed then our lord, our sovereign king.
So should we you, if you should be our king.

RICHARD
If I should be? I had rather be a pedlar.
Far be it from my heart, the thought thereof.

QUEEN ELIZABETH
As little joy, my lord, as you suppose   150
You should enjoy, were you this country's king,
As little joy may you suppose in me
That I enjoy, being the Queen thereof.

QUEEN MARGARET
[*Aside*] As little joy enjoys the Queen thereof,
For I am she, and altogether joyless.   155
I can no longer hold me patient.
                                          [Coming forward]
Hear me, you wrangling pirates, that fall out
In sharing that which you have pilled from me.
Which of you trembles not that looks on me?
If not, that I am queen, you bow like subjects,   160
Yet that, by you deposed, you quake like rebels.
[*To RICHARD*] Ah gentle villain, do not turn away.

RICHARD
Foul, wrinkled witch, what mak'st thou in my sight?

QUEEN MARGARET
But repetition of what thou hast marred,
That will I make, before I let thee go.   165

166: Wert thou not banished on pain of death: In fact, Margaret was *not* banished and was dead by the time of these events; see note for 1.3.108. "Pain" here means to require something under threat of penalty; Margaret plays with its more common meaning in the next line.

168: abode: abiding, being here

170: "And thou a kingdom; all of you allegiance": Jennifer Harmon as Queen Margaret, David Sabin as Lord Hastings, Diana LaMar as Queen Elizabeth, and Wallace Acton as Richard in the 2003 Shakespeare Theatre Company production directed by Gale Edwards

Photo: Carol Rosegg

173-179: The curse...fallen upon thee: Richard here recounts the events in *Henry VI, Part 3*, 1.4.

176: clout: cloth or rag

177: Rutland: see note 1.2.158-160

182: babe: i.e., Rutland. In point of fact, Rutland was seventeen, one year younger than Edward IV and nine years older than Richard, when he was killed at the Battle of Wakefield in 1460.

RICHARD
    Wert thou not banished on pain of death?

QUEEN MARGARET
    I was; but I do find more pain in banishment
    Than death can yield me here by my abode.
    A husband and a son thou ow'st to me;
    [*To QUEEN ELIZABETH*] And thou a kingdom; all of you allegiance.
    The sorrow that I have by right is yours,
    And all the pleasures you usurp are mine.

RICHARD
    The curse my noble father laid on thee,
    When thou didst crown his warlike brows with paper,
    And with thy scorns drew'st rivers from his eyes,   175
    And then, to dry them, gav'st the duke a clout
    Steeped in the faultless blood of pretty Rutland—
    His curses, then from bitterness of soul,
    Denounced against thee, are all fallen upon thee;
    And God, not we, hath plagued thy bloody deed.   180

QUEEN ELIZABETH
    So just is God, to right the innocent.

HASTINGS
    O, 'twas the foulest deed to slay that babe,
    And the most merciless that e'er was heard of.

RIVERS
    Tyrants themselves wept when it was reported.

DORSET
    No man but prophesied revenge for it.   185

BUCKINGHAM
    Northumberland, then present, wept to see it.

QUEEN MARGARET
    What, were you snarling all before I came,
    Ready to catch each other by the throat,

193: **peevish:** foolish or silly, frequently applied to small children

195: **quick:** lively

196: **surfeit:** overindulgence, usually to the point of sickness

198: **Edward:** i.e., the eldest son of Edward IV and Elizabeth Woodville; **Prince of Wales:** From 1301, when Edward I gave this title to the future Edward II, to the present day, the heir to the English throne is invested with this title.

200: **like:** similar; **untimely:** before his time, i.e., to die young

205: **stalled:** installed

211: **God, I pray Him:** I pray to God

213: **unlooked:** unlooked for

214: **charm:** curse

218: **them:** heaven

221: **still:** continue to

And turn you all your hatred now on me?
Did York's dread curse prevail so much with heaven   190
That Henry's death, my lovely Edward's death,
Their kingdom's loss, my woeful banishment,
Should all but answer for that peevish brat?
Can curses pierce the clouds and enter heaven?
Why then give way dull clouds to my quick curses.   195
Though not by war, by surfeit die your King,
As ours by murder, to make him a king.
Edward thy son, which now is Prince of Wales,
For Edward our son, that was Prince of Wales,
Die in his youth, by like untimely violence.   200
Thyself a queen, for me that was a queen,
Outlive thy glory, like my wretched self.
Long mayst thou live, to wail thy children's death,
And see another, as I see thee now,
Decked in thy rights, as thou art stalled in mine.   205
Long die thy happy days before thy death,
And after many lengthened hours of grief,
Die neither mother, wife, nor England's Queen.
Rivers and Dorset, you were standers by,
And so wast thou, Lord Hastings, when my son   210
Was stabbed with bloody daggers. God, I pray Him,
That none of you may live his natural age,
But by some unlooked accident cut off.

RICHARD
    Have done thy charm, thou hateful withered hag.

QUEEN MARGARET
    And leave out thee? Stay, dog, for thou shalt hear me.   215
    If heaven have any grievous plague in store
    Exceeding those that I can wish upon thee,
    O let them keep it, till thy sins be ripe,
    And then hurl down their indignation
    On thee, the troubler of the poor world's peace.   220
    The worm of conscience still begnaw thy soul,
    Thy friends suspect for traitors while thou liv'st,
    And take deep traitors for thy dearest friends.

227: **elvish-marked:** marked at birth by elves or fairies; **abortive:** prematurely born; **hog:** Richard's heraldic symbol

228: **sealed:** stamped at birth

229: **slave of nature:** physically deformed

230: **heavy:** 1) heavily pregnant, and 2) sad

234: **cry thee mercy:** beg your pardon

237: **period:** conclusion

240: **painted:** imitation; **vain flourish:** useless decoration

241: **strew'st thou sugar:** spread sweet words; **bottled spider:** spider appearing to be hunchbacked because it is swollen with venom

No sleep close up that deadly eye of thine,
Unless it be whilst some tormenting dream   225
Affrights thee with a hell of ugly devils.
Thou elvish-marked, abortive, rooting hog,
Thou that wast sealed in thy nativity
The slave of nature and the son of hell.
Thou slander of thy mother's heavy womb.   230
Thou loathèd issue of thy father's loins,
Thou rag of honor, thou detested—

RICHARD
                              Margaret.

QUEEN MARGARET
  Richard!

RICHARD
                    Ha!

QUEEN MARGARET
                              I call thee not.

RICHARD
  I cry thee mercy, then, for I did think
  That thou hadst called me all these bitter names.   235

QUEEN MARGARET
  Why so I did, but looked for no reply.
  O let me make the period to my curse.

RICHARD
  'Tis done by me, and ends in "Margaret."

QUEEN ELIZABETH
  Thus have you breathed your curse against yourself.

QUEEN MARGARET
  Poor painted queen, vain flourish of my fortune,   240
  Why strew'st thou sugar on that bottled spider,
  Whose deadly web ensnareth thee about?

245: **bunch-backed:** humpbacked

246: **False-boding:** falsely prophesying; **frantic:** mad or exaggerated

249: **well served:** properly advised

250: **do me duty:** do me homage, i.e., bow

Tana Hicken as Queen Margaret in the 2007 Shakespeare Theatre Company production directed by Michael Kahn

Photo: Carol Rosegg

254: **malapert:** impudent

255: **fire-new stamp:** recently cast, a reference to the newness of Dorset's title; **scarce:** hardly or barely

261: **touches:** applies to

262: **but:** for or because

263: **aerie:** nest of an eagle, also a brood of young eagles; i.e., the sons of the Duke of York; **buildeth:** is built

264: **dallies:** plays; **scorns:** treats disdainfully

Fool, fool, thou whet'st a knife to kill thyself.
The day will come that thou shalt wish for me
To help thee curse that poisonous bunch-backed toad.   245

HASTINGS
False-boding woman, end thy frantic curse,
Lest to thy harm thou move our patience.

QUEEN MARGARET
Foul shame upon you, you have all moved mine.

RIVERS
Were you well served, you would be taught your duty.

QUEEN MARGARET
To serve me well, you all should do me duty,   250
Teach me to be your queen, and you my subjects.
O, serve me well, and teach yourselves that duty.

DORSET
Dispute not with her; she is lunatic.

QUEEN MARGARET
Peace, master Marquess, you are malapert,
Your fire-new stamp of honor is scarce current.   255
O, that your young nobility could judge
What 'twere to lose it, and be miserable.
They that stand high have many blasts to shake them,
And if they fall, they dash themselves to pieces.

RICHARD
Good counsel, marry, learn it, learn it, Marquess.   260

DORSET
It touches you, my lord, as much as me.

RICHARD
Ay, and much more, but I was born so high,
Our aerie buildeth in the cedar's top,
And dallies with the wind, and scorns the sun.

265: **turns the sun to shade:** makes overcast or darkens

270: **suffer:** allow

271: **was:** from the First Quarto, the First Folio reads "is"

272: **charity:** see note 1.2.68

278-293: Scene: **Have done...attend on him:** In Alexander's production (RSC, 1984), Margaret spoke to Buckingham in the center of the stage, but it was not clear whether or not the others heard what was being said since they did not move.

281: **fair befall:** good fortune happen to

283: **compass:** circle or scope

286: **not think but:** believe

288: **dog:** i.e., Richard

289: **Look when:** whenever

290: **venom:** envenomed; **rankle:** infect

QUEEN MARGARET

    And turns the sun to shade. Alas, alas,   265
    Witness my son, now in the shade of death,
    Whose bright out-shining beams thy cloudy wrath
    Hath in eternal darkness folded up.
    Your aerie buildeth in our aerie's nest.
    O God, that seest it, do not suffer it.   270
    As it was won with blood, lost be it so.

BUCKINGHAM

    Peace, peace, for shame, if not for charity.

QUEEN MARGARET

    Urge neither charity nor shame to me.
    Uncharitably with me have you dealt,
    And shamefully my hopes, by you, are butchered.   275
    My charity is outrage, life my shame,
    And in that shame still live my sorrow's rage.

BUCKINGHAM

    Have done, have done.

QUEEN MARGARET

    O princely Buckingham I'll kiss thy hand,
    In sign of league and amity with thee.   280
    Now fair befall thee and thy noble house.
    Thy garments are not spotted with our blood,
    Nor thou within the compass of my curse.

BUCKINGHAM

    Nor no one here, for curses never pass
    The lips of those that breathe them in the air.   285

QUEEN MARGARET

    I will not think but they ascend the sky,
    And there awake God's gentle sleeping peace.
    O Buckingham, take heed of yonder dog.
    Look when he fawns, he bites; and when he bites,
    His venom tooth will rankle to the death.   290

293: **attend on:** wait upon or serve

294: Scene: **What...Buckingham:** Because of this line, some editors have marked part or all of Margaret's lines that are addressed to Buckingham as an aside to him. In performance, it is clearly the case that she is speaking to Buckingham, but there is no textual evidence that the others do not hear her words. Richard's line is as likely to be a scornful comment as it is a literal question. On stage, if Richard chooses to turn away after line 264, then he is in a physical position to pretend not to hear her.

302: **My...end:** Bogdanov (1989) gave this line to Hastings rather than Buckingham.

308: Speech Prefix: **QUEEN ELIZABETH:** In the First Folio, the speech prefix is *"Mar.",* Queen Margaret's prefix hitherto.

309: **vantage:** advantage or benefit; **her wrong:** i.e., the wrong done to her

310: **somebody:** i.e., Edward IV, his brother

313: **franked up to fatting:** penned up like cattle being fattened for slaughter; **pains:** efforts (for Edward IV, his brother)

Have not to do with him, beware of him.
Sin, death, and hell have set their marks on him,
And all their ministers attend on him.

RICHARD
What doth she say, my Lord of Buckingham?

BUCKINGHAM
Nothing that I respect, my gracious lord.   295

QUEEN MARGARET
What, dost thou scorn me for my gentle counsel?
And soothe the devil that I warn thee from?
O but remember this another day,
When he shall split thy very heart with sorrow,
And say, poor Margaret, was a prophetess.   300
Live each of you the subjects to his hate,
And he to yours, and all of you to God's.

                                                                    Exit

BUCKINGHAM
My hair doth stand on end to hear her curses.

RIVERS
And so doth mine. I muse why she's at liberty.

RICHARD
I cannot blame her, by God's holy mother,   305
She hath had too much wrong, and I repent
My part thereof, that I have done to her.

QUEEN ELIZABETH
I never did her any, to my knowledge.

RICHARD
Yet you have all the vantage of her wrong.
I was too hot to do somebody good   310
That is too cold in thinking of it now.
Marry, as for Clarence, he is well repaid.
He is franked up to fatting for his pains.
God pardon them that are the cause thereof.

316: **scathe:** harm
317: **ever:** always; **well advised:** careful, wary

317: Stage Direction: The First Folio's direction, "*Speakes to himselfe.*", is set between 1.3.317 and 1.3.318.

Costume rendering for Catesby from the 1953 production at the Shakespeare Memorial Theatre in Stratford-upon-Avon directed by Glen Byam Shaw
Rare Book and Special Collection Library, University of Illinois at Urbana-Champaign

320: **lords:** the First Folio reads "Lord" and the First Quarto "Lo". However, since only the Queen and Richard are referred to in the remainder of the speech, Catesby must be addressing the others (i.e., the lords) here.

322: Scene: ***Exeunt all but RICHARD:*** In the Alexander production (RSC, 1984), Margaret's crown was thrown on the floor as all others exit.

323: **brawl:** noisy quarrel
324: **mischiefs:** evil actions or suggestions; **set abroach:** propagated or published abroad
325: **lay:** attribute
327: **gulls:** fools or gullible people
331: **withal:** in addition to; **whet:** urge
336: **odd old ends:** random bits and pieces
339: **mates:** fellows

RIVERS
> A virtuous, and a Christian-like conclusion,   315
> To pray for them that have done scathe to us.

RICHARD
> So do I ever—*speaks to himself*—being well advised,
> For had I cursed now, I had cursed myself.

Enter Catesby

CATESBY
> Madam, his Majesty doth call for you,
> And for your Grace, and yours, my gracious lords.   320

QUEEN ELIZABETH
> Catesby, I come, lords will you go with me?

RIVERS
> We wait upon your Grace.

Exeunt all but RICHARD

RICHARD
> I do the wrong, and first begin to brawl.
> The secret mischiefs that I set abroach
> I lay unto the grievous charge of others.   325
> Clarence, who I indeed have cast in darkness,
> I do beweep to many simple gulls,
> Namely to Derby, Hastings, Buckingham,
> And tell them 'tis the Queen and her allies
> That stir the King against the duke my brother.   330
> Now they believe it and withal whet me
> To be revenged on Rivers, Dorset, Grey.
> But then I sigh, and with a piece of scripture,
> Tell them that God bids us do good for evil;
> And thus I clothe my naked villainy   335
> With odd old ends stolen forth of holy writ,
> And seem a saint, when most I play the devil.

Enter two MURDERERS

> But soft, here come my executioners.
> How now, my hardy stout resolvèd mates,
> Are you now going to dispatch this thing?   340

341: Speech Prefix: **MURDERER:** The speech prefix in the First Folio for this character is "*Viline*" for Villain. In the First Quarto, he is called Executioner and given the speech prefix "*Execue.*"

345: **sudden:** immediate

346: **Withal:** moreover

348: **mark him:** pay attention to him

349: **stand to prate:** stand around and chat

352: **Your...tears:** proverbial expression communicating a lack of compassion

353: **straight:** immediately

MURDERER

  We are, my lord; and come to have the warrant
  That we may be admitted where he is.

RICHARD

  Well thought upon. I have it here about me.

  [Gives the warrant]

  When you have done, repair to Crosby Place.
  But sirs be sudden in the execution,   345
  Withal obdurate, do not hear him plead;
  For Clarence is well spoken, and perhaps
  May move your hearts to pity if you mark him.

MURDERER

  Tut, tut, my lord, we will not stand to prate.
  Talkers are no good doers be assured.   350
  We go to use our hands, and not our tongues.

RICHARD

  Your eyes drop millstones, when fools' eyes drop tears.
  I like you, lads, about your business straight.
  Go, go, dispatch.

MURDERER

                    We will, my noble lord.

                                                            [Exeunt]

0: Scene: This scene was cut by Cibber, most unfortunately for Clarence, since it leaves him with only seven speeches for a total of sixteen and a half lines. Without this scene, Clarence's character is largely determined by what others say about him. With this scene (restored to performances in the middle of the nineteenth century), it becomes obvious that Clarence is something of a performance poet, and several of his speeches (e.g., lines 1.4.2-74, barring the short interruptions by the Keeper) were applauded much in the way a tenor might be when finishing a very grand aria.

0: Stage Direction: *KEEPER*: Jailer. In the First Quarto (and almost all modern productions) the Keeper's lines are given to Brakenbury, thus combining the two roles.

tracks 11-13

9-75:
Tenniel Evans as Clarence
Clifford Rose as Clarence

13: **hatches:** raised openings on the deck
14: **cited up:** remembered
19: **stay:** catch or support
24: **wracks:** wrecks

Set rendering for 1953 production at the Shakespeare Memorial Theatre in Stratford-upon-Avon directed by Glen Byam Shaw
Rare Book and Special Collection Library, University of Illinois at Urbana-Champaign

Act 1, Scene 4]

KEEPER
Why looks your Grace so heavily today?

CLARENCE
O, I have passed a miserable night,
So full of fearful dreams, of ugly sights,
That as I am a Christian faithful man,
I would not spend another such a night   5
Though 'twere to buy a world of happy days,
So full of dismal terror was the time.

KEEPER
What was your dream, my lord? I pray you tell me.

CLARENCE
Methoughts that I had broken from the Tower,
And was embarked to cross to Burgundy;   10
And in my company my brother Gloucester,
Who from my cabin tempted me to walk
Upon the hatches. There we looked toward England,
And cited up a thousand heavy times,
During the wars of York and Lancaster   15
That had befall'n us. As we paced along
Upon the giddy footing of the hatches,
Methought that Gloucester stumbled, and, in falling
Struck me, that thought to stay him, overboard
Into the tumbling billows of the main.   20
O Lord, methought what pain it was to drown,
What dreadful noise of water in mine ears,
What sights of ugly death within mine eyes.
Methoughts, I saw a thousand fearful wracks,
A thousand men that fishes gnawed upon,   25

tracks 11-13

9–75:
Tenniel Evans as Clarence
Clifford Rose as Clarence

27: **Inestimable...unvalued:** valuable beyond the ability to assign value

37: **yield the ghost:** die, as in the expression, "give up the ghost"; **envious flood:** malicious water of the ocean

38: **Stopped:** closed up, as a stopper in a bottle

41: **Who:** which

45: **melancholy flood:** i.e., the River Styx of the classical underworld

46: **sour ferryman:** Charon, who ferried dead souls across Styx into Hades; **poets:** Virgil in his *Aeneid* and Dante in his *Inferno*

48: **stranger-soul:** newly arrived soul

50: **scourge:** punishment

51: **afford:** provide for

53: **shadow:** ghost or shade, this one of Edward, the son of Henry VI

54: **Dabbled in:** spattered with

55: **fleeting:** fickle

Wedges of gold, great anchors, heaps of pearl,
Inestimable stones, unvalued jewels,
All scattered in the bottom of the sea.
Some lay in dead men's skulls, and in those holes
Where eyes did once inhabit, there were crept,   30
As 'twere in scorn of eyes, reflecting gems,
Which wooed the slimy bottom of the deep
And mocked the dead bones that lay scattered by.

KEEPER
Had you such leisure in the time of death
To gaze upon these secrets of the deep?   35

CLARENCE
Methought I had, and often did I strive
To yield the ghost, but still the envious flood
Stopped my soul and would not let it forth
To find the empty, vast, and wand'ring air,
But smothered it within my panting bulk,   40
Who almost burst to belch it in the sea.

KEEPER
Awaked you not with this sore agony?

CLARENCE
No, no, my dream was lengthened after life.
O, then began the tempest to my soul.
I passed, methought, the melancholy flood,   45
With that sour ferryman which poets write of,
Unto the kingdom of perpetual night.
The first that there did greet my stranger-soul
Was my great father-in-law, renownèd Warwick,
Who spake aloud "What scourge for perjury   50
Can this dark monarchy afford false Clarence?"
And so he vanished. Then came wand'ring by
A shadow like an angel, with bright hair
Dabbled in blood, and he shrieked out aloud,
"Clarence is come; false, fleeting, perjured Clarence,   55
That stabbed me in the field by Tewkesbury.

9-75:
Tenniel Evans as Clarence
Clifford Rose as Clarence

57: **Furies:** The Furies, or Erinyes, in Greek and Roman mythology were the three daughters of Mother Earth. They represented conscience and punished crimes against kindred, pursuing their victims until they died in a "furor" of madness or torment.

58: **foul fiends:** devils

59: **Environed:** surrounded

61: **season:** period of time

74: **fain would:** desire to

76: **breaks seasons:** interrupts normality; **reposing hours:** normal periods of sleep

76-83: Scene: **Sorrow...fame:** In the BBC version (Howells, 1983) this was delivered by Brakenbury (Derek Farr) as a soliloquy directly to the camera.

80: **for unfelt imagination:** for pleasures that are only imaginary

82: **between...name:** between those of high rank and those of low rank

83: Stage Direction: ***Enter two MURDERERS:*** From the restoration of this scene in the middle of the nineteenth century to well into the twentieth century, the two Murderers were played as comic characters, more as Dogberry and Verges in *Much Ado About Nothing* than as the Murderers in *Macbeth*, even though reviewers and observers objected to this. George Bernard Shaw, commenting on Henry Irving's 1897 production, thought the two were pantomime characters from *Babes in the Wood*. As inappropriate as it may seem, "Look behind you, my lord" (line 243), shouted just before Clarence is stabbed, can be, and usually is, a comic turn.

Seize on him, Furies, take him unto torment."
With that, methought, a legion of foul fiends
Environed me, and howlèd in mine ears
Such hideous cries, that with the very noise   60
I trembling, waked, and for a season after
Could not believe but that I was in hell,
Such terrible impression made my dream.

KEEPER
No marvel, lord, though it affrighted you,
I am afraid, methinks, to hear you tell it.   65

CLARENCE
Ah, Keeper, Keeper, I have done these things,
That now give evidence against my soul,
For Edward's sake, and see how he requites me.
O God, if my deep prayers cannot appease Thee,
But Thou wilt be avenged on my misdeeds,   70
Yet execute Thy wrath in me alone.
O, spare my guiltless wife and my poor children.
Keeper, I prithee sit by me awhile.
My soul is heavy, and I fain would sleep.

KEEPER
I will, my lord. God give your Grace good rest.   75
                                            [CLARENCE sleeps]
                            Enter BRAKENBURY, THE LIEUTENANT

BRAKENBURY
Sorrow breaks seasons and reposing hours,
Makes the night morning, and the noontide night.
Princes have but their titles for their glories,
An outward honor for an inward toil,
And, for unfelt imagination,   80
They often feel a world of restless cares,
So that between their titles, and low name,
There's nothing differs but the outward fame.
                                    Enter two MURDERERS

FIRST MURDERER
Ho, who's here?

85: **how...hither:** by what authority did you enter here

89: **commission:** warrant

93: **will be:** wish to be; **from:** of

95: **signify:** tell or confirm

99- 135, 139-245: Scene: **What...Strike, In God's...within:** Olivier (1955) cut this line in his film. Loncraine (1995) cut a good deal of the Murderers' chat, and they killed Clarence in his bath by cutting his throat.

Costume rendering for Brakenbury from the 1953 production at the Shakespeare Memorial Theatre in Stratford-upon-Avon directed by Glen Byam Shaw

BRAKENBURY
What wouldst thou, fellow? And how cam'st thou hither?   85

SECOND MURDERER
I would speak with Clarence, and I came hither on my legs.

BRAKENBURY
What, so brief?

FIRST MURDERER
'Tis better, sir, than to be tedious.
Let him see our commission, and talk no more.

[BRAKENBURY] reads

BRAKENBURY
I am in this commanded to deliver   90
The noble Duke of Clarence to your hands.
I will not reason what is meant hereby
Because I will be guiltless from the meaning.
There lies the duke asleep, and there the keys.
I'll to the King; and signify to him   95
That thus I have resigned to you my charge.

FIRST MURDERER
You may, sir, 'tis a point of wisdom.
Fare you well.

Exit [BRAKENBURY and KEEPER]

SECOND MURDERER
What, shall we stab him as he sleeps?

FIRST MURDERER
No. He'll say 'twas done cowardly, when he wakes.   100

SECOND MURDERER
Why, he shall never wake, until the great judgment day.

FIRST MURDERER
Why then he'll say we stabbed him sleeping.

103: **remorse:** pity or compassion

111: **passionate:** compassionate; **humor:** disposition

112: **was wont:** was usually; **tells:** counts to

Costume rendering for First Murderer from the 1953 production at the Shakespeare Memorial Theatre in Stratford-upon-Avon directed by Glen Byam Shaw

Rare Book and Special Collection Library, University of Illinois at Urbana-Champaign

116: **'Zounds:** This oath ("God's wounds") is found in the First Quarto; the First Folio reads "Come". This and other oaths were removed from printings that occurred after the "Act to Restrain the Abuses of Players" of May 27, 1606. We assume that this change also occurred on stage as well as in print.

SECOND MURDERER
The urging of that word "judgment" hath bred a kind of remorse in me.

FIRST MURDERER
What, art thou afraid?   105

SECOND MURDERER
Not to kill him, having a warrant, but to be damned for killing him, from which no warrant can defend me.

FIRST MURDERER
I thought thou hadst been resolute.

SECOND MURDERER
So I am, to let him live.

FIRST MURDERER
I'll back to the Duke of Gloucester and tell him so.   110

SECOND MURDERER
Nay, I prithee stay a little. I hope this passionate humor of mine will change. It was wont to hold me but while one tells twenty.

FIRST MURDERER
How dost thou feel thyself now?

SECOND MURDERER
Some certain dregs of conscience are yet within me.

FIRST MURDERER
Remember our reward, when the deed's done.   115

SECOND MURDERER
'Zounds, he dies. I had forgot the reward.

FIRST MURDERER
Where's thy conscience now?

SECOND MURDERER
O, in the Duke of Gloucester's purse.

121: **entertain:** receive or accept

132: **'Zounds:** oath ("God's wounds") removed under the "Act to Restrain the Abuses of Players"; see note 1.4.116

134: **him:** i.e., your conscience

137: **tall:** brave

139: **Take him:** attack him; **costard:** head

FIRST MURDERER
When he opens his purse to give us our reward, thy conscience
flies out.   120

SECOND MURDERER
'Tis no matter, let it go. There's few or none will entertain it.

FIRST MURDERER
What if it come to thee again?

SECOND MURDERER
I'll not meddle with it. It makes a man a coward: a man cannot
steal but it accuseth him; a man cannot swear but it checks him;
a man cannot lie with his neighbor's wife but it detects him. 'Tis   125
a blushing, shamefaced spirit that mutinies in a man's bosom. It
fills one full of obstacles. It made me once restore a purse of gold
that, by chance, I found. It beggars any man that keeps it. It is
turned out of towns and cities for a dangerous thing, and every
man that means to live well endeavors to trust to himself and to   130
live without it.

FIRST MURDERER
'Zounds, it is even now at my elbow, persuading me not to kill the
duke.

SECOND MURDERER
Take the devil in thy mind, and believe him not. He would
insinuate with thee but to make thee sigh.   135

FIRST MURDERER
I am strong framed, he cannot prevail with me.

SECOND MURDERER
Spoke like a tall man that respects his reputation. Come, shall we
fall to work?

FIRST MURDERER
Take him on the costard, with the hilts of thy sword, and then

140: **malmsey butt:** barrel of malmsey wine, a sweet strong wine

141: **sop:** a cake or wafer dipped in wine

142: **Soft:** look

145: **anon:** soon

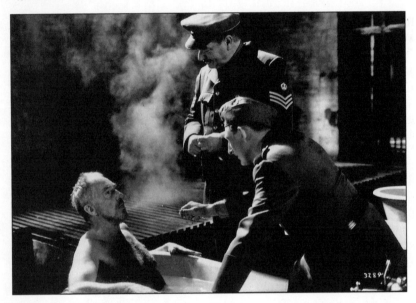

146: "In God's name, what art thou?": Nigel Hawthorne as Clarence and Andy Rashleigh and Adrian Dunbar as Murderers in the 1995 film directed by Richard Loncraine
Courtesy of Douglas Lanier

152: **darkly...deadly:** ominously

throw him into the malmsey butt in the next room.   140

SECOND MURDERER
O excellent devise; and make a sop of him.

FIRST MURDERER
Soft, he wakes.

SECOND MURDERER
                    Strike!

FIRST MURDERER
No, we'll reason with him.

CLARENCE
Where art thou Keeper? Give me a cup of wine.

SECOND MURDERER
You shall have wine enough, my lord, anon.   145

CLARENCE
In God's name, what art thou?

FIRST MURDERER
A man, as you are.

CLARENCE
But not as I am, royal.

FIRST MURDERER
Nor you as we are, loyal.

CLARENCE
Thy voice is thunder, but thy looks are humble.   150

FIRST MURDERER
My voice is now the King's, my looks mine own.

CLARENCE
How darkly and how deadly dost thou speak?

154: **Wherefore:** why

164: **drawn...men:** selected out of all mankind

167: **quest:** inquest

170: **convict:** convicted

172: **charge:** order

172-173: **to have...sins:** This passage is taken from the First Quarto; the First Folio reads "for any goodnesse". Modern editors usually adopt this reading because we suspect that the First Folio reading is the result of censorship of the mention of Christ's blood (see note 1.4.116).

175: **damnable:** both terrible and bringing damnation upon one

Your eyes do menace me. Why look you pale?
Who sent you hither? Wherefore do you come?

SECOND MURDERER
To, to, to—   155

CLARENCE
To murder me?

BOTH MURDERERS
Ay, ay.

CLARENCE
You scarcely have the hearts to tell me so,
And therefore cannot have the hearts to do it.
Wherein, my friends, have I offended you?   160

FIRST MURDERER
Offended us you have not, but the King.

CLARENCE
I shall be reconciled to him again.

SECOND MURDERER
Never, my lord, therefore prepare to die.

CLARENCE
Are you drawn forth among a world of men
To slay the innocent? What is my offense?   165
Where is the evidence that doth accuse me?
What lawful quest have given their verdict up
Unto the frowning judge? Or who pronounced
The bitter sentence of poor Clarence' death,
Before I be convict by course of law?   170
To threaten me with death is most unlawful.
I charge you, as you hope to have redemption,
By Christ's dear blood shed for our grievous sins,
That you depart and lay no hands on me.
The deed you undertake is damnable.   175

FIRST MURDERER
What we will do, we do upon command.

178: **Erroneous:** deluded

179: **table:** Ten Commandments

181: **Spurn:** contemptuously reject

185: **false forswearing:** breaking an oath

186: **receive the sacrament:** swore solemnly at mass upon the sacrament

187: **In...Lancaster:** to fight for Henry VI (House of Lancaster) against his brothers Edward IV and Richard (House of York)

188-190: **And...son:** First Murderer describes Clarence violating his solemn and sacred vow and fighting with his brothers against Henry VI and helping to kill Edward, Henry's son.

190: **Unrippedst:** all the early editions read "Vnrip'st"; ripped open

193: **dear degree:** great extent

201: **indirect:** secret or hidden

203: **minister:** agent or officer

SECOND MURDERER
  And he that hath commanded is our King.

CLARENCE
  Erroneous vassals, the great King of kings
  Hath in the table of His law commanded
  That thou shalt do no murder. Will you then   180
  Spurn at His edict, and fulfil a man's?
  Take heed for He holds vengeance in His hand,
  To hurl upon their heads that break His law.

SECOND MURDERER
  And that same vengeance doth He hurl on thee
  For false forswearing and for murder too.   185
  Thou didst receive the sacrament, to fight
  In quarrel of the House of Lancaster.

FIRST MURDERER
  And, like a traitor to the name of God,
  Didst break that vow, and with thy treacherous blade
  Unrippedst the bowels of thy sovereign's son.   190

SECOND MURDERER
  Whom thou wast sworn to cherish and defend.

FIRST MURDERER
  How canst thou urge God's dreadful law to us,
  When thou hast broke it in so dear degree?

CLARENCE
  Alas! For whose sake did I that ill deed?
  For Edward, for my brother, for his sake.   195
  He sends you not to murder me for this,
  For in this sin he is as deep as I.
  If God will be avengèd for the deed,
  O, know you yet He doth it publicly.
  Take not the quarrel from His powerful arm;   200
  He needs no indirect, or lawless, course
  To cut off those that have offended Him.

FIRST MURDERER
  Who made thee then a bloody minister,

204: **gallant-springing:** valiant and lively; **Plantagenet:** i.e., Edward, Henry VI's son

James Ricks and Carl Palmer as the murderers and Andrew Long as Clarence in the 2007 Shakespeare Theatre Company production directed by Michael Kahn
Photo: Carol Rosegg

211: **meed:** reward

219: **arm:** the First Quarto adds the line, "And charged us from his soul to love each other"

222: **millstones:** see note 1.3.352; **lessoned:** taught

When gallant-springing brave Plantagenet,
That princely novice, was struck dead by thee?   205

CLARENCE
My brother's love, the devil, and my rage.

FIRST MURDERER
Thy brother's love, our duty, and thy faults,
Provoke us hither now to slaughter thee.

CLARENCE
If you do love my brother, hate not me.
I am his brother, and I love him well.   210
If you be hired for meed, go back again,
And I will send you to my brother Gloucester,
Who shall reward you better for my life
Than Edward will for tidings of my death.

SECOND MURDERER
You are deceived. Your brother Gloucester hates you.   215

CLARENCE
O no, he loves me, and he holds me dear.
Go you to him from me.

FIRST MURDERER
                              Ay, so we will.

CLARENCE
Tell him, when that our princely father York
Blessed his three sons with his victorious arm,
He little thought of this divided friendship.   220
Bid Gloucester think on this, and he will weep.

FIRST MURDERER
Ay, millstones, as he lessoned us to weep.

CLARENCE
O do not slander him, for he is kind.

FIRST MURDERER
Right, as snow in harvest. Come, you deceive yourself.

226: **bewept:** wept for; **fortune:** misfortune

228: **labor:** labor for

230: **thraldom:** enslavement

239-243: **Which...distress:** These lines are found only in the First Folio; no comparable passage is in the First Quarto, where Clarence has only the last half of 1.4.231.

240: **pent:** shut up

'Tis he that sends us to destroy you here.   225

CLARENCE
It cannot be, for he bewept my fortune,
And hugged me in his arms, and swore with sobs
That he would labor my delivery.

FIRST MURDERER
Why so he doth, when he delivers you
From this earth's thraldom to the joys of heaven.   230

SECOND MURDERER
Make peace with God, for you must die, my lord.

CLARENCE
Have you that holy feeling in your souls
To counsel me to make my peace with God,
And are you yet to your own souls so blind,
That you will war with God by murd'ring me?   235
O sirs consider, they that set you on
To do this deed will hate you for the deed.

SECOND MURDERER
What shall we do?

CLARENCE
                    Relent, and save your souls.
Which of you, if you were a prince's son,
Being pent from liberty, as I am now,   240
If two such murderers as yourselves came to you,
Would not entreat for life, as you would beg
Were you in my distress.

FIRST MURDERER
Relent? No. 'Tis cowardly and womanish.

CLARENCE
Not to relent is beastly, savage, devilish.   245

251: Stage Direction: *Stabs him*: Ann Ogbomo and Liza Hayden as murderers, and Rachel Sanders and Clarence in the 2003 Shakespeare's Globe production directed by Barry Kyle
Photo: Donald Cooper

254: **Pilate:** Pontius Pilate, see Matthew 27:24

265: **will out:** will become known

My friend, I spy some pity in thy looks.
O, if thine eye be not a flatterer,
Come thou on my side and entreat for me,
A begging prince, what beggar pities not?

SECOND MURDERER
Look behind you, my lord.   250

FIRST MURDERER
Take that, and that. If all this will not do,

Stabs him

I'll drown you in the malmsey butt within.

Exit[, with the body]

SECOND MURDERER
A bloody deed, and desperately dispatched.
How fain, like Pilate, would I wash my hands
Of this most grievous murder.   255

[Reenter] FIRST MURDERER

FIRST MURDERER
How now? what mean'st thou that thou help'st me not? By
heaven, the duke shall know how slack you have been.

SECOND MURDERER
I would he knew that I had saved his brother.
Take thou the fee, and tell him what I say,
For I repent me that the duke is slain.   260

Exit

FIRST MURDERER
So do not I. Go, coward as thou art.
Well, I'll go hide the body in some hole
Till that the duke give order for his burial.
And when I have my meed, I must away,
For this will out, and here I must not stay.   265

Exit

[Richard III

Act 2

0: Scene: This scene was cut by Cibber. Even when the scene was restored, the role of Edward IV was not much noticed until at least Henry Cass's production at the Old Vic in 1936. In Olivier's productions in the 1940s and in his film in 1955, Jane Shore was among the *"and others"* in the entry and eyed Hastings, her new lover, from behind Edward's bed. Loncraine (1995) set this as a picnic in a garden of what appeared to be the Royal Pavilion at Brighton.

1-42: Scene: **Why, so...sickly heart:** Since nearly every word in these lines is ironic actors can, and often have, assumed all sorts of expressions and bodily movements to indicate their lack of true goodwill. Edward, often played as an ill and dissipated old man (*"Enter . . . sick"*), usually takes them at their word.

2: **united league:** mutual compact
3: **embassage:** message or ambassador
5: **in:** from the First Quarto, the First Folio reads "to"
7: **Rivers and Hastings:** from the First Quarto, the First Folio reads, *"Dorset* and *Rivers"*. However, it is Rivers and Hastings who first speak in answer to the King's request. Also, with Rivers being Queen Elizabeth's brother and Dorset her son, it is not likely they are in need of reconciliation.
9: **from:** of
12: **dally:** trifle
14: **award:** cause

Set rendering for the 1953 production at the Shakespeare Memorial Theatre in Stratford-upon-Avon directed by Glen Byam Shaw
Rare Book and Special Collection Library, University of Illinois at Urbana-Champaign

Act 2, Scene 1]

Flourish. Enter KING [EDWARD IV] sick,
QUEEN [ELIZABETH], DORSET,
RIVERS, HASTINGS, CATESBY,
BUCKINGHAM, GREY, [and others]

KING EDWARD IV
  Why, so. Now have I done a good day's work.
  You peers, continue this united league.
  I every day expect an embassage
  From my Redeemer to redeem me hence.
  And more in peace my soul shall part to heaven,   5
  Since I have made my friends at peace on earth.
  Rivers and Hastings, take each other's hand,
  Dissemble not your hatred. Swear your love.

RIVERS
  By heaven, my soul is purged from grudging hate,
  And with my hand I seal my true heart's love.   10

HASTINGS
  So thrive I, as I truly swear the like.

KING EDWARD IV
  Take heed you dally not before your king,
  Lest he that is the supreme king of kings
  Confound your hidden falsehood, and award
  Either of you to be the other's end.   15

HASTINGS
  So prosper I, as I swear perfect love.

RIVERS
  And I, as I love Hastings with my heart.

19: **son:** i.e., stepson

20: **been factious:** formed factions against each other

22: **unfeignedly:** sincerely

25: **Marquess:** i.e., Dorset

Costume rendering for King Edward IV from the 1953 production at the Shakespeare Memorial Theatre in Stratford-upon-Avon directed by Glen Byam Shaw
Rare Book and Special Collection Library, University of Illinois at Urbana-Champaign

30: **embracements to:** embraces of

32-35: **Whenever...love:** the construction is not coherent; "but" is probably meant to be taken as "nor" or "and not"

39: **God:** from the First Quarto, the First Folio reads "heaven"

KING EDWARD IV
>Madam, yourself is not exempt in this.
>Nor you, son Dorset, Buckingham, nor you.
>You have been factious one against the other.   20
>Wife, love Lord Hastings, let him kiss your hand,
>And what you do, do it unfeignedly.

QUEEN ELIZABETH
>There, Hastings; I will never more remember
>Our former hatred, so thrive I and mine.

KING EDWARD IV
>Dorset, embrace him. Hastings, love Lord Marquess.   25

DORSET
>This interchange of love, I here protest,
>Upon my part shall be inviolable.

HASTINGS
>And so swear I.

KING EDWARD IV
>Now princely Buckingham, seal thou this league
>With thy embracements to my wife's allies,   30
>And make me happy in your unity.

BUCKINGHAM
>[*To QUEEN ELIZABETH*] Whenever Buckingham doth turn his hate
>Upon your Grace, but with all duteous love
>Doth cherish you and yours, God punish me
>With hate in those where I expect most love.   35
>When I have most need to employ a friend,
>And most assurèd that he is a friend,
>Deep, hollow, treacherous, and full of guile,
>Be he unto me. This do I beg of God,
>When I am cold in love to you or yours.   40

41: **cordial:** restoring drink
44: **period:** conclusion

46: Scene: ***Enter RATCLIFF:*** Jane Howell (1983) had the character of Ratcliff (Anthony Brown) played throughout as a rather superior civil servant, always observing, always with a folder of papers in his hand, always reserved. He was a presence even in scenes where he did not speak or where he speaks little. Loncraine (1995) had Richard accompanied by Anne. He combined parts of the roles of Ratcliff, Lovell, and Tyrrel so that only two actors performed the three roles.

The Ensemble in the 1990 Shakespeare Theatre Company production directed by Michael Kahn

Photo: Joan Marcus

47: **morrow:** morning
52: **swelling:** indignant; **wrong-incensèd:** mistakenly angry
54: **heap:** large assemblage, used ironically
57: **unwittingly:** from the First Quarto, the First Folio reads "unwillingly"
58: **hardly borne:** resented
59: **By:** from the First Quarto, the First Folio reads "To"
67: **Lord Rivers and of Dorset:** see note for 1.3.37
68: **desert:** deserving
69: **Of...you:** line omitted from the quartos; see note for 1.3.37

KING EDWARD IV
> A pleasing cordial, princely Buckingham,
> Is this thy vow unto my sickly heart.
> There wanteth now our brother Gloucester here,
> To make the blessèd period of this peace.

BUCKINGHAM
> And, in good time   45
> Here comes Sir Richard Ratcliff and the duke.
>> *Enter RATCLIFF and [RICHARD OF] GLOUCESTER*

RICHARD
> Good morrow to my sovereign king and queen.
> And princely peers, a happy time of day.

KING EDWARD IV
> Happy indeed, as we have spent the day.
> Gloucester, we have done deeds of charity,   50
> Made peace of enmity, fair love of hate,
> Between these swelling wrong-incensèd peers.

RICHARD
> A blessed labor my most sovereign lord.
> Among this princely heap, if any here
> By false intelligence, or wrong surmise,   55
> Hold me a foe,
> If I unwittingly, or in my rage,
> Have aught committed that is hardly borne
> By any in this presence, I desire
> To reconcile me to his friendly peace.   60
> 'Tis death to me to be at enmity;
> I hate it, and desire all good men's love.
> First, madam, I entreat true peace of you,
> Which I will purchase with my duteous service.
> Of you, my noble cousin Buckingham,   65
> If ever any grudge were lodged between us;
> Of you and you, Lord Rivers and of Dorset,
> That all without desert have frowned on me;
> Of you, Lord Woodville, and Lord Scales, of you;

75-92: Scene: **A holy...him burièd:** The effect of Richard's announcement at line 81 is by its very nature theatrical. Richard can make it in anger, in feigned sadness, or in various ways demonstrating low cunning. That it works is shown in the exchange between Buckingham and Dorset at lines 85-87.

76: **compounded:** settled
78: **to your grace:** into your favor
80: **flouted:** mocked
82: **scorn:** disdain
83: Speech Prefix: **KING EDWARD IV:** This speech is assigned to Rivers in the First Quarto.

83: Scene: **Who knows...is:** Olivier (1955) gave this line to Rivers as did Howell (1983) and Bogdanov (1989), who also cut lines 84-87.

89: "But he, poor man, by your first order died": Tom Nelis as Edward IV and Peter Dinklage as Richard in the 2004 Public Theater production directed by Peter DuBois
Photo: Michal Daniel

90: **wingèd Mercury:** very speedy. Mercury was the messenger of the gods and was usually depicted with winged heels.

Dukes, earls, lords, gentlemen; indeed, of all.   70
I do not know that Englishman alive
With whom my soul is any jot at odds
More than the infant that is born tonight.
I thank my God for my humility.

QUEEN ELIZABETH
A holy day shall this be kept hereafter.   75
I would to God all strifes were well compounded.
My sovereign lord, I do beseech your Highness
To take our brother Clarence to your grace.

RICHARD
Why madam, have I offered love for this
To be so flouted in this royal presence?   80
Who knows not that the gentle duke is dead?

They all start

You do him injury to scorn his corse.

KING EDWARD IV
Who knows not he is dead? Who knows he is?

QUEEN ELIZABETH
All-seeing heaven, what a world is this?

BUCKINGHAM
Look I so pale, Lord Dorset, as the rest?   85

DORSET
Ay, my good lord, and no man in this presence
But his red color hath forsook his cheeks.

KING EDWARD IV
Is Clarence dead? The order was reversed.

RICHARD
But he, poor man, by your first order died,
And that a wingèd Mercury did bear.   90
Some tardy cripple bore the countermand,

92: **lag:** late

93-94: **some less...blood:** a veiled suggestion that the Queen's family ("less noble," "not in blood") is perhaps guilty of Clarence's death ("bloody thoughts")

95: **not worse than:** at least what

96: **go current:** are taken for true (pun on "current" and "currency")

96: Stage Direction: ***Enter...DERBY:*** As Stanley's statement at line 99 indicates, he either prostrates himself before Edward, or at the very least, kneels. Olivier (1955) and Loncraine (1995), though having Stanley present in the chamber, cut his begging speeches and Edward's responses to them.

97: **boon:** favor

101: **The forfeit...life:** the release from the death penalty for my servant

102: **riotous:** troublesome or difficult, given to violent actions

103: **Duke of Norfolk:** probably meant to be John Howard, Duke of Norfolk from June 28, 1483. However, the actual Duke of Norfolk at the date supposed in the play is Richard, Duke of York, the younger of the two sons of Edward IV (whom Richard has murdered).

104: **doom:** condemn, in this case to death

105: **slave:** servant or bond servant

108: **sued:** begged; **in:** during

109: **at:** from the First Quarto, the First Folio reads "and"; **be advised:** take advice

111-115: Scene: **Who...king:** Shakespeare does not include this scene in any of his history plays.

114: **Oxford:** John de Vere, thirteenth Earl of Oxford (1442–1513) was not present at the Battle of Tewkesbury (May 4, 1471), having been on the losing side at the Battle of Barnet (April 14) and fled from there to Scotland.

117: **lap:** wrap

That came too lag to see him burièd.
God grant, that some less noble, and less loyal,
Nearer in bloody thoughts, and not in blood,
Deserve not worse than wretched Clarence did,   95
And yet go current from suspicion.

Enter [LORD STANLEY,] EARL OF DERBY

STANLEY
A boon, my sovereign, for my service done.

KING EDWARD IV
I prithee, peace. My soul is full of sorrow.

STANLEY
I will not rise unless your Highness hear me.

KING EDWARD IV
Then say at once, what is it thou requests.   100

STANLEY
The forfeit, sovereign, of my servant's life,
Who slew today a riotous gentleman,
Lately attendant on the Duke of Norfolk.

KING EDWARD IV
Have I a tongue to doom my brother's death,
And shall that tongue give pardon to a slave?   105
My brother killed no man, his fault was thought,
And yet his punishment was bitter death.
Who sued to me for him? Who, in my wrath,
Kneeled at my feet, and bid me be advised?
Who spoke of brotherhood? Who spoke of love?   110
Who told me how the poor soul did forsake
The mighty Warwick, and did fight for me?
Who told me, in the field by Tewkesbury,
When Oxford had me down, he rescued me,
And said "Dear brother, live, and be a king"?   115
Who told me, when we both lay in the field,
Frozen almost to death, how he did lap me

119: **thin:** thinly covered, wearing only thin clothing; **numb:** numbingly
120: **brutish:** furious
123: **carters:** cart drivers or low uncultured men; **waiting vassals:** servants

133-136: Scene: **O God...Clarence:** These lines imply that Edward's illness is worsened by what has happened and that he needs help, in this case, from Hastings, to get off stage. There is a fine irony in asking Hastings since they both share Jane Shore as a mistress.

135: **closet:** private room
137: Scene: **This is the fruit of rashness:** In the Branagh recording (Naxos, 1999) a bell starts tolling just after this line, indicating the death of Edward.

143: Stage Direction: ***Exeunt:*** Sher (Alexander, 1984) remained on stage here, got on the plinth where Edward's throne had just been, and raised his crutches in a sign of triumph.

143: "We wait upon your Grace": Stacy Keach as Richard and Ted van Griethuysen as Buckingham in the 1990 Shakespeare Theatre Company production directed by Michael Kahn

Photo: Joan Marcus

Even in his own garments and gave himself,
All thin and naked, to the numb cold night?
All this from my remembrance brutish wrath   120
Sinfully plucked, and not a man of you
Had so much grace to put it in my mind.
But when your carters or your waiting vassals
Have done a drunken slaughter, and defaced
The precious image of our dear Redeemer,   125
You straight are on your knees for pardon, pardon;
And I, unjustly too, must grant it you.
But for my brother not a man would speak,
Nor I, ungracious, speak unto myself
For him, poor soul. The proudest of you all   130
Have been beholding to him in his life;
Yet none of you would once beg for his life.
O God, I fear Thy justice will take hold
On me and you, and mine and yours for this.
Come, Hastings, help me to my closet.   135
Ah, poor Clarence.
          Exeunt some with KING EDWARD IV and QUEEN ELIZABETH

RICHARD
This is the fruit of rashness. Marked you not
How that the guilty kindred of the Queen
Looked pale when they did hear of Clarence' death?
O! They did urge it still unto the King.   140
God will revenge it. Come lords, will you go
To comfort Edward with our company.

BUCKINGHAM
We wait upon your Grace.

                                              Exeunt

1: Speech Prefix: **BOY**: This speech prefix is in the First Quarto; the First Folio reads "*Edw.*" in this line and "*Boy*" thereafter. Clarence's son and heir was Edward, later Earl of Warwick, who was executed for treason by Henry VII in 1599.

1-33: Scene: **Good grandam...this:** Cibber cut these lines and almost all productions since have done the same. The Hall/Barton production (Royal Shakespeare Theatre, 1963) ran 2.1 and 2.2 together going straight on from 2.1.141 to 2.2.33 with Richard saying, "Hark, what noise is this?". Bogdanov (1989), having cut the first 33 lines, also removed all of the Duchess of York's speeches up to line 100, when she entered and seated herself in a chair stage right.

3: **you:** the First Folio omits the word, the First Quarto supplies it
4: **unhappy:** unfortunate
8: **cousins:** "Cousin" was used to refer to almost any relative, no matter the degree of relationship.
11: **lost:** wasted
14: **importune:** constantly solicit

Costume rendering for son of Clarence from the 1953 production at the Shakespeare Memorial Theatre in Stratford-upon-Avon directed by Glen Byam Shaw

Act 2, Scene 2]

Enter the old DUCHESS OF YORK,
with the two children of CLARENCE

BOY
  Good grandam tell us, is our father dead?

DUCHESS OF YORK
  No, boy.

DAUGHTER
  Why do you weep so oft? And beat your breast?
  And cry "O Clarence, my unhappy son"?

BOY
  Why do you look on us, and shake your head,   5
  And call us orphans, wretches, castaways,
  If that our noble father were alive?

DUCHESS OF YORK
  My pretty cousins, you mistake me both,
  I do lament the sickness of the King,
  As loath to lose him, not your father's death;   10
  It were lost sorrow to wail one that's lost.

BOY
  Then you conclude, my grandam, he is dead.
  The King mine uncle is to blame for it.
  God will revenge it; whom I will importune
  With earnest prayers, all to that effect.   15

DAUGHTER
  And so will I.

18: **shallow:** inexperienced

22: **impeachments:** charges

26: **And he:** and he said

27: **shape:** appearance or role

28: **visor:** mask

30: **dugs:** breasts, also nipples

31: **Think:** believe

33: Stage Direction: ***with her hair about her ears:*** from the First Folio. In pre-1660 English drama, this was the standard way to portray extreme grief, madness, or distress. Cibber cut this direction, as did productions for most of the eighteenth century, since it would have been impossible to achieve given the elaborate hair arrangements of the period. The direction is not restored to acting editions or prompt books until the twentieth century, and by this time, the theatrical convention had disappeared.

34-100: Scene: **Ah...living Edward's throne:** Most productions considerably shorten these lamentations.

38: **rude:** violent

DUCHESS OF YORK
> Peace, children, peace, the King doth love you well.
> Incapable and shallow innocents,
> You cannot guess who caused your father's death.

BOY
> Grandam, we can, for my good uncle Gloucester   20
> Told me, the King, provoked to it by the Queen,
> Devised impeachments to imprison him;
> And when my uncle told me so, he wept,
> And pitied me, and kindly kissed my cheek,
> Bade me rely on him as on my father,   25
> And he would love me dearly as a child.

DUCHESS OF YORK
> Ah! that deceit should steal such gentle shape,
> And with a virtuous visor hide deep vice.
> He is my son, ay, and therein my shame,
> Yet from my dugs he drew not this deceit.   30

BOY
> Think you my uncle did dissemble, grandam?

DUCHESS OF YORK
> Ay, boy.

BOY
> I cannot think it. Hark, what noise is this?
> > *Enter QUEEN [ELIZABETH] with her hair about her ears,*
> > *RIVERS and DORSET after her*

QUEEN ELIZABETH
> Ah! who shall hinder me to wail and weep,
> To chide my fortune, and torment myself?   35
> I'll join with black despair against my soul,
> And to myself become an enemy.

DUCHESS OF YORK
> What means this scene of rude impatience?

39: **act of tragic violence:** perform violence as found in tragedies

42: **want:** lack

43: **brief:** quick about it

47: **interest:** legal right; **I:** the First Folio omits the word, the First Quarto supplies it

48: **title:** ownership, as in title deed

49: **bewept:** wept for; **husband's death:** i.e., the death of Richard, Duke of York

50: **images:** i.e., Edward IV, Clarence, and Richard

53: **glass:** mirror

60: **moiety:** smaller portion

61: **overgo:** exceed

62: **aunt:** i.e., Queen Elizabeth

63: **kindred tears:** 1) tears of a relative, and 2) similar tears

65: **widow-dolor:** sorrow of a widow

68: **reduce their currents to:** channel or flow into

QUEEN ELIZABETH

To make an act of tragic violence.
Edward, my lord, thy son, our King, is dead.   40
Why grow the branches when the root is gone?
Why wither not the leaves that want their sap?
If you will live, lament. If die, be brief,
That our swift-wingèd souls may catch the King's,
Or, like obedient subjects, follow him   45
To his new kingdom of ne'er-changing night.

DUCHESS OF YORK

Ah, so much interest have I in thy sorrow
As I had title in thy noble husband.
I have bewept a worthy husband's death,
And lived with looking on his images;   50
But now two mirrors of his princely semblance
Are cracked in pieces by malignant death,
And I for comfort have but one false glass,
That grieves me when I see my shame in him.
Thou art a widow, yet thou art a mother,   55
And hast the comfort of thy children left,
But death hath snatched my husband from mine arms,
And plucked two crutches from my feeble hands,
Clarence and Edward. O, what cause have I,
Thine being but a moiety of my moan,   60
To overgo thy woes and drown thy cries.

BOY

Ah, aunt, you wept not for our father's death!
How can we aid you with our kindred tears?

DAUGHTER

Our fatherless distress was left unmoaned.
Your widow-dolor likewise be unwept.   65

QUEEN ELIZABETH

Give me no help in lamentation,
I am not barren to bring forth complaints.
All springs reduce their currents to mine eyes,

69: **watery moon:** the moon, because it controls the tides, is watery. The image in this and the next line seems to envisage her tears becoming a tidal wave.

71: Scene: **Ah...Edward:** Olivier (1955) began the scene with this line and then went on with line 89. Jane Shore was prominent at the death bed.

81: **parceled:** divided into smaller portions; **general:** not divided, all-inclusive

83: **weep:** from the First Quarto, the First Folio reads "weepes"

84-85: **and so...weep:** These words are from the First Quarto; the First Folio nonsensically reads "These Babes for *Clarence* weepe, so do not they."

87: **nurse:** wet-nurse

That I, being governed by the watery moon,
May send forth plenteous tears to drown the world.   70
Ah, for my husband, for my dear lord Edward.

CHILDREN
Ah, for our father, for our dear lord Clarence.

DUCHESS OF YORK
Alas for both, both mine Edward and Clarence.

QUEEN ELIZABETH
What stay had I but Edward, and he's gone?

CHILDREN
What stay had we but Clarence? And he's gone.   75

DUCHESS OF YORK
What stays had I but they? And they are gone.

QUEEN ELIZABETH
Was never widow had so dear a loss.

CHILDREN
Were never orphans had so dear a loss.

DUCHESS OF YORK
Was never mother had so dear a loss.
Alas, I am the mother of these griefs!   80
Their woes are parceled, mine are general.
She for an Edward weeps, and so do I;
I for a Clarence weep, so doth not she;
These babes for Clarence weep, and so do I;
I for an Edward weep, so do not they.   85
Alas, you three, on me, threefold distressed,
Pour all your tears! I am your sorrow's nurse,
And I will pamper it with lamentations.

DORSET
[*To QUEEN ELIZABETH*] Comfort, dear mother. God is much displeased

94: **opposite with:** opposed to

96: **bethink:** think

100: Stage Direction: ***Enter RICHARD:*** Cibber had Richard enter "behind," and many other productions have brought him on stage in various indirect ways, but there seems to be no reason to see this as other than another of Richard's bustling entrances, designed to put others off their guard.

101: **Sister:** i.e., sister-in-law

104: **I do cry you mercy:** I beg your pardon

104-106: Scene: **I do...blessing:** Irving (1877), in a spirit of mockery, spread a hand-kerchief in front of his mother and knelt on it until he rose for his aside at line 109.

107: **breast:** heart

109-111: Scene: **And make...it out:** It is not clear to whom, besides the audience, this aside is addressed. It could be to all those on stage, in which case it is a tremendous insult to his mother. If it is to Buckingham, a likely recipient, then there must be a short pause before Buckingham begins line 112. Ron Cook (Howell, 1983) delivered it directly to the camera.

110: **butt end:** conclusion

111: **I marvel:** I am surprised

112: **cloudy:** darkened by clouds of sorrow; **heart-sorrowing:** heart-sick with grief

113: **moan:** grief

115: **spent:** used up

That you take with unthankfulness His doing.   90
In common worldly things, 'tis called ungrateful,
With dull unwilligness to repay a debt,
Which with a bounteous hand was kindly lent;
Much more to be thus opposite with heaven,
For it requires the royal debt it lent you.   95

RIVERS
Madam, bethink you, like a careful mother,
Of the young prince your son. Send straight for him,
Let him be crowned. In him your comfort lives.
Drown desperate sorrow in dead Edward's grave,
And plant your joys in living Edward's throne.   100
          Enter RICHARD, BUCKINGHAM, [LORD STANLEY, EARL OF]
                    DERBY, HASTINGS, and RATCLIFF

RICHARD
Sister, have comfort, all of us have cause
To wail the dimming of our shining star,
But none can help our harms by wailing them.
Madam, my mother, I do cry you mercy;
I did not see your Grace. Humbly on my knee   105
I crave your blessing.

DUCHESS OF YORK
God bless thee, and put meekness in thy breast,
Love, charity, obedience, and true duty.

RICHARD
Amen. [*Aside*] And make me die a good old man,
That is the butt end of a mother's blessing;   110
I marvel that her Grace did leave it out.

BUCKINGHAM
You cloudy princes and heart-sorrowing peers
That bear this heavy mutual load of moan,
Now cheer each other in each other's love.
Though we have spent our harvest of this king,   115
We are to reap the harvest of his son.

RICHARD III [150

117-119: The broken...and kept: Buckingham is referring to the oaths of friendship extracted by Edward IV from the various court factions in 2.1.

120: Meseemeth: it seems to me; **little train:** small company of people

121: Ludlow: town and castle in Shropshire near the Welsh border; **fet:** fetched

124: Marry: indeed

127: By how much...yet ungoverned: given that Edward V's reign is young, as he is, and the government is newly in place; **estate:** state

128-131: Where...prevented: the image and the language of the obscure. Buckingham seems to be saying that when every horse is in control and goes where it wants, there is potential as well as promise of harm, and they should take steps to prevent it.

132: I hope: I trust

137: haply: perhaps; **urged:** encouraged

139: meet: right, fitting

142: post: go swiftly; **Ludlow:** from the First Quarto. The First Folio reads "London", which does not make sense since this scene is taking place in London.

144: censures: judgments

[T H E   S O U R C E B O O K S   S H A K E S P E A R E]   1392-1423

The broken rancor of your high-swoll'n hates,
But lately splintered, knit, and joined together,
Must gently be preserved, cherished, and kept.
Meseemeth good, that, with some little train,   120
Forthwith from Ludlow the young prince be fet
Hither to London, to be crowned our king.

RIVERS
Why "with some little train," my Lord of Buckingham?

BUCKINGHAM
Marry, my lord, lest by a multitude
The new-healed wound of malice should break out,   125
Which would be so much the more dangerous
By how much the estate is green and yet ungoverned.
Where every horse bears his commanding rein,
And may direct his course as please himself,
As well the fear of harm, as harm apparent,   130
In my opinion, ought to be prevented.

RICHARD
I hope the King made peace with all of us;
And the compact is firm and true in me.

RIVERS
And so in me, and so, I think, in all.
Yet since it is but green, it should be put   135
To no apparent likelihood of breach,
Which haply by much company might be urged.
Therefore I say with noble Buckingham,
That it is meet so few should fetch the prince.

HASTINGS
And so say I.   140

RICHARD
Then be it so, and go we to determine
Who they shall be that straight shall post to Ludlow.
Madam, and you, my sister, will you go
To give your censures in this business?

145: QUEEN...hearts: from the First Quarto, this line is not in the First Folio

145: Stage Direction: *Exeunt*: Several recent productions (e.g., Hands and Alexander, both RSC, 1970 and 1984) keep the children (Clarence's children and the Duke of York) on stage until the end of the scene. Hands had Richard fooling around with them to the irritation of Buckingham, and Alexander had them playing with Richard's crutches so that he had to limp out without them.

147: God's: from the First Quarto, the First Folio reads "God" (removed under the "Act to Restrain the Abuses of Players"; see note 1.4.116)

148: sort occasion: find an opportunity

149: index: preface

151: consistory: meeting room

153: thy direction: your instructions

QUEEN ELIZABETH and DUCHESS OF YORK
   With all our hearts.   145
                    Exeunt, manet BUCKINGHAM and RICHARD

BUCKINGHAM
   My lord, whoever journeys to the Prince,
   For God's sake let not us two stay at home.
   For by the way, I'll sort occasion,
   As index to the story we late talked of,
   To part the Queen's proud kindred from the prince.   150

RICHARD
   My other self, my counsel's consistory,
   My oracle, my prophet, my dear cousin,
   I, as a child, will go by thy direction.
   Towards Ludlow then, for we'll not stay behind.

                                                    Exeunt

o: **Scene:** Most productions cut this scene, though some do retain it. Margaret Webster at the City Center in New York (1953) had Richard's secret police enter at the very end so that lines 46-47 were spoken for their benefit; Michael Bogdanov at the Young Vic (1978) and with the English Shakespeare Company (1989) made his Citizens newspaper sellers and other working class types. For most others who retain this scene, the characters are respectably-dressed citizens of London.

o: **Stage Direction: *one door...the other [door]*:** This direction describes the common practice on the early stage; modern productions effect the entry of these characters as best suits their venue. The point behind using both doors is to indicate that the Citizens come from all over the city.

Scene rendering for the 1953 production at the Shakespeare Memorial Theatre in Stratford-upon-Avon directed by Glen Byam Shaw

Rare Book and Special Collection Library, University of Illinois at Urbana-Champaign

4: **by'r Lady:** by our Lady (the Virgin Mary), a mild oath typically used by the lower classes
5: **giddy:** 1) dizzy or 2) unsettled
6: **God speed:** God make you prosper, a conventional greeting; **Give:** I give
7: **Doth this news hold:** is the report confirmed
8: **God help the while:** an exclamation of grief
9: **troublous:** unsettled or troublesome

Act 2, Scene 3]

FIRST CITIZEN
Good morrow neighbor, whither away so fast?

SECOND CITIZEN
I promise you, I scarcely know myself.
Hear you the news abroad?

FIRST CITIZEN
                              Yes, that the King is dead.

SECOND CITIZEN
Ill news, by'r Lady, seldom comes the better.
I fear, I fear,'twill prove a giddy world.   5

Enter another citizen

THIRD CITIZEN
Neighbors, God speed.

FIRST CITIZEN
                              Give you good morrow, sir.

THIRD CITIZEN
Doth this news hold of good King Edward's death?

SECOND CITIZEN
Ay, sir, it is too true, God help the while.

THIRD CITIZEN
Then masters look to see a troublous world.

FIRST CITIZEN
No, no, by God's good grace his son shall reign.   10

13: **nonage:** minority

18: **wot:** knows

19: **enriched:** supplied

20: **politic:** prudent, sagacious; **grave:** serious

23: **they all came by his father:** i.e., that they are of the royal blood

23-24: **Better...all:** i.e., better that they be of the royal blood or there be none at all. The Citizen shows the same dislike for Queen Elizabeth's family that Richard and Clarence have manifested.

25: **emulation:** attempting to surpass the others

28: **haught:** haughty

30: **solace:** take comfort

THIRD CITIZEN
>   Woe to the land that's governed by a child.

SECOND CITIZEN
>   In him there is a hope of government,
>   Which in his nonage, council under him,
>   And, in his full and ripened years, himself
>   No doubt shall then, and till then, govern well.   15

FIRST CITIZEN
>   So stood the state when Henry the Sixth
>   Was crowned in Paris, but at nine months old.

THIRD CITIZEN
>   Stood the state so? No, no, good friends, God wot,
>   For then this land was famously enriched
>   With politic grave counsel; then the King   20
>   Had virtuous uncles to protect his Grace.

FIRST CITIZEN
>   Why, so hath this, both by his father and mother.

THIRD CITIZEN
>   Better it were they all came by his father,
>   Or by his father there were none at all,
>   For emulation who shall now be nearest,   25
>   Will touch us all too near if God prevent not.
>   O, full of danger is the Duke of Gloucester,
>   And the Queen's sons and brothers, haught and proud,
>   And were they to be ruled, and not to rule,
>   This sickly land might solace as before.   30

FIRST CITIZEN
>   Come, come, we fear the worst. All will be well.

THIRD CITIZEN
>   When clouds are seen, wise men put on their cloaks;
>   When great leaves fall, then winter is at hand;
>   When the sun sets, who doth not look for night?

35: **Untimely:** unseasonable

36: **sort:** arrange or order

39: **reason:** talk to

40: **That:** who; **heavily:** sad

41: **still:** always

43: **Ensuing:** from the First Quarto, the First Folio reads "Pursuing"; **proof:** experience

45: **Whither away:** where are you going

46: **justices:** there is nothing in the text to explain why they are going to the justices

Untimely storms makes men expect a dearth.   35
All may be well; but if God sort it so,
'Tis more than we deserve, or I expect.

SECOND CITIZEN
Truly, the hearts of men are full of fear.
You cannot reason, almost, with a man
That looks not heavily and full of dread.   40

THIRD CITIZEN
Before the days of change, still is it so,
By a divine instinct, men's minds mistrust
Ensuing danger, as by proof, we see
The water swell before a boisterous storm.
But leave it all to God. Whither away?   45

SECOND CITIZEN
Marry, we were sent for to the justices.

THIRD CITIZEN
And so was I. I'll bear you company.

                                                       Exeunt

0: Scene: Cibber also cut this scene, as did Macready, Booth, and Irving. Most modern productions either cut it entirely or reduce it drastically. Bogdanov (1989) did not have the Cardinal enter at the opening of the scene and gave Queen Elizabeth his opening speech. The Cardinal entered in place of the Messenger at line 39, the previous line being cut. Loncraine, going outside the text, cut much of this scene and had Stanley and Richmond enter and deliver much of the information instead of the Archbishop. The death of Rivers (Grey and Vaughan do not appear in this film), shown just before this scene, occurred while he was having sex with an air stewardess in his bedroom.

1: **hear:** from the First Quarto, the First Folio reads "heard"

1-2: **Stony Stratford...Northampton:** The First Folio has these two locations in this order whereas the First Quarto reverses them. While it is true that geographically, a trip from Ludlow to London should proceed first to Northampton and then to Stony Stratford, Shakespeare's sources indicate that Richard, as part of his plotting to destroy the family and supporters of Queen Elizabeth, forced his party to backtrack in their journey, and so the reading of the First Folio is correct. Apparently the First Quarto was corrected solely on the grounds of geography without any apparent knowledge of the historical sources.

9: **cousin:** kinsman (see note 2.2.8)
13: **grace:** an individual virtue or sense of propriety; **apace:** quickly
17: **object the same:** make that argument

Costume rendering for young Duke of York from the 1953 production at the Shakespeare Memorial Theatre in Stratford-upon-Avon directed by Glen Byam Shaw

Act 2, Scene 4]

Enter ARCHBISHOP [OF YORK], young [DUKE OF] YORK,
QUEEN [ELIZABETH], and the DUCHESS [OF YORK]

ARCHBISHOP OF YORK
Last night, I hear, they lay at Stony Stratford,
And at Northampton they do rest tonight.
Tomorrow, or next day, they will be here.

DUCHESS OF YORK
I long with all my heart to see the prince.
I hope he is much grown since last I saw him.   5

QUEEN ELIZABETH
But I hear, no. They say my son of York
Has almost overta'en him in his growth.

YORK
Ay, mother, but I would not have it so.

DUCHESS OF YORK
Why, my young cousin, it is good to grow.

YORK
Grandam, one night as we did sit at supper,   10
My uncle Rivers talked how I did grow
More than my brother. "Ay," quoth my uncle Gloucester,
"Small herbs have grace, great weeds do grow apace.'"
And since, methinks, I would not grow so fast,
Because sweet flowers are slow, and weeds make haste.   15

DUCHESS OF YORK
Good faith, good faith, the saying did not hold
In him that did object the same to thee.
He was the wretched'st thing when he was young,
So long a-growing and so leisurely,
That if his rule were true, he should be gracious.   20

21: Speech Prefix: **YORK:** All the early quartos and many later editions assign this speech to the Archbishop of York.
23: **troth:** truth, faith; **if I had been remembered:** if I had known that
24: **flout:** insult

Set design by Rachel Hauck for the 2005 Oregon Shakespeare Festival production directed by Libby Appel
Courtesy of Oregon Shakespeare Festival

35: **parlous:** shrewd or clever
37: **Pitchers have ears:** proverbial expression, little pitchers have big ears

37: Stage Direction: ***Enter a MESSENGER:*** In the First Quarto, there is no Messenger, and the person who enters and speaks the Messenger's lines is the Earl of Dorset, the Queen's son. However, there is nothing in his lines or in the others' reactions to them that would indicate that he is supposed to be a person of that rank or relationship.

YORK
  And so no doubt he is, my gracious madam.

DUCHESS OF YORK
  I hope he is, but yet let mothers doubt.

YORK
  Now, by my troth, if I had been remembered,
  I could have given my uncle's grace a flout,
  To touch his growth nearer than he touched mine.   25

DUCHESS OF YORK
  How, my young York? I prithee let me hear it.

YORK
  Marry, they say, my uncle grew so fast
  That he could gnaw a crust at two hours old
  'Twas full two years ere I could get a tooth.
  Grandam, this would have been a biting jest.   30

DUCHESS OF YORK
  I prithee, pretty York, who told thee this?

YORK
  Grandam, his nurse.

DUCHESS OF YORK
  His nurse? Why, she was dead ere thou wast born.

YORK
  If 'twere not she, I cannot tell who told me.

QUEEN ELIZABETH
  A parlous boy. Go to, you are too shrewd.   35

DUCHESS OF YORK
  Good madam, be not angry with the child.

QUEEN ELIZABETH
  Pitchers have ears.

                                    Enter a MESSENGER

Costume rendering for the Duchess of York from the 1953 production at the Shakespeare Memorial Theatre in Stratford-upon-Avon directed by Glen Byam Shaw
Rare Book and Special Collection Library, University of Illinois at Urbana-Champaign

42: Pomfret: Pontefract, in West Yorkshire, the reference here is probably to the castle. Richard II was killed, or died, here in 1400 (see Shakespeare's *Richard II* 5.5).

43: Sir Thomas Vaughan: was an ardent Yorkist during his career as a royal servant, but had the misfortune to be with Prince Edward (Edward V) at Ludlow when Edward IV died and therefore to be in Richard's way. He has only one line in this play while alive (3.3.7) and two while a ghost (5.3.143-144).

44: committed: ordered their imprisonment

46: sum of all I can: all I know

51: Insulting: triumphing; **jut:** strike

52: aweless: weak, inspiring no reverence or dread

ARCHBISHOP OF YORK
Here comes a messenger. What news?

MESSENGER
Such news, my lord, as grieves me to report.

QUEEN ELIZABETH
How doth the prince?

MESSENGER
                    Well, madam, and in health.   40

DUCHESS OF YORK
What is thy news?

MESSENGER
Lord Rivers and Lord Grey are sent to Pomfret,
And, with them, Sir Thomas Vaughan, prisoners.

DUCHESS OF YORK
Who hath committed them?

MESSENGER
                         The mighty dukes
Gloucester and Buckingham.

ARCHBISHOP OF YORK
                         For what offense?   45

MESSENGER
The sum of all I can, I have disclosed.
Why, or for what, these nobles were committed
Is all unknown to me, my gracious lord.

QUEEN ELIZABETH
Ay me! I see the ruin of my house.
The tiger now hath seized the gentle hind;   50
Insulting tyranny begins to jut
Upon the innocent and aweless throne.
Welcome, destruction, blood, and massacre.
I see, as in a map, the end of all.

55-65: Scene: **Accursèd and...death no more:** Bogdanov (1989) cut a few lines and left the Duchess of York on stage after the rest exited. She closed the scene with this speech.

60: **seated:** on the English throne; **broils:** quarrels

61: **Clean overblown:** completely blown away`

63: **preposterous:** monstrous, perverse

64: **spleen:** violent illness

66: **sanctuary:** By old English custom and accepted by Anglo-Norman law, churches and churchyards were recognized as sanctuaries from the law for a period of time, not permanently. The right of sanctuary was restricted by statute in 1540 and abolished entirely in 1624.

DUCHESS OF YORK

> Accursèd and unquiet wrangling days,   55
> How many of you have mine eyes beheld?
> My husband lost his life to get the crown,
> And often up and down my sons were tossed,
> For me to joy and weep their gain and loss.
> And being seated, and domestic broils   60
> Clean overblown, themselves the conquerors.
> Make war upon themselves, brother to brother,
> Blood to blood, self against self. O, preposterous
> And frantic outrage, end thy damnèd spleen,
> Or let me die, to look on death no more.   65

QUEEN ELIZABETH

> [*To YORK*] Come, come, my boy. We will to sanctuary.
> Madam, farewell.

DUCHESS OF YORK

> Stay, I will go with you.

QUEEN ELIZABETH

> You have no cause.

ARCHBISHOP OF YORK

> My gracious lady, go,
> And thither bear your treasure and your goods.
> For my part, I'll resign unto your Grace   70
> The seal I keep; and so betide to me
> As well I tender you and all of yours.
> Go, I'll conduct you to the sanctuary.

> *Exeunt*

[Richard III

Act 3

0: Scene: From Charles Kean in 1848 onward through the nineteenth century, this entry was used for a great procession with many lords and ladies, Beefeaters as guards, trumpet fanfares, courtly dances, and richly decorated costumes. In some productions, the Lord Mayor and his train also enter here instead of at line 17.

1-166: **Welcome...against him:** This portion of the text follows the First Quarto as the copy-text rather than the First Folio (see "About the Text").

1: **chamber:** royal residence, perhaps meaning London itself

4: **crosses:** difficulties, and perhaps an allusion to the circuitous route devised by Richard (see note 2.4.1-2)

10: **God He knows:** God knows, a typical expression of the times

11: **jumpeth:** accords

17: **Mayor of London:** i.e., Edmund Shaa, or Shaw, and brother of the Ralph Shaa later mentioned in the play (see note 3.5.103)

17: Stage Direction: ***Enter LORD MAYOR:*** From at least Cibber, if not before, until the nineteenth century, the Lord Mayor was played as a buffoon. Then he became a low stage comic until Tyrone Guthrie's production in 1953. In more modern times he seems to have become a combination of the two, but he has almost never been a serious and important figure of civic authority.

Set rendering from the 1953 production at the Shakespeare Memorial Theatre in Stratford-upon-Avon directed by Glen Byam Shaw

Act 3, Scene 1]

The trumpets sound. Enter young PRINCE [EDWARD],
[RICHARD] DUKE OF GLOUCESTER, and BUCKINGHAM,
[the] LORD CARDINAL, [and CATESBY,] with others

BUCKINGHAM
Welcome, sweet prince, to London, to your chamber.

RICHARD
Welcome, dear cousin, my thoughts' sovereign.
The weary way hath made you melancholy.

PRINCE EDWARD
No, uncle, but our crosses on the way
Have made it tedious, wearisome, and heavy.   5
I want more uncles here to welcome me.

RICHARD
Sweet prince, the untainted virtue of your years
Hath not yet dived into the world's deceit;
Nor more can you distinguish of a man
Than of his outward show, which, God He knows,   10
Seldom or never jumpeth with the heart.
Those uncles which you want were dangerous.
Your Grace attended to their sugared words
But looked not on the poison of their hearts.
God keep you from them, and from such false friends.   15

PRINCE EDWARD
God keep me from false friends, but they were none.

RICHARD
My lord, the Mayor of London comes to greet you.
                              Enter LORD MAYOR [and his train]

22: **Fie:** exclamation of disgust or reproach, sometimes used in jest; **slug:** lazy person

26: **what occasion:** for what reason

29: **fain:** gladly

30: **perforce:** forcibly

31: **indirect:** devious

35: **deny:** refuse

Costume rendering for the Cardinal from the 1953 production at the Shakespeare Memorial Theatre in Stratford-upon-Avon directed by Glen Byam Shaw

Rare Book and Special Collection Library, University of Illinois at Urbana-Champaign

LORD MAYOR
God bless your Grace with health and happy days.

PRINCE EDWARD
I thank you, good my lord, and thank you all.
I thought my mother, and my brother York   20
Would long ere this have met us on the way.
Fie, what a slug is Hastings, that he comes not
To tell us whether they will come or no.

Enter LORD HASTINGS

BUCKINGHAM
And, in good time, here comes the sweating lord.

PRINCE EDWARD
Welcome, my lord. What, will our mother come?   25

HASTINGS
On what occasion, God He knows, not I,
The Queen your mother, and your brother York,
Have taken sanctuary. The tender prince
Would fain have come with me to meet your Grace,
But by his mother was perforce withheld.   30

BUCKINGHAM
Fie, what an indirect and peevish course
Is this of hers? Lord Cardinal, will your Grace
Persuade the Queen to send the Duke of York
Unto his princely brother presently?
If she deny, Lord Hastings, go with him,   35
And from her jealous arms pluck him perforce.

CARDINAL
My Lord of Buckingham, if my weak oratory
Can from his mother win the Duke of York,
Anon expect him here. But if she be obdurate
To mild entreaties, God in heaven forbid   40
We should infringe the holy privilege
Of blessed sanctuary. Not for all this land
Would I be guilty of so great a sin.

44: **senseless:** unreasonably

45: **Too ceremonious and traditional:** too careful about observing correct form and custom

46: **grossness:** lack of enlightenment

50: **wit:** good sense

54: **charter:** publicly recognized right

60: Stage Direction: *[Exeunt...HASTINGS]:* The stage direction appears one line earlier in the First Folio; it is not in the First Quarto.

65: **Tower:** Although it is more famous as a prison, the Tower of London was also a royal residence. Whether in 1483 the Tower was thought of as a place of death and torture or as a royal residence and fortress, by the time Shakespeare wrote this play, it had become a byword for fatal imprisonment. Consequently, from the 1590s onward when Richard says, "repose you at the Tower," and Edward replies, "I do not like the Tower, of any place," the audience would feel a chill. Indeed, Richard's words are often accompanied with various sorts of somber sound effects.

69: **Julius Caesar:** invaded Britain in 55 and 54 BCE. He does not, in fact, have any connection to the Tower of London, which was begun by William the Conqueror in the late 1070s.

BUCKINGHAM
> You are too senseless obstinate, my lord,
> Too ceremonious and traditional.   45
> Weigh it but with the grossness of this age,
> You break not sanctuary in seizing him.
> The benefit thereof is always granted
> To those whose dealings have deserved the place,
> And those who have the wit to claim the place.   50
> This prince hath neither claimed it, nor deserved it,
> And therefore, in mine opinion, cannot have it.
> Then taking him from thence that is not there,
> You break no privilege nor charter there.
> Oft have I heard of sanctuary men,   55
> But sanctuary children, never till now.

CARDINAL
> My lord, you shall o'errule my mind for once.
> Come on, Lord Hastings, will you go with me?

HASTINGS
> I go, my lord.

PRINCE EDWARD
> Good lords, make all the speedy haste you may.   60
>   *[Exeunt CARDINAL and HASTINGS]*
> Say, Uncle Gloucester, if our brother come,
> Where shall we sojourn till our coronation?

RICHARD
> Where it seems best unto your royal self.
> If I may counsel you, some day or two
> Your Highness shall repose you at the Tower;   65
> Then where you please, and shall be thought most fit
> For your best health and recreation.

PRINCE EDWARD
> I do not like the Tower, of any place.
> Did Julius Caesar build that place, my lord?

71: **re-edified:** restored, maintained, or rebuilt with additions

72-73: **Is it upon record...age:** i.e., is there a written record or has this only been reported by word of mouth

75: **registered:** written down

Peter Vack as Prince Edward, Peter Dinklage as Richard, and the Ensemble in the 2004 Public Theater production directed by Peter DuBois

Photo: Michal Daniel

78: **general all-ending day:** end of the world, doomsday

81: **without characters:** without being written, literally the characters of the alphabet

82: **formal Vice:** conventional Vice character in the Morality plays of the previous two to three centuries. The Vice was a stock figure, and sometimes "Vice" was the character's name. **Iniquity:** this is the Vice's name in at least two contemporary morality plays, *Nice Wanton* (c. 1560) and *King Darius* (c. 1565)

83: **moralize:** interpret

85: **what:** that with which

86: **set down:** wrote

86: Scene: **His...valor live:** Olivier inserts 3.5.86-94 here before resuming the scene.

BUCKINGHAM

    He did, my gracious lord, begin that place,   70

    Which since, succeeding ages have re-edified.

PRINCE EDWARD

    Is it upon record, or else reported

    Successively from age to age, he built it?

BUCKINGHAM

    Upon record, my gracious lord.

PRINCE EDWARD

    But say, my lord, it were not registered,   75

    Methinks the truth should live from age to age,

    As 'twere retailed to all posterity,

    Even to the general all-ending day.

RICHARD

    [*Aside*] So wise so young, they say, do never live long.

PRINCE EDWARD

    What say you, uncle?   80

RICHARD

    I say, without characters, fame lives long.

    [*Aside*] Thus, like the formal Vice, Iniquity,

    I moralize two meanings in one word.

PRINCE EDWARD

    That Julius Caesar was a famous man,

    With what his valor did enrich his wit,   85

    His wit set down to make his valor live.

    Death makes no conquest of this conqueror,

    For now he lives in fame, though not in life.

    I'll tell you what, my cousin Buckingham—

BUCKINGHAM

    What, my gracious lord?   90

91: **An if:** if

94: **lightly:** commonly; **forward:** early

98: **our:** the royal plural, he means himself

99. **late:** recently

101: "How fares our cousin, noble Lord of York?": Wallace Acton as Richard, Christopher Luggiero as York, and Patrick Collins as Prince Edward in the 2003 Shakespeare Theatre Company production directed by Gale Edwards
Photo: Carol Rosegg

101-131: Scene: **How fares...shoulders:** This fooling between young York and Richard, ending with the reference to bearing the boy upon his shoulders, is often one of the more chilling incidents in the play. Olivier (1955) had York point at Richard's shoulder and Richard turned on him a look which terrified York and startled most of those in the chamber. In many productions York leaps, or tries to leap, on Richard's shoulders at lines 130-131, and he is either shrugged off or whirled around with great fury (Olivier, 1955; Bogdanov, 1989). Eyre/Loncraine/McKellen (1990, 1995) made the deformity of Richard's shoulder something that gave him considerable pain, so when little York leapt on his shoulder, Richard collapsed in agony. It is, under almost any circumstances, a tense moment and Buckingham's speech (lines 132-35) is clearly intended to defuse it.

PRINCE EDWARD
    An if I live until I be a man,
    I'll win our ancient right in France again,
    Or die a soldier, as I lived a king.

RICHARD
    [*Aside*] Short summers lightly have a forward spring.
                    Enter young YORK, HASTINGS, [and] CARDINAL

BUCKINGHAM
    Now, in good time, here comes the Duke of York.   95

PRINCE EDWARD
    Richard of York, how fares our loving brother?

YORK
    Well, my dread lord; so must I call you now.

PRINCE EDWARD
    Ay, brother, to our grief, as it is yours.
    Too late he died that might have kept that title,
    Which by his death hath lost much majesty.   100

RICHARD
    How fares our cousin, noble Lord of York?

YORK
    I thank you, gentle uncle. O, my lord,
    You said that idle weeds are fast in growth.
    The prince my brother hath outgrown me far.

RICHARD
    He hath, my lord.

YORK
                    And therefore is he idle?   105

RICHARD
    O my fair cousin, I must not say so.

113: **that**: who

114: **toy**: trifle

115: "A greater gift than that I'll give my cousin": Simon Russell Beale as Richard with the two young princes, Annabelle Apsion and Kate Duchene, in the 1992 Royal Shakespeare Company production directed by Sam Mendes
Photo: Donald Cooper

116: **that's the sword to it**: the sword that belongs with it. Swords and daggers were normally worn, and often manufactured, in sets.

118: **light**: trivial; York is playing with the meanings of "light"

121: **I weigh...heavier**: I would think it light even if it were heavier

YORK
Then he is more beholding to you than I.

RICHARD
He may command me as my sovereign,
But you have power in me as in a kinsman.

YORK
I pray you, uncle, give me this dagger.   110

RICHARD
My dagger, little cousin? With all my heart.

PRINCE EDWARD
A beggar, brother?

YORK
Of my kind uncle, that I know will give,
And being but a toy, which is no grief to give.

RICHARD
A greater gift than that I'll give my cousin.   115

YORK
A greater gift? O that's the sword to it.

RICHARD
Ay, gentle cousin, were it light enough.

YORK
O, then I see you will part but with light gifts.
In weightier things you'll say a beggar nay.

RICHARD
It is too heavy for your Grace to wear.   120

YORK
I weigh it lightly, were it heavier.

126: **cross:** contrary, perverse

130: **ape:** Professional fools and jesters often had monkeys (apes) on their shoulders; in some cases a bear would have been mounted on their shoulders.

132: **sharp-provided:** quick or ready

136: **pass along:** continue on your way

RICHARD
  What, would you have my weapon, little lord?

YORK
  I would, that I might thank you as you call me.

RICHARD
  How?

YORK
  Little.   125

PRINCE EDWARD
  My Lord of York will still be cross in talk.
  Uncle, your Grace knows how to bear with him.

YORK
  You mean, to bear me, not to bear with me.
  Uncle, my brother mocks both you and me,
  Because that I am little, like an ape,   130
  He thinks that you should bear me on your shoulders.

BUCKINGHAM
  With what a sharp-provided wit he reasons.
  To mitigate the scorn he gives his uncle,
  He prettily and aptly taunts himself.
  So cunning and so young is wonderful.   135

RICHARD
  My lord, will't please you pass along?
  Myself and my good cousin Buckingham
  Will to your mother, to entreat of her
  To meet you at the Tower and welcome you.

YORK
  What, will you go unto the Tower, my lord?   140

PRINCE EDWARD
  My Lord Protector needs will have it so.

150: Stage Direction: [*A Sennet.*]: from the First Folio, not in the First Quarto. A sennet is set of notes on the trumpet or cornet that signals a ceremonial entrance or exit. Productions that opened this scene with an elaborate processional closed this section of it with an equally elaborate recessional.

151: **prating:** chattering

152: **incensèd:** incited, encouraged

154: **parlous:** dangerously cunning or clever

155: **quick:** lively; **forward:** impertinent; **capable:** clever, intelligent

158: **deeply:** thoroughly

YORK
> I shall not sleep in quiet at the Tower.

RICHARD
> Why, what should you fear?

YORK
> Marry, my uncle Clarence' angry ghost.
> My grandam told me he was murdered there.   145

PRINCE EDWARD
> I fear no uncles dead.

RICHARD
> Nor none that live, I hope.

PRINCE EDWARD
> An if they live, I hope I need not fear.
> [*To YORK*] But come, my lord. With a heavy heart,
> Thinking on them, go I unto the Tower.   150

> *[A Sennet. Exeunt,] manet RICHARD,*
> *BUCKINGHAM [and CATESBY]*

BUCKINGHAM
> Think you, my lord, this little prating York
> Was not incensèd by his subtle mother
> To taunt and scorn you thus opprobriously?

RICHARD
> No doubt, no doubt. O, 'tis a parlous boy.
> Bold, quick, ingenious, forward, capable.   155
> He is all the mother's, from the top to toe.

BUCKINGHAM
> Well, let them rest. Come hither, Catesby.
> Thou art sworn as deeply to effect what we intend,
> As closely to conceal what we impart.
> Thou knowest our reasons urged upon the way.   160

165: **his father's:** i.e., Edward V's father, Edward IV

166: **aught:** anything

Costume rendering for Buckingham from the 1953 production at the Shakespeare Memorial Theatre in Stratford-upon-Avon directed by Glen Byam Shaw

Rare Book and Special Collection Library, University of Illinois at Urbana-Champaign

171: **affected:** disposed

173: **sit:** sit in council

179: **divided councils:** two separate councils

182: **ancient knot:** old group

183: **let blood:** to be executed; the term comes from the medical bleeding of patients by barber-surgeons

What thinkest thou? Is it not an easy matter
To make William Lord Hastings of our mind
For the installment of this noble duke
In the seat royal of this famous isle?

CATESBY
He, for his father's sake, so loves the prince   165
That he will not be won to aught against him.

BUCKINGHAM
What thinkst thou then of Stanley? Will not he?

CATESBY
He will do all in all as Hastings doth.

BUCKINGHAM
Well, then, no more but this. Go, gentle Catesby,
And, as it were far off, sound thou Lord Hastings   170
How doth he stand affected to our purpose,
And summon him tomorrow to the Tower
To sit about the coronation.
If thou dost find him tractable to us,
Encourage him, and show him all our reasons.   175
If he be leaden, icy, cold, unwilling,
Be thou so too, and so break off your talk,
And give us notice of his inclination;
For we tomorrow hold divided councils,
Wherein thyself shalt highly be employed.   180

RICHARD
Commend me to Lord William. Tell him, Catesby,
His ancient knot of dangerous adversaries
Tomorrow are let blood at Pomfret Castle,
And bid my lord, for joy of this good news,
Give Mistress Shore one gentle kiss the more.   185

BUCKINGHAM
Good Catesby, go effect this business soundly.

192: **complots:** devious plans, conspiracies

193: Scene: **Chop off his head:** These words are, or can be, four quite terrible syllables. They can be said with menace, glee, or relish. Olivier (1955) and Sher (Alexander, 1984) both said this with a kind of surprise, causing Buckingham to ask about such an obvious solution. Andrew Jarvis (Bogdanov, 1989) said the words in a quiet, almost pondering, manner. The full stop after the four monosyllabic words followed by the disyllabic "Something" and concluding in the trisyllabic "determine" serves to set it off effectively.

195: **moveables:** household property and therefore moveable from place to place, as opposed to real estate

196: **Whereof...possessed:** A portion of this earldom came into the crown's possession through Henry IV and remained there.

199: **betimes:** early

200: **digest:** discuss, consider

CATESBY
    My good lords both, with all the heed I can.

RICHARD
    Shall we hear from you, Catesby, ere we sleep?

CATESBY
    You shall, my lord.

RICHARD
    At Crosby House, there shall you find us both.   190

                                                    Exit CATESBY

BUCKINGHAM
    Now, my lord, what shall we do if we perceive
    Lord Hastings will not yield to our complots?

RICHARD
    Chop off his head. Something we will determine.
    And, look when I am King, claim thou of me
    The earldom of Hereford, and the moveables   195
    Whereof the King my brother stood possessed.

BUCKINGHAM
    I'll claim that promise at your Grace's hand.

RICHARD
    And look to have it yielded with all kindness.
    Come, let us sup betimes, that afterwards
    We may digest our complots in some form.   200

                                                    Exeunt

0: Scene: Again, Cibber, and all those who follow his adaptation, omit this scene. In Olivier's film (1955) and Alexander's production (RSC, 1984), Jane Shore was much in evidence from the start of the scene through about line 85; Olivier actually opened the scene with the two of them in bed kissing. In Alexander's production, Shore brought Hastings water and a towel, and Hastings toyed with not only Jane Shore but also another woman throughout the scene. Jane Howell (BBC, 1983) had Shore enter at line 57 with Hastings' outer garments and sword, all of which she helps him put on. At line 79 and again at line 88, he gave her a long kiss, much to the distaste of Stanley.

0: Stage Direction: ***Enter a MESSENGER to the door of HASTINGS:*** In the early theaters (e.g., Globe and Blackfriars) the Messenger would have entered from one of the two stage doors and crossed to the other stage door, thus establishing the second one as the door to Hastings's lodging. The others (Catesby, Stanley, the Pursuivant, the Priest, and Buckingham) would therefore have entered and exited through the first door, as would Buckingham and Hastings at the end of the scene. With the advent of proscenium-arch theaters and representational sets after 1660, these actors could now enter from the wings and the door of Hastings' lodgings would have been represented in the flats and/or sets.

4: **What is't o'clock?:** What time is it?

10: **certifies:** tells

11: **boar:** Richard's heraldic emblem was the white boar; **razèd off his helm:** struck off his helmet, literally, cut off his head

Act 3, Scene 2]

Enter a MESSENGER to the door of HASTINGS

MESSENGER
[*Knocking*] My lord, my lord!

HASTINGS
[*Within*] Who knocks?

MESSENGER
One from the Lord Stanley.

HASTINGS
[*Within*] What is't o'clock?

MESSENGER
Upon the stroke of four.   5

Enter LORD HASTINGS

HASTINGS
Cannot my Lord Stanley sleep these tedious nights?

MESSENGER
So it appears by that I have to say.
First, he commends him to your noble self.

HASTINGS
What then?

MESSENGER
Then certifies your lordship that this night   10
He dreamt the boar had razèd off his helm.
Besides, he says there are two councils kept;
And that may be determined at the one,
Which may make you and him to rue at th' other.

Set design by Rachel Hauck for the 2005 Oregon Shakespeare Festival production directed by Libby Appel
Courtesy of Oregon Shakespeare Festival

24: **intelligence:** information

25: **instance:** cause

26: **simple:** foolish, simple minded

30: **mean:** intend

Therefore he sends to know your lordship's pleasure,   15
If you will presently take horse with him,
And with all speed post with him toward the north,
To shun the danger that his soul divines.

HASTINGS
Go, fellow, go, return unto thy lord,
Bid him not fear the separated council.   20
His honor and myself are at the one,
And at the other is my good friend Catesby,
Where nothing can proceed that toucheth us
Whereof I shall not have intelligence.
Tell him his fears are shallow, without instance.   25
And for his dreams, I wonder he's so simple
To trust the mock'ry of unquiet slumbers.
To fly the boar before the boar pursues
Were to incense the boar to follow us
And make pursuit where he did mean no chase.   30
Go, bid thy master rise and come to me,
And we will both together to the Tower,
Where he shall see the boar will use us kindly.

MESSENGER
I'll go, my lord, and tell him what you say.

Exit
Enter CATESBY

CATESBY
Many good morrows to my noble lord.   35

HASTINGS
Good morrow, Catesby, you are early stirring.
What news, what news, in this our tott'ring state?

CATESBY
It is a reeling world, indeed, my lord.
And I believe will never stand upright
Till Richard wear the garland of the realm.   40

43: **crown:** crown of his head

44: **crown:** crown of England

59: **tragedy:** their execution; the term is used to describe the downfall of their house, in this case the Woodvilles

60: **Well, Catesby:** The First Quarto inserts a response by Catesby, "What, my lord", after this prompt.

HASTINGS
How "wear the garland"? Dost thou mean the crown?

CATESBY
Ay, my good lord.

HASTINGS
I'll have this crown of mine cut from my shoulders
Before I'll see the crown so foul misplaced.
But canst thou guess that he doth aim at it?   45

CATESBY
Ay, on my life, and hopes to find you forward
Upon his party for the gain thereof.
And thereupon he sends you this good news,
That this same very day your enemies,
The kindred of the Queen, must die at Pomfret.   50

HASTINGS
Indeed, I am no mourner for that news,
Because they have been still my adversaries.
But, that I'll give my voice on Richard's side,
To bar my master's heirs in true descent,
God knows I will not do it, to the death.   55

CATESBY
God keep your lordship in that gracious mind.

HASTINGS
But I shall laugh at this a twelve-month hence,
That they who brought me in my master's hate,
I live to look upon their tragedy.
Well, Catesby, ere a fortnight make me older,   60
I'll send some packing that yet think not on't.

CATESBY
'Tis a vile thing to die, my gracious lord,
When men are unprepared, and look not for it.

70: **account:** reckon; **head upon the bridge:** Heads of traitors were displayed on pikes on London Bridge.

71-94: Scene: **I know...good fellow:** Olivier (1955) cut Stanley and this exchange with Hastings.

75: **holy rood:** holy cross, a crucifix

76: **several:** separate

77: **you do:** from the First Quarto, these words are not in the First Folio

80: **state:** condition

87: **a needless coward:** to be afraid without need

88: **spent:** well advanced

HASTINGS

    O monstrous, monstrous! And so falls it out

    With Rivers, Vaughan, Grey; and so 'twill do   65

    With some men else, that think themselves as safe

    As thou and I, who, as thou know'st, are dear

    To princely Richard and to Buckingham.

CATESBY

    The princes both make high account of you;

    [*Aside*] For they account his head upon the bridge.   70

HASTINGS

    I know they do, and I have well deserved it.

                                  Enter LORD STANLEY

    Come on, come on. Where is your boar-spear, man?

    Fear you the boar, and go so unprovided?

STANLEY

    My lord, good morrow. Good morrow, Catesby.

    You may jest on, but by the holy rood,   75

    I do not like these several councils, I.

HASTINGS

    My lord, I hold my life as dear as you do yours,

    And never in my days, I do protest,

    Was it more precious to me as 'tis now.

    Think you, but that I know our state secure,   80

    I would be so triumphant as I am?

STANLEY

    The lords at Pomfret, when they rode from London,

    Were jocund, and supposed their state was sure,

    And they indeed had no cause to mistrust;

    But yet you see how soon the day o'ercast.   85

    This sudden stab of rancor I misdoubt.

    Pray God, I say, I prove a needless coward!

    What, shall we toward the Tower? The day is spent.

89: **have with you:** let us go; **Wot:** know

93-123: Scene: ***Enter a PURSUIVANT...your lordship:*** This material is frequently cut and so too are Hastings's lines at 3.4.86-90, which recall the incident. Olivier (1955) and Bogdanov (1989) cut the Pursuivant but retained the Priest; Bogdanov had the Priest enter as Jane Shore appeared naked at the window from which Hastings has been speaking. He then encountered Hastings on the stage.

93: Stage Direction: ***PURSUIVANT:*** a royal or government messenger. The First Quarto calls him Hastings, and some editors include this, but it is likely that this identification was a printing error.

95: **sirrah:** term of address to men of lesser rank; accented on first syllable

104: **hold:** preserve

105: **Gramercy:** thank you

HASTINGS
Come, come, have with you. Wot you what, my lord?
Today the lords you talk of are beheaded.   90

STANLEY
They, for their truth, might better wear their heads
Than some that have accused them wear their hats.
But come, my lord, let's away.

Enter a PURSUIVANT

HASTINGS
Go on before; I'll talk with this good fellow.

Exeunt LORD STANLEY and CATESBY

How now, sirrah? How goes the world with thee?   95

PURSUIVANT
The better that your lordship please to ask.

HASTINGS
I tell thee, man, 'tis better with me now
Than when thou met'st me last where now we meet.
Then was I going prisoner to the Tower
By the suggestion of the Queen's allies.   100
But now, I tell thee—keep it to thyself—
This day those enemies are put to death,
And I in better state than e'er I was.

PURSUIVANT
God hold it, to your honor's good content.

HASTINGS
Gramercy, fellow. There, drink that for me.   105

Throws him his purse

PURSUIVANT
I thank your honor.

*Exit PURSUIVANT
Enter a PRIEST*

PRIEST
Well met, my lord. I am glad to see your honor.

108: **Sir John:** A priest who had taken his first university degree was given the title Sir, although he was not a knight.

109: **exercise:** prayers or sermon

110: **content:** reward or pay

114: **shriving work:** confession and absolution

120: **like:** likely; **stay:** remain for

HASTINGS
I thank thee, good Sir John, with all my heart.
I am in your debt for your last exercise.
Come the next Sabbath, and I will content you.   110

PRIEST
I'll wait upon your lordship.

[Exit PRIEST]
Enter BUCKINGHAM

BUCKINGHAM
What, talking with a priest, Lord Chamberlain?
Your friends at Pomfret, they do need the priest.
Your honor hath no shriving work in hand.

HASTINGS
Good faith, and when I met this holy man,   115
The men you talk of came into my mind.
What, go you toward the Tower?

BUCKINGHAM
I do, my lord, but long I cannot stay there.
I shall return before your lordship thence.

HASTINGS
Nay, like enough, for I stay dinner there.   120

BUCKINGHAM
[Aside] And supper too, although thou know'st it not.—
Come, will you go?

HASTINGS
I'll wait upon your lordship.

Exeunt

o: Scene: This scene was omitted by Cibber and all productions through the end of the nineteenth century. When it was brought back in the twentieth century, it was almost always played to present the extreme cruelty of the scene and of Richard's administration, even before he becomes king. For example, at line 6, Hands (1970, 1980) had Ratcliff kick Grey, and in the Hall/Barton production (1963), Ratcliff struck Rivers across the face with his glove while two soldiers held him. Alexander (1984) was unusual in not emphasizing the violence; he merely had Grey and Rivers (Vaughan was cut from the scene) hooded and led off stage.

If, in the early theaters, this scene were played to one side of the stage or aloft, it would allow time and space for the council table to be brought on for the next scene (see note for Stage Direction in 3.4.0).

o: Stage Direction: *carrying*: leading. As used in the First Folio, the only text in which the verb appears, this means to bring on stage under guard and, usually, under restraint. It does not mean they are physically carried on stage.

1: **RATCLIFF Come...prisoners:** from the First Quarto, not in the First Folio
8: **Dispatch:** make haste
11: **closure:** enclosure
13: **slander:** disgrace; **dismal:** sinister

Costume rendering for Grey from the 1953 production at the Shakespeare Memorial Theatre in Stratford-upon-Avon directed by Glen Byam Shaw

Act 3, Scene 3]

Enter SIR RICHARD RATCLIFF, with Halberds, carrying the nobles
[RIVERS, GREY, and VAUGHAN] to death at Pomfret

RATCLIFF
  Come, bring forth the prisoners.

RIVERS
  Sir Richard Ratcliff, let me tell thee this,
  Today shalt thou behold a subject die
  For truth, for duty, and for loyalty.

GREY
  God keep the prince from all the pack of you.   5
  A knot you are of damnèd bloodsuckers.

VAUGHAN
  You live that shall cry woe for this hereafter.

RATCLIFF
  Dispatch, the limit of your lives is out.

RIVERS
  O Pomfret, Pomfret! O thou bloody prison,
  Fatal and ominous to noble peers!   10
  Within the guilty closure of thy walls,
  Richard the Second here was hacked to death,
  And, for more slander to thy dismal seat,
  We give to thee our guiltless blood to drink.

GREY
  Now Margaret's curse is fall'n upon our heads,   15
  When she exclaimed on Hastings, you, and I,
  For standing by when Richard stabbed her son.

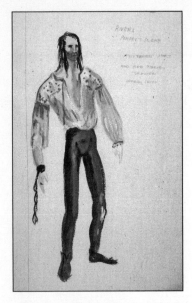

Costume rendering for Rivers from the 1953 production at the Shakespeare Memorial
Theatre in Stratford-upon-Avon directed by Glen Byam Shaw

Rare Book and Special Collection Library, University of Illinois at Urbana-Champaign

24: **expiate:** fully come

RIVERS

Then cursed she Richard. Then cursed she Buckingham.
Then cursed she Hastings. O, remember, God
To hear her prayers for them, as now for us.   20
And for my sister and her princely sons,
Be satisfied, dear God, with our true blood,
Which, as Thou know'st, unjustly must be spilt.

RATCLIFF

Make haste. The hour of death is expiate.

RIVERS

Come, Grey. Come, Vaughan. Let us all embrace.   25
Farewell until we meet in heaven.

Exeunt

0: Scene: Cibber cut this scene, though his cut was not completely adopted by productions in the two centuries that followed. The scene was acted as part of act four of Nicholas Rowe's play *Jane Shore* (1714), with Cibber taking the role of Richard. By the beginning of the nineteenth century, certainly by the time of Macready, the scene had been restored to general critical approval. Lovell was not present in the Loncraine production, his lines being taken by the character Ratcliff/Tyrrel.

0: Stage Direction: *at a table*: In the early theaters, the table and seats could either have been thrust out from the center discovery space or could have been carried in by "*others*" at the beginning or end of 3.3. There would probably have been enough time to bring on the table and seats quickly during the first twelve lines of 3.4. After 1660, with the use of a stage curtain and later the dimming and raising of artificial lights, the placement of the furniture would present no particular problem.

8: **inward**: intimate

Costume rendering for the Bishop of Ely from 1953 production at the Shakespeare Memorial Theatre in Stratford-upon-Avon directed by Glen Byam Shaw

Rare Book and Special Collection Library, University of Illinois at Urbana-Champaign

Act 3, Scene 4]

Enter BUCKINGHAM, [LORD STANLEY, EARL OF] DERBY,
HASTINGS, BISHOP OF ELY, NORFOLK,
RATCLIFF, LOVELL, with others, at a table

HASTINGS
Now, noble peers, the cause why we are met
Is to determine of the coronation.
In God's name speak, when is the royal day?

BUCKINGHAM
Is all things ready for that royal time?

STANLEY
It is, and wants but nomination. 5

BISHOP OF ELY
Tomorrow, then, I judge a happy day.

BUCKINGHAM
Who knows the Lord Protector's mind herein?
Who is most inward with the noble duke?

BISHOP OF ELY
Your Grace, we think, should soonest know his mind.

BUCKINGHAM
We know each other's faces; for our hearts, 10
He knows no more of mine, than I of yours,
Or I of his, my lord, than you of mine.
Lord Hastings, you and he are near in love.

HASTINGS
I thank his Grace, I know he loves me well.
But for his purpose in the coronation, 15

21: **happy:** fortunate

22: **cousins all:** When used by the monarch, "cousin" includes all the nobility; Richard may already be using the royal form of address or he may be only referring to his actual kinsmen in the group.

24: **neglect:** cause the neglect of

30: **His lordship...loves me well:** After this line, the First Quarto has this exchange: "*Hast.* I thank your Grace. / *Glo.* My Lord of Ely! *Bish.* My lord?" The last question shares a line with Richard's speech, which then continues as it is found in the First Folio.

31–34-Stage Direction and 45-Stage Direction–47: **My Lord of Ely...*Exit BISHOP*** and ***Enter the BISHOP OF ELY*...these strawberries:** Samuel Phelps (1837-61) and Irving (c. 1877) cut out the strawberries, as have several other productions including Eyre/Loncraine/McKellen (1990, 1995) (in which the cut ran all the way to line 58). The purpose of this business has always been unclear, since although it removes Ely from the council chamber, it does not remove him from any important discussions. Edwin Booth (1878) had strawberries appear at line 57 when a Page enters with a dish, and Ely rises to receive them, but Catesby intercepts; later productions have often made much of this interaction.

31: **Holborn:** The Bishop of Ely's London palace was at Ely Place in the district of Holborn, just outside the City of London to the west. It was noted for its extensive gardens.

32: **strawberries:** As Edward IV died on April 9, 1483, and Richard III seated himself on the king's bench in Westminster Hall on June 26 of that year, these strawberries might have been notable because they were early. Strawberries were associated with serpents and with hypocrisy in popular lore and iconography.

34: **Marry, and will:** indeed I will

39: **worshipfully:** respectfully

I have not sounded him, nor he delivered
His gracious pleasure any way therein.
But you, my honorable lords, may name the time,
And in the duke's behalf I'll give my voice,
Which I presume he'll take in gentle part.   20

Enter RICHARD

BISHOP OF ELY
In happy time, here comes the duke himself.

RICHARD
My noble lords, and cousins all, good morrow.
I have been long a sleeper; but, I trust
My absence doth neglect no great design,
Which by my presence might have been concluded.   25

BUCKINGHAM
Had not you come upon your cue, my lord,
William, Lord Hastings, had pronounced your part—
I mean your voice — for crowning of the King.

RICHARD
Than my Lord Hastings no man might be bolder.
His lordship knows me well, and loves me well.   30
My Lord of Ely, when I was last in Holborn,
I saw good strawberries in your garden there;
I do beseech you, send for some of them.

BISHOP OF ELY
Marry, and will, my lord, with all my heart.

Exit BISHOP

RICHARD
Cousin of Buckingham, a word with you.   35

[Draws him aside]

Catesby hath sounded Hastings in our business,
And finds the testy gentleman so hot,
That he will lose his head ere give consent
His master's child, as worshipfully he terms it,
Shall lose the royalty of England's throne.   40

42: **triumph:** public celebration

43: **sudden:** soon

45: **As else:** as otherwise; **prolonged:** delayed

48: **smooth:** agreeable

49: **conceit:** 1) idea or 2) piece of wit

55: **livelihood:** liveliness of appearance

58-59: "I pray you all, tell me what they deserve / That do conspire my death": Antony Sher as Richard and Brian Blessed as Hastings in the 1984 Royal Shakespeare Company production directed by Bill Alexander

Photo: Donald Cooper

57: **For...looks:** the First Quarto follows this with a line for Stanley, "I pray God he be not, I say."

58-74: Scene: **I pray you all...traitor:** Richard, with Buckingham, enters in his usual abrupt fashion but with a good deal of verbal and, by implication, physical violence. This is true whether or not he is entering from one of the two stage doors, from the wings, or from the far side of the stage where he has withdrawn with Buckingham. .

59: **conspire:** conspire to cause

61: **charms:** spells

BUCKINGHAM
Withdraw yourself awhile. I'll go with you.
Exeunt [RICHARD and BUCKINGHAM]

STANLEY
We have not yet set down this day of triumph.
Tomorrow, in my judgment, is too sudden,
For I myself am not so well provided
As else I would be, were the day prolonged.   45
Enter the BISHOP OF ELY

BISHOP OF ELY
Where is my lord, the Duke of Gloucester?
I have sent for these strawberries.

HASTINGS
His Grace looks cheerfully and smooth this morning.
There's some conceit or other likes him well,
When he doth bid good morrow with such spirit.   50
I think there's never a man in Christendom
Can less hide his love, or hate, than he,
For by his face straight shall you know his heart.

STANLEY
What of his heart perceive you in his face
By any livelihood he showed today?   55

HASTINGS
Marry, that with no man here he is offended,
For were he, he had shown it in his looks.
Enter RICHARD and BUCKINGHAM

RICHARD
I pray you all, tell me what they deserve
That do conspire my death with devilish plots
Of damnèd witchcraft, and that have prevailed   60
Upon my body with their hellish charms?

63: **forward:** ready; **presence:** company
70: **Consorted:** conspired

74: "Thou art a traitor": Tom Nelis as the Cardinal, Peter Dinklage as Richard,
Stephen Barker Turner as Hastings and Harry Barandes as Catesby in the 2004
Public Theater production directed by Peter DuBois
Photo: Michal Daniel

74-76: Scene: **Talk'st thou...same:** From Burbage until today, this is one of the most
dramatic of moments in English drama. It is frequently done with a dismissive gesture of the arm, sometimes the withered arm about which Richard has just been
speaking. Sometimes Richard makes a throat-cutting motion with his hand; other
times he bangs the table.

78: Stage Direction: ***Exeunt, manet RATCLIFF and LOVELL with the LORD HASTINGS:*** In
the First Folio the direction "*Exeunt*" appears at the end of line 77 and "*Manet Louell
and Ratcliffe, with the Lord Hastings*" appears after line 78; here they are combined
since they both describe what must be one set of actions.

80: **fond:** foolish
81: **raze his helm:** From the First Quarto, the First Folio reads "rowse our Helmes".
Although both readings are possible it seems much more likely that Hastings, by
referring to the earlier exchanges with Stanley and Stanley's Messenger (3.2.10-34
and 72-76), is thinking of the boar as being only Richard and therefore singular.
83: **foot-cloth horse:** horse with hangings over its sides as far down as and covering
the rider's feet. Such adornment of the horse was a sign of the rider's high rank.

HASTINGS
> The tender love I bear your Grace, my lord,
> Makes me most forward in this princely presence
> To doom th' offenders, whatsoe'er they be.
> I say, my lord, they have deservèd death.   65

RICHARD
> Then be your eyes the witness of their evil.
> Look how I am bewitched. Behold mine arm
> Is like a blasted sapling, withered up.
> And this is Edward's wife, that monstrous witch,
> Consorted with that harlot, strumpet Shore,   70
> That by their witchcraft thus have markèd me.

HASTINGS
> If they have done this deed, my noble lord—

RICHARD
> If? Thou protector of this damnèd strumpet,
> Talk'st thou me of "ifs"? Thou art a traitor.
> Off with his head! Now by Saint Paul I swear,   75
> I will not dine until I see the same.
> Lovell and Ratcliff, look that it be done.
> The rest that love me, rise and follow me.

Exeunt, manet RATCLIFF and LOVELL with the LORD HASTINGS

HASTINGS
> Woe, woe for England, not a whit for me,
> For I, too fond, might have prevented this.   80
> Stanley did dream the boar did raze his helm,
> And I did scorn it, and disdain to fly.
> Three times today my foot-cloth horse did stumble,
> And started, when he looked upon the Tower,
> As loath to bear me to the slaughterhouse.   85
> O, now I need the priest that spake to me.
> I now repent I told the Pursuivant,
> As too triumphing, how mine enemies
> Today at Pomfret bloodily were butchered,

93: **dispatch:** hurry; **would be:** wishes to be

94: **short shrift:** speedy confession

95: **grace:** favor

95-loo: Scene: **O momentary...deep:** Olivier (1955) replaced this speech with "The Cat, the Rat, and Lovell the Dog, rule all of England under the Hog," a rhyme supposedly written by William Collingham in the fifteenth century who was put to death for it; the Cat is Catesby, the Rat is Ratcliff, and Lovell is Lord Lovell, whose emblem was a hound, and, of course, Richard's badge was the white boar.

101: **bootless:** useless

106: Stage Direction: ***Exeunt:*** Olivier (1955) showed the beheading of Hastings. Bogdanov (1989) had Ratcliff produce a knife and cut Hastings's throat and then the lights went down. Loncraine (1995) showed the hanging, not beheading, of Hastings.

And I myself secure in grace and favor.   90
O Margaret, Margaret, now thy heavy curse
Is lighted on poor Hastings' wretched head.

RATCLIFF
Come, come, dispatch. The duke would be at dinner.
Make a short shrift. He longs to see your head.

HASTINGS
O momentary grace of mortal men,   95
Which we more hunt for than the grace of God!
Who builds his hope in air of your good looks,
Lives like a drunken sailor on a mast,
Ready with every nod to tumble down
Into the fatal bowels of the deep.   100

LOVELL
Come, come, dispatch, 'tis bootless to exclaim.

HASTINGS
O bloody Richard! Miserable England,
I prophesy the fearfull'st time to thee
That ever wretched age hath looked upon.
Come, lead me to the block. Bear him my head.   105
They smile at me who shortly shall be dead.

Exeunt

0: Scene: Neither the First Quarto nor the First Folio mark a new scene here; however, since the clearing of the stage and the entry of other characters is one of the conventions of scene division in Shakespearean drama, a new scene is marked here.

Cibber and almost all following productions, even into the twentieth century, cut nearly all of this scene, moving only those lines needed for the plot to other points in the play (e.g., lines 3.5.72-109 to the end of 3.1 [Cibber] or as part of the aside at 3.4.35 [Edwin Booth]). When it is retained, it can be done as almost a play-within-a-play as Hands did in 1980, with Richard and Buckingham on a table beating drums and trying on clothes out of a property basket. This sort of playacting is possible up to line 21 when Hastings's head is brought on. The cries of false alarms and feigned watching against the mythical attackers offer Richard, the consummate actor, considerable scope. In Alexander's 1984 production, Sher was atop one of the tombs, perched like a bird of prey.

0: Stage Direction: ***rotten...ill-favored***: rusty armor, extremely ugly

1-22: Scene: **Come....Hastings:** Eyre/Loncraine/McKellen (1990, 1995) cut these lines and inserted a cut version of Buckingham's lines 33-39.

1: **change thy color:** be pale or flushed

2: **Murder thy breath:** gasp

5: **counterfeit:** imitate

6: **pry on every side:** look all around

8: **Intending:** signifying

[Act 3, Scene 5]

Enter RICHARD and BUCKINGHAM,
in rotten armor, marvelous ill-favored

RICHARD
    Come, cousin, canst thou quake and change thy color,
    Murder thy breath in the middle of a word,
    And then begin again, and stop again,
    As if thou wert distraught and mad with terror?

BUCKINGHAM
    Tut, I can counterfeit the deep tragedian,   5
    Speak, and look back, and pry on every side,
    Tremble and start at wagging of a straw,
    Intending deep suspicion. Ghastly looks
    Are at my service, like enforcèd smiles;
    And both are ready in their offices,   10
    At any time, to grace my stratagems.
    But what, is Catesby gone?

RICHARD
    He is; and see he brings the Mayor along.
                            Enter the [LORD] MAYOR and CATESBY

BUCKINGHAM
    Lord Mayor—

RICHARD
    Look to the drawbridge there!   15

BUCKINGHAM
    Hark, a drum!

RICHARD
    Catesby, o'erlook the walls.

                                            [Exit CATESBY]

21 Stage Direction-72: ***Enter LOVELL...farewell:*** It is typical of *Richard III* that the entry of a severed head, an event usually redolent of pity, lamentation, terror, and fear, has often been an event of comedy, albeit sinister comedy, in productions of this play, at least in the twentieth century. Donald Wolfit (Strand, St. James, and Scala theatres, 1942, 1944) gloated over the head of Hastings while eating the Bishop of Ely's strawberries. In Michael Bogdanov's production (1989) the head was brought in a gladstone bag (a rectangular, leather suitcase) and never taken out, though the bag was peered into by all present. More typical of recent years has perhaps been the use of Hastings's head as a football. In Hands's productions (1970, 1980) it was tossed about among those on stage, and Richard tosses it to the Lord Mayor who fainted (in the 1980 version the Lord Mayor hid in a property basket), then Buckingham threw it to Lovell who caught it in his helmet. In Alexander's production (1984) the head was also thrown about until line 40 when the Lord Mayor says, "Had he done so?" and Richard responds with "What, think you we are Turks and infidels?" while pushing the head into the Lord Mayor's hands, at which point all fell back, leaving him holding it alone.

27: **book:** journal or commonplace book

30: **apparent:** obvious

31: **conversation:** sexual intercourse

32: **attainder of suspects:** dishonor of suspicion

33: **covert'st sheltered:** secret protected

35: Scene: **Would you imagine:** Olivier began the scene at about this line with the Lord Mayor, Buckingham, Catesby, Ratcliff, and Lovell riding through the streets of London in a wagon, but cut most of the remainder going straight to 3.7 without a scene break.

BUCKINGHAM
Lord Mayor, the reason we have sent—

RICHARD
Look back, defend thee, here are enemies.

BUCKINGHAM
God and our innocency defend and guard us.   20

RICHARD
Be patient, they are friends, Ratcliff and Lovell.
          Enter LOVELL and RATCLIFF, with HASTINGS's head

LOVELL
Here is the head of that ignoble traitor,
The dangerous and unsuspected Hastings.

RICHARD
So dear I loved the man, that I must weep.
I took him for the plainest harmless creature   25
That breathed upon this earth a Christian;
Made him my book, wherein my soul recorded
The history of all her secret thoughts.
So smooth he daubed his vice with show of virtue,
That, his apparent open guilt omitted,   30
I mean his conversation with Shore's wife,
He lived from all attainder of suspects.

BUCKINGHAM
Well, well, he was the covert'st sheltered traitor
That ever lived.—
Would you imagine, or almost believe,   35
Were't not that, by great preservation
We live to tell it, that the subtle traitor
This day had plotted, in the council house,
To murder me and my good Lord of Gloucester?

LORD MAYOR
Had he done so?   40

44: **But:** except
47: **fair befall you:** good fortune be yours

Costume rendering for Lord Mayor from the 1953 production at the Shakespeare Memorial Theatre in Stratford-upon-Avon directed by Glen Byam Shaw

Rare Book and Special Collection Library, University of Illinois at Urbana-Champaign

50-51: **I never...Mistress Shore:** In the First Quarto, these two lines are part of the Lord Mayor's preceding speech.
54: **friends:** i.e., Lovell and Ratcliff
55: **Something:** somewhat
59: **signified:** told
60: **haply:** perhaps
61: **Misconster us in him:** misconstrue what we did to him
68: **carping:** fault-finding

RICHARD

    What, think you we are Turks or infidels?
    Or that we would, against the form of law,
    Proceed thus rashly to the villain's death,
    But that the extreme peril of the case,
    The peace of England, and our persons' safety,   45
    Enforced us to this execution?

LORD MAYOR

    Now fair befall you! He deserved his death,
    And your good Graces both have well proceeded,
    To warn false traitors from the like attempts.

BUCKINGHAM

    I never looked for better at his hands,   50
    After he once fell in with Mistress Shore.
    Yet had not we determined he should die
    Until your lordship came to see his end,
    Which now the loving haste of these our friends,
    Something against our meanings, have prevented.   55
    Because, my lord, I would have had you heard
    The traitor speak and timorously confess
    The manner and the purpose of his treasons,
    That you might well have signified the same
    Unto the citizens, who haply may   60
    Misconster us in him, and wail his death.

LORD MAYOR

    But, my good lord, your Graces' words shall serve
    As well as I had seen and heard him speak.
    And doubt you not, right noble princes both,
    But I'll acquaint our duteous citizens   65
    With all your just proceedings in this case.

RICHARD

    And to that end we wished your lordship here,
    T' avoid the censures of the carping world.

69: **of our intent:** for our purposes

73: **Guildhall:** the center of civic government for the City of London. It is in the center of the City, northeast of St. Paul's Cathedral.

74: **meetest:** most suitable

76-79: **Tell them...termèd so:** Shakespeare takes this story from Sir Thomas More's *History of Richard III*, which appeared in English and Latin printed editions in the 1540s and 1550s but was written much earlier. In the story, a man is executed for treason for saying his son would be heir to his house, called The Crown because of the sign hanging in front of it.

80: **luxury:** lechery

86: **went with:** was with

96: **golden fee:** the Crown

98: **Baynard's Castle:** Richard's residence on the north bank of the Thames between Blackfriars and London Bridge, it had been a royal residence since the time of Henry V.

BUCKINGHAM

> Which since you come too late of our intent,
> Yet witness what you hear we did intend.   70
> And so, my good Lord Mayor, we bid farewell.

Exit [LORD] MAYOR

RICHARD

> Go, after, after, cousin Buckingham.
> The Mayor towards Guildhall hies him in all post.
> There, at your meetest vantage of the time,
> Infer the bastardy of Edward's children.   75
> Tell them how Edward put to death a citizen,
> Only for saying he would make his son
> Heir to the Crown, meaning indeed his house,
> Which by the sign thereof was termèd so.
> Moreover, urge his hateful luxury   80
> And bestial appetite in change of lust,
> Which stretched unto their servants, daughters, wives,
> Even where his raging eye or savage heart,
> Without control, lusted to make his prey.
> Nay, for a need, thus far come near my person: 85
> Tell them, when that my mother went with child
> Of that insatiate Edward, noble York
> My princely father then had wars in France,
> And, by true computation of the time,
> Found that the issue was not his begot,   90
> Which well appearèd in his lineaments,
> Being nothing like the noble duke my father.
> Yet touch this sparingly, as 'twere far off,
> Because, my lord, you know my mother lives.

BUCKINGHAM

> Doubt not, my lord, I'll play the orator   95
> As if the golden fee for which I plead
> Were for myself. And so, my lord, adieu.

RICHARD

> If you thrive well, bring them to Baynard's Castle,
> Where you shall find me well accompanied
> With reverend fathers and well-learnèd bishops.   100

103: **Doctor Shaw:** Ralph Shaa or Shaw, was the brother of the Edmund Shaa, the Lord Mayor of London (see note 3.1.17). He was a Doctor of Theology from Cambridge University and, in 1483, at the time of these events, he was a Canon of St. Paul's Cathedral, London. He preached a sermon in this year at Paul's Cross, the popular open-air pulpit outside the Cathedral, covering the points made by Richard in lines 72-45 and claiming Richard was the only valid claimant to the crown. His sermon was coldly received by the populace, and his death the following year was said to have been caused by his embarrassment at the reception of his sermon. Friar Penker in the next line has not been positively identified, though Sir Thomas More says he was the Provincial of the Augustine Friars.

103–105-Stage Direction and 109-Stage Direction: **Go, Lovell...*[Exeunt, manet RICHARD]*** and ***[Exit]*:** Lines 103 to 105 do not appear in the First Quarto, and the First Folio has the stage direction "*Exit,*" though clearly Lovell and Ratcliff both exit and Richard remains, since he continues speaking. When he does exit at 3.5.109, the First Folio provides "*Exeunt*" as a stage direction, although by this time Richard is the only one left on stage.

106: **take:** issue; **privy order:** secret command

108: **no manner person:** no one whatsoever

109: **any:** at any

BUCKINGHAM
    I go; and towards three or four o'clock
    Look for the news that the Guildhall affords.

Exit BUCKINGHAM

RICHARD
    Go, Lovell, with all speed to Doctor Shaw—
    [*To RATCLIFF*] Go thou to Friar Penker. Bid them both
    Meet me within this hour at Baynard's Castle.   105

[Exeunt, manet RICHARD]

    Now will I go to take some privy order,
    To draw the brats of Clarence out of sight,
    And to give order that no manner person
    Have any time recourse unto the princes.

[Exit]

0: Scene: As with the previous scene (3.5), neither the First Folio nor the First Quarto have a new scene here, though it conforms to the convention for scene division. This scene was cut by Cibber and nearly all productions thereafter, though not by Alexander (1984).

0: Stage Direction: **SCRIVENER:** a professional penman, in this case a copyist of legal documents

1: **indictment:** bill of indictment
2: **set hand:** style of handwriting specifically used for legal documents; **fairly is engrossed:** properly transcribed
3: **read o'er in Paul's:** proclaimed at Paul's Cross outside St. Paul's Cathedral
4: **sequel:** sequence
7: **precedent:** original, from which he copied
9: **Untainted:** without charges against him
10: **gross:** stupid
13: **naught:** evil
14: **must be seen in thought:** may not be spoken but only thought about

Costume rendering for Scrivener from the 1953 production at the Shakespeare Memorial Theatre in Stratford-upon-Avon directed by Glen Byam Shaw

Act 3, Scene 6]

Enter a SCRIVENER

SCRIVENER
    This is the indictment of the good Lord Hastings,
    Which in a set hand fairly is engrossed,
    That it may be this day read o'er in Paul's.
    And mark how well the sequel hangs together:
    Eleven hours I spent to write it over,   5
    For yesternight by Catesby was it sent me;
    The precedent was full as long a-doing,
    And yet within these five hours Hastings lived,
    Untainted, unexamined, free, at liberty.
    Here's a good world the while. Who is so gross,   10
    That cannot see this palpable device?
    Yet who so bold but says he sees it not?
    Bad is the world, and all will come to naught,
    When such ill dealing must be seen in thought.

Exit

0: Scene: Again, this scene division is marked in neither the First Folio nor the First Quarto. For once, Cibber did not cut this scene but expanded it, and it has come to be known as the Gothic Chamber scene. Using material he found in Shakespeare's sources, notably Holinshed, he created a scene to fill the time while Buckingham is speaking to the Lord Mayor and citizens at Guildhall. The scene is a meeting between Richard and Anne, who enters at the close of 3.5 or, in later versions, is discovered. She demands of Richard why she is so ill used; Richard tells her he does not love her and wishes she would kill herself. He wants to marry his niece Elizabeth because she is young and fair. The scene ends with this exchange: "*Rich.* Your absence, Madam, will be necessary. *Anne.* Would my death were so. *Rich.* It may be shortly." At this point Buckingham enters and the scene proceeds generally as it does in the usual text. This way of opening 3.7 held the stage until well after the middle of the nineteenth century.

0: Stage Direction: ***several doors:*** two doors; the two doors on either side of most early stages

4: **Touched you:** did you mention
5: **Lady Lucy:** i.e., Elizabeth Lucy, one of two women (the other being Eleanor Butler) with whom it was suggested that Edward IV had contracted marriage before he met Elizabeth Woodville
6: **by deputy in France:** Edward IV had also arranged to marry Bona of Savoy using a proxy in his place, quite a common custom at the time. (This arrangement is described in Shakespeare's *Henry VI, Part 3*.)
7: **unsatiate:** insatiable
8: **enforcement:** compelled sexual favors
9: **tyranny for trifles:** extreme penalties for small offenses
10: **got:** conceived; **your father:** meaning Richard, Duke of York
12: **Withal:** in addition
13: **right idea:** accurate image
15: **victories in Scotland:** In 1482, Richard led the capture of Berwick.
20: **mine:** from the First Quarto, the First Folio reads "my"

Act 3, Scene 7]

Enter RICHARD and BUCKINGHAM, at several doors

RICHARD
How now, how now, what say the citizens?

BUCKINGHAM
Now, by the holy mother of our Lord,
The citizens are mum, say not a word.

RICHARD
Touched you the bastardy of Edward's children?

BUCKINGHAM
I did; with his contract with Lady Lucy,   5
And his contract by deputy in France;
Th' unsatiate greediness of his desire,
And his enforcement of the city wives;
His tyranny for trifles; his own bastardy,
As being got, your father then in France,   10
And his resemblance being not like the duke.
Withal, I did infer your lineaments,
Being the right idea of your father,
Both in your form and nobleness of mind;
Laid open all your victories in Scotland,   15
Your discipline in war, wisdom in peace,
Your bounty, virtue, fair humility;
Indeed, left nothing fitting for your purpose
Untouched or slightly handled in discourse.
And when mine oratory drew toward end,   20
I bid them that did love their country's good
Cry "God save Richard, England's royal king!"

RICHARD
And did they so?

30: **Recorder:** civil magistrate of the City. At this time he was Thomas Fitzwilliam.
33: **in warrant from himself:** by his own authority
37: **vantage:** advantage
40: **wisdoms:** from the First Quarto, the First Folio reads "wisdom"

Set design by William Bloodgood for the 1993 Oregon Shakespeare Festival production directed by James Edmondson
Courtesy of Oregon Shakespeare Festival

41: **brake:** broke
44: **Intend:** pretend
45: **by mighty suit:** for a great reason
47: **two churchmen:** see stage direction 3.7.93
48: **ground:** subject, in this case the sight of Richard between the clergymen; **holy descant:** a melody accompanying a simple musical line, such as the plainsong, often extemporized
50: **Play...it:** proverb expression, "maids say nay and take it"
51: **An if:** if

BUCKINGHAM
    No. So God help me, they spake not a word;
    But like dumb statues, or breathing stones,   25
    Stared each on other, and looked deadly pale.
    Which when I saw, I reprehended them,
    And asked the Mayor what meant this willful silence.
    His answer was, the people were not used
    To be spoke to but by the Recorder.   30
    Then he was urged to tell my tale again:
    "Thus saith the duke, thus hath the duke inferred"—
    But nothing spake in warrant from himself.
    When he had done, some followers of mine own,
    At lower end of the hall, hurled up their caps,   35
    And some ten voices cried "God save King Richard!"
    And thus I took the vantage of those few.
    "Thanks, gentle citizens and friends," quoth I.
    "This general applause and cheerful shout
    Argues your wisdoms and your love to Richard."   40
    And even here brake off, and came away.

RICHARD
    What tongueless blocks were they! Would not they speak?
    Will not the Mayor then and his brethren come?

BUCKINGHAM
    The Mayor is here at hand. Intend some fear;
    Be not you spoke with but by mighty suit.   45
    And look you get a prayer book in your hand
    And stand between two churchmen, good my lord,
    For on that ground I'll make a holy descant.
    And be not easily won to our requests,
    Play the maid's part: still answer "nay," and take it.   50

RICHARD
    I go. An if you plead as well for them
    As I can say "nay" to thee for myself,
    No doubt we bring it to a happy issue.

                                  [Knocking within]

54: **leads:** the roof, though in this case, probably meaning the upper stage. Strips of lead were a common roof covering in large buildings

55: **dance attendance:** tap my foot or kick my heels while waiting for Richard

56: **withal:** with

62: **worldly suits:** secular requests; **moved:** persuaded

63: **holy exercise:** devotions

66: **deep designs:** serious concerns

70: Scene: **Ah ha:** At this point Sher (Alexander, 1984) and the two clergymen passed across the gallery aloft as Buckingham pointed them out to the Mayor and Citizens, but Sher exited and entered at line 93.

74: **deep:** learned

76: **watchful:** awake, unsleeping

BUCKINGHAM
Go, go, up to the leads. The Lord Mayor knocks.

[Exit RICHARD]
Enter the [LORD] MAYOR and CITIZENS
Welcome my lord, I dance attendance here.   55
I think the duke will not be spoke withal.

Enter CATESBY
Now, Catesby, what says your lord to my request?

CATESBY
He doth entreat your Grace, my noble lord,
To visit him tomorrow or next day.
He is within, with two right reverend fathers,   60
Divinely bent to meditation,
And in no worldly suits would he be moved,
To draw him from his holy exercise.

BUCKINGHAM
Return, good Catesby, to the gracious duke.
Tell him, myself, the Mayor and Aldermen,   65
In deep designs, in matter of great moment,
No less importing than our general good,
Are come to have some conference with his Grace.

CATESBY
I'll signify so much unto him straight.

Exit

BUCKINGHAM
Ah ha, my lord, this prince is not an Edward!   70
He is not lolling on a lewd love-bed,
But on his knees at meditation;
Not dallying with a brace of courtesans,
But meditating with two deep divines;
Not sleeping, to engross his idle body,   75
But praying, to enrich his watchful soul.
Happy were England would this virtuous prince
Take on his Grace the sovereignty thereof.
But sure I fear we shall not win him to it.

80: **defend:** forbid

92: **beads:** prayers, with perhaps a passing allusion to the rosary; **'tis much:** it requires something serious

93: Stage Direction: **between two bishops:** If we are to assume that these two clergymen are Canon Dr. Shaw and Friar Penker (see lines 105-106) then they certainly are not bishops of any kind. If bishops are really intended (perhaps because of the distinctiveness of their dress) then some other unidentified, or generic, bishops enter with Richard. It is very unlikely, almost impossible, that they can be any of the three bishops with speaking roles in the play (the Archbishops of Canterbury and York and the Bishop of Ely), especially since two of the three (York and Ely) are strong members of the anti-Richard faction.

Both F1 and Q1 indicate that Richard and the bishops are to be aloft (Q1 actually reads, "*Enter Rich. with two bishops a loste.*" but the last two words are no doubt a typesetting error). In a theater such as the Globe, the gallery would be certainly large enough to contain these three with room to spare. The point is that all others will be put in the position of having to look up at them. However, directors, actors, and even some editors, try to avoid the very clear direction that Richard and the clergymen are to be aloft. Cibber seems to have feared being charged with blasphemy for bringing two clergymen on in such a situation, and he has the Lord Mayor and Buckingham look off stage and comment on them (lines 94-102) and then Richard enters, bowing in thanks to the clergymen and not aloft. Although the early editions clearly specify bishops (costumed as clergy wearing mitres), it has become almost universal for them simply to be generic clergymen, often monks.

tracks 14-15

94–154:
Peter Yapp as Lord Mayor, Nicholas Farrell as Buckingham,
and Kenneth Branagh as Richard

LORD MAYOR
   Marry, God defend his Grace should say us nay.   80

BUCKINGHAM
   I fear he will. Here Catesby comes again.

                                              Enter CATESBY

   Now, Catesby, what says his Grace?

CATESBY
   He wonders to what end you have assembled
   Such troops of citizens to come to him,
   His Grace not being warned thereof before.   85
   He fears, my lord, you mean no good to him.

BUCKINGHAM
   Sorry I am my noble cousin should
   Suspect me that I mean no good to him.
   By heaven, we come to him in perfect love,
   And so once more return and tell his Grace.   90
                                              Exit CATESBY

   When holy and devout religious men
   Are at their beads, 'tis much to draw them thence,
   So sweet is zealous contemplation.
                     Enter RICHARD aloft, between two bishops,
                                        [and CATESBY below]

LORD MAYOR
   See where his Grace stands, 'tween two clergymen.

BUCKINGHAM
   Two props of virtue for a Christian prince,   95
   To stay him from the fall of vanity;
   And see, a book of prayer in his hand,
   True ornaments to know a holy man.
   Famous Plantagenet, most gracious prince,
   Lend favorable ear to our requests,   100
   And pardon us the interruption
   Of thy devotion and right Christian zeal.

tracks 14-15

94–154:
Peter Yapp as Lord Mayor, Nicholas Farrell as Buckingham,
and Kenneth Branagh as Richard

105-106: Who...friends: I put my religious duties before meeting with my friends; see note 3.7.93

107: leaving this: putting this aside

111: disgracious: ungracious, displeasing

115: Else wherefore: why else

116-216: Scene: Know then...your house: Buckingham and Richard's argument, though we know them to be play-acting, can be vigorous. In Alexander's production (1984) Buckingham so forces himself on Richard that at one point (lines 172-99), he has him on the floor and pushed against the wall, and almost all those on stage are eventually in a heap on the floor as the pleading ends. At lines 238-239, Buckingham comes back to kiss Richard's hand three times.

119: state of fortune: position of greatness

124: want: lack; **her:** from Q1-Q2, the First Folio and Q3-Q6 read "his"; **proper:** own

125: Her: from Q1-Q6, the First Folio reads "His"

126: Her: The first editor to make this emendation was Alexander Pope (1725); the First Folio reads "His", and the line does not appear in Q1-Q6.

127: in: into

129: recure: restore

RICHARD
  My lord, there needs no such apology.
  I do beseech your Grace to pardon me,
  Who, earnest in the service of my God,   105
  Deferred the visitation of my friends.
  But, leaving this, what is your Grace's pleasure?

BUCKINGHAM
  Even that, I hope, which pleaseth God above,
  And all good men of this ungoverned isle.

RICHARD
  I do suspect I have done some offense   110
  That seems disgracious in the City's eye,
  And that you come to reprehend my ignorance.

BUCKINGHAM
  You have, my lord. Would it might please your Grace,
  On our entreaties, to amend that fault.

RICHARD
  Else wherefore breathe I in a Christian land?   115

BUCKINGHAM
  Know then, it is your fault that you resign
  The supreme seat, the throne majestical,
  The sceptered office of your ancestors,
  Your state of fortune, and your due of birth,
  The lineal glory of your royal house,   120
  To the corruption of a blemished stock;
  Whiles in the mildness of your sleepy thoughts,
  Which here we waken to our country's good,
  This noble isle doth want her proper limbs;
  Her face defaced with scars of infamy,   125
  Her royal stock graft with ignoble plants,
  And almost shouldered in the swallowing gulf
  Of dark forgetfulness and deep oblivion.
  Which to recure, we heartily solicit
  Your gracious self to take on you the charge   130

tracks 14-15

94–154:
Peter Yapp as Lord Mayor, Nicholas Farrell as Buckingham,
and Kenneth Branagh as Richard

133: **factor:** agent
134: **successively...blood:** in true succession of your family line
135: **empery:** sole rule
137: **worshipful:** honorable
139: **move:** convince

Ian McKellen as Richard with Bishops in the 1990 National Theatre production
directed by Richard Eyre

Photo: Donald Cooper

142: **fitteth:** suits; **degree:** rank; **condition:** standing in society
143: **not to:** I do not; **haply:** perhaps
144-145: **Tongue-tied...sovereignty:** not speaking implies consent
146: **fondly:** foolishly
148: **seasoned:** made tasty or agreeable
149: **checked:** reproved
153-154: **desert / Unmeritable:** unworthiness
156: **that:** if; **even:** level or direct
160: **my greatness:** my title to the crown
161: **bark:** boat; **brook:** endure
167: **stealing:** quietly passing

And kingly government of this your land,
Not as Protector, steward, substitute,
Or lowly factor for another's gain,
But as successively from blood to blood,
Your right of birth, your empery, your own.   135
For this, consorted with the citizens,
Your very worshipful and loving friends,
And by their vehement instigation,
In this just cause come I to move your Grace.

RICHARD
    I cannot tell if to depart in silence   140
Or bitterly to speak in your reproof
Best fitteth my degree or your condition.
If not to answer, you might haply think
Tongue-tied ambition, not replying, yielded
To bear the golden yoke of sovereignty,   145
Which fondly you would here impose on me.
If to reprove you for this suit of yours,
So seasoned with your faithful love to me,
Then on the other side I checked my friends.
Therefore, to speak, and to avoid the first,   150
And then, in speaking, not to incur the last,
Definitively thus I answer you.
Your love deserves my thanks; but my desert
Unmeritable shuns your high request.
First, if all obstacles were cut away   155
And that my path were even to the crown
As the ripe revenue and due of birth,
Yet so much is my poverty of spirit,
So mighty and so many my defects,
That I would rather hide me from my greatness,   160
Being a bark to brook no mighty sea,
Than in my greatness covet to be hid
And in the vapor of my glory smothered.
But, God be thanked, there is no need of me,
And much I need to help you, were there need.   165
The royal tree hath left us royal fruit,
Which, mellowed by the stealing hours of time,

173: **conscience:** conscientiousness

174: **nice:** overscrupulous

176: **Edward:** i.e., Prince Edward, or Edward V, as he was from April 9 through June 25, 1483

178: **Lady Lucy:** see note 3.7.5

181: **Bona:** see note 3.7.6

182: **put off:** delayed or set aside; **poor petitioner:** meaning Elizabeth Grey, Queen Elizabeth

186: **prize and purchase:** plunder and booty

187: **pitch:** highest elevation (a term from falconry); **degree:** rank

188: **declension:** falling away from eminence

190: **manners:** politeness

192: **some alive:** perhaps a reference to the Duchess of York, see 3.5.95

196: **withal:** as well

Will well become the seat of majesty,
And make, no doubt, us happy by his reign.
On him I lay what you would lay on me,   170
The right and fortune of his happy stars,
Which God defend that I should wring from him.

BUCKINGHAM
My lord, this argues conscience in your Grace,
But the respects thereof are nice and trivial,
All circumstances well considerèd.   175
You say that Edward is your brother's son;
So say we too, but not by Edward's wife.
For first he was contract to Lady Lucy—
Your mother lives a witness to that vow—
And afterward by substitute betrothed   180
To Bona, sister to the King of France.
These both put off, a poor petitioner,
A care-crazed mother of a many sons,
A beauty-waning and distressèd widow,
Even in the afternoon of her best days,   185
Made prize and purchase of his wanton eye,
Seduced the pitch and height of his degree
To base declension and loathed bigamy.
By her in his unlawful bed he got
This Edward, whom our manners call the prince.   190
More bitterly could I expostulate,
Save that, for reverence to some alive,
I give a sparing limit to my tongue.
Then, good my lord, take to your royal self
This proffered benefit of dignity,   195
If not to bless us and the land withal,
Yet to draw forth your noble ancestry
From the corruption of abusing times,
Unto a lineal true-derivèd course.

LORD MAYOR
Do, good my lord, your citizens entreat you.   200

BUCKINGHAM
Refuse not, mighty lord, this proffered love.

204: **state:** dignity or pomp

207: **as:** as being

210: **effeminate:** compassionate

212: **egally:** evenly or equally, with regard to justice. Shakespeare used the word in 4.4 of *Titus Andronicus* (written at about the same time as *Richard III*): "Confronted thus, and for the extent / Of egall justice, us'd in such contempt?"; **all estates:** all ranks of people

218: **'Zounds! I'll:** from Q1-Q6; the First Folio reads only "we will" (removed under the "Act to Restrain the Abuses of Players")

219: **RICHARD...Buckingham:** from Q1-Q6; not in the First Folio

219: Stage Direction: ***Exeunt [BUCKINGHAM with the LORD MAYOR and CITIZENS]:*** Because line 219 does not appear in the First Folio, this follows line 218. In Cibber's version only Buckingham exits at this point, and the Lord Mayor is one of those calling Buckingham back.

CATESBY
  O, make them joyful, grant their lawful suit.

RICHARD
  Alas, why would you heap this care on me?
  I am unfit for state and majesty.
  I do beseech you, take it not amiss;   205
  I cannot, nor I will not, yield to you.

BUCKINGHAM
  If you refuse it, as in love and zeal
  Loath to depose the child, your brother's son—
  As well we know your tenderness of heart
  And gentle, kind, effeminate remorse,   210
  Which we have noted in you to your kindred
  And egally indeed to all estates—
  Yet know, whether you accept our suit or no,
  Your brother's son shall never reign our king;
  But we will plant some other in the throne,   215
  To the disgrace and downfall of your house.
  And in this resolution here we leave you.—
  Come citizens. 'Zounds! I'll entreat no more.

RICHARD
  O, do not swear, my Lord of Buckingham.
                    Exeunt [BUCKINGHAM with the
                    LORD MAYOR and CITIZENS]

CATESBY
  Call him again, sweet prince, accept their suit.   220
  If you deny them all the land will rue it.

RICHARD
  Will you enforce me to a world of cares?
  Call them again, I am not made of stones,
  But penetrable to your kind entreaties,
  Albeit against my conscience and my soul.   225
                    Enter BUCKINGHAM, and the rest
  Cousin of Buckingham, and you sage, grave men,
  Since you will buckle fortune on my back,

232: **mere:** absolute; **acquittance:** acquit

246: **cousin:** from the First Quarto, the First Folio reads "Cousins". Since there is only one person present that Richard might call cousin (Buckingham), even in the archaic sense, the word should be singular.

245: "Come, let us to our holy work again": Kevin Kline as Richard in the 1983 Public Theater production directed by Jane Howell

Photo: George E. Joseph

245-246: Scene: **Come…friends:** Cibber reversed these two lines so that Richard bids farewell to all the others and, with a revised line 245 ("I must to my holy Work agen"), was left in triumph to deliver a soliloquy of Cibber's devising. David Garrick (1741), playing Cibber's version, flung away the prayer book he was holding on the last line. This was so well received that every actor playing the Cibber version followed Garrick's example, including even most modern productions adhering to the Shakespearean text. Frank Benson at the Memorial Theatre in Stratford (1901-15) used this staging and added the shout "King!". Starting with Richard Mansfield (Globe Theatre, London, 1889), a tradition of throwing the prayer book straight up in the air, typically as high as the actor could manage also developed . Ian Holm (Hall/Barton, 1963) threw the prayer book to Buckingham.

To bear her burden, whe'er I will or no,
I must have patience to endure the load;
But if black scandal or foul-faced reproach   230
Attend the sequel of your imposition,
Your mere enforcement shall acquittance me
From all the impure blots and stains thereof;
For God doth know, and you may partly see,
How far I am from the desire of this.   235

LORD MAYOR
God bless your Grace, we see it, and will say it.

RICHARD
In saying so, you shall but say the truth.

BUCKINGHAM
Then I salute you with this kingly title:
Long live Richard, England's royal King!

ALL
Amen.   240

BUCKINGHAM
Tomorrow may it please you to be crowned?

RICHARD
Even when you please, for you will have it so.

BUCKINGHAM
Tomorrow, then, we will attend your Grace,
And so most joyfully we take our leave.

RICHARD
[*To Bishops*] Come, let us to our holy work again.—   245
Farewell, my cousin. Farewell, gentle friends.

Exeunt

[Richard III

Act 4

0: Scene: There has been a tendency, perhaps amounting to a wish, to cut this scene or to diminish it considerably. Booth and Irving cut it, Phelps shortened it, and Cibber wrote his own version of it. It is a scene of marking time, since one would not normally expect 4.2 ("*Enter RICHARD [III,] in pomp, [crowned,]*") to immediately follow 3.7. However, many feel that at 103 lines long, the scene may mark too much time. Bogdanov (1989) kept the scene but opened it with only Queen Elizabeth and Dorset entering, with Anne following at the end of line 1; the Duchess of York's lines are merely cut. Alexander (1984) inserted a full-blown coronation scene at this point just before the interval; Sher, without crutches, struggled downstage with Anne beside him, and as they turned and knelt, their cloaks slipped to reveal their bare backs and, especially, Richard's hump. Loncraine (1995) used the device of starting with a real coronation and then fading into Richard and his court watching newsreel footage of the coronation.

0: Stage Direction: *[at one door]* and *[at the other door]*: from the First Quarto, the First Folio does not specify this.

1: **My niece Plantagenet:** i.e., Clarence's daughter, the Duchess of York is using "niece" in one of its older senses to mean granddaughter

5: **Daughter:** i.e., daughter-in-law

7: **sister:** i.e., sister-in-law

9: **devotion:** pious act

10: **gratulate:** greet, salute

15: **By your patience:** by your leave

16: **suffer:** permit

17: **charged:** ordered

Act 4, Scene 1]

\

Enter [at one door] QUEEN [ELIZABETH with the] DUCHESS OF
YORK [and the LORD MARQUESS
DORSET; [at the other door] ANNE, DUCHESS OF GLOUCESTER
[with CLARENCE'S daughter]

DUCHESS OF YORK
Who meets us here? My niece Plantagenet
Led in the hand of her kind aunt of Gloucester?
Now, for my life, she's wandering to the Tower,
On pure heart's love, to greet the tender prince.
Daughter, well met.

LADY ANNE
               God give your Graces both   5
A happy and a joyful time of day.

QUEEN ELIZABETH
As much to you, good sister. Whither away?

LADY ANNE
No farther than the Tower; and, as I guess,
Upon the like devotion as yourselves,
To gratulate the gentle princes there.   10

QUEEN ELIZABETH
Kind sister, thanks. We'll enter all together.
               Enter [BRAKENBURY,] THE LIEUTENANT
And in good time, here the lieutenant comes.
Master lieutenant, pray you, by your leave,
How doth the Prince, and my young son of York?

BRAKENBURY
Right well, dear madam. By your patience,   15
I may not suffer you to visit them.
The King hath strictly charged the contrary.

25: **office:** duty; **on:** at

26: **leave it so:** thus abandon my duty

29: **mother:** i.e., mother-in-law

30: **two fair Queens:** i.e., Queen Elizabeth, widow of Edward IV, and Queen Anne, wife of Richard III

31: **Westminster:** i.e., Westminster Abbey

33: **lace:** cord that fastens the bodice of a dress

Annette Bening as Queen Elizabeth and Kristin Scott Thomas as Lady Anne in the 1995 film directed by Richard Loncraine

Courtesy of Douglas Lanier

QUEEN ELIZABETH
    The King? Who's that?

BRAKENBURY
                    I mean the Lord Protector.

QUEEN ELIZABETH
    The Lord protect him from that kingly title!
    Hath he set bounds between their love and me?   20
    I am their mother. Who shall bar me from them?

DUCHESS OF YORK
    I am their father's mother. I will see them.

LADY ANNE
    Their aunt I am in law, in love their mother.
    Then bring me to their sights. I'll bear thy blame
    And take thy office from thee, on my peril.   25

BRAKENBURY
    No, madam, no. I may not leave it so.
    I am bound by oath, and therefore pardon me.
                    Exit [BRAKENBURY, THE] LIEUTENANT
                    Enter STANLEY

STANLEY
    Let me but meet you ladies one hour hence,
    And I'll salute your Grace of York as mother,
    And reverend looker-on of two fair Queens.   30
    [*To ANNE*] Come madam, you must straight to Westminster,
    There to be crownèd Richard's royal queen.

QUEEN ELIZABETH
    Ah, cut my lace asunder
    That my pent heart may have some scope to beat,
    Or else I swoon with this dead-killing news!   35

LADY ANNE
    Despiteful tidings! O, unpleasing news!

43: hie thee: make haste

46: counted: accepted, accounted

51: ta'en tardy: caught (by being slow)

52: ill-dispersing: evil spreading

54: cockatrice: mythical bird whose look was deadly; often a synonym for the basilisk

58-59: the inclusive...metal: i.e., the Crown

DORSET
    [To QUEEN ELIZABETH] Be of good cheer, mother. How fares your Grace?

QUEEN ELIZABETH
    O Dorset, speak not to me, get thee gone.
    Death and destruction dogs thee at thy heels.
    Thy mother's name is ominous to children.   40
    If thou wilt outstrip death, go cross the seas,
    And live with Richmond, from the reach of hell.
    Go, hie thee, hie thee from this slaughterhouse,
    Lest thou increase the number of the dead,
    And make me die the thrall of Margaret's curse,   45
    Nor mother, wife, nor England's counted Queen.

STANLEY
    Full of wise care is this your counsel, madam.
    [To DORSET] Take all the swift advantage of the hours.
    You shall have letters from me to my son
    In your behalf to meet you on the way.   50
    Be not ta'en tardy by unwise delay.

DUCHESS OF YORK
    O ill-dispersing wind of misery!
    O my accursèd womb, the bed of death!
    A cockatrice hast thou hatched to the world,
    Whose unavoided eye is murderous.   55

LORD STANLEY
    [To ANNE] Come, madam, come. I in all haste was sent.

LADY ANNE
    And I with all unwillingness will go.
    O, would to God that the inclusive verge
    Of golden metal that must round my brow
    Were red-hot steel, to sear me to the brains.   60
    Anointed let me be with deadly venom,
    And die ere men can say "God save the Queen!"

64: **humor:** mental state

81: **hitherto:** ever since

87: **complaining:** cause of complaint

QUEEN ELIZABETH
Go, go, poor soul, I envy not thy glory.
To feed my humor, wish thyself no harm.

LADY ANNE
No? Why? When he that is my husband now   65
Came to me, as I followed Henry's corse,
When scarce the blood was well washed from his hands
Which issued from my other angel husband
And that dear saint which then I weeping followed—
O, when, I say, I looked on Richard's face,   70
This was my wish: "Be thou," quoth I, "accursed
For making me, so young, so old a widow;
And, when thou wedd'st, let sorrow haunt thy bed;
And be thy wife, if any be so mad,
More miserable by the life of thee   75
Than thou hast made me by my dear lord's death."
Lo, ere I can repeat this curse again,
Within so small a time, my woman's heart
Grossly grew captive to his honey words
And proved the subject of mine own soul's curse,   80
Which hitherto hath held mine eyes from rest.
For never yet one hour in his bed
Did I enjoy the golden dew of sleep,
But with his timorous dreams was still awaked.
Besides, he hates me for my father Warwick,   85
And will, no doubt, shortly be rid of me.

QUEEN ELIZABETH
Poor heart, adieu. I pity thy complaining.

LADY ANNE
No more than from my soul I mourn for yours.

QUEEN ELIZABETH
Farewell, thou woeful welcomer of glory.

90: "Adieu, poor soul": Aysan Celik as Duchess of York and Jenn Miller Cribbs as Queen Elizabeth in the 2004 Acting Company production directed by Eve Shapiro

Photo: Richard Termine

95: **Eighty odd years:** The Duchess of York was, in fact, 68 years of age in 1483; however, she did die at age 80 in 1495.

96: **wracked:** wrecked; **teen:** trouble, grief, or woe

LADY ANNE
Adieu, poor soul, that tak'st thy leave of it.   90

DUCHESS OF YORK
[*To DORSET*] Go thou to Richmond, and good fortune guide thee.
[*To ANNE*] Go thou to Richard, and good angels tend thee.
[*To QUEEN ELIZABETH*] Go thou to sanctuary, and good thoughts
    possess thee.
I to my grave, where peace and rest lie with me.
Eighty odd years of sorrow have I seen,   95
And each hour's joy wracked with a week of teen.

QUEEN ELIZABETH
Stay, yet look back with me unto the Tower.
Pity, you ancient stones, those tender babes
Whom envy hath immured within your walls,
Rough cradle for such little pretty ones,   100
Rude ragged nurse, old sullen playfellow
For tender princes. Use my babies well.
So foolish sorrows bids your stones farewell.

                                                    Exeunt

0: Stage Direction: *Enter RICHARD [III,] in pomp, [crowned,]*: The First Folio has him in coronation robes ("*pomp*") and the First Quarto has him crowned; productions have worked their elaborations on these very bare statements.

1: **Stand all apart:** disperse or spread yourselves; this is actually a verbal stage direction indicating that those who have entered should stand aside from Richard

3: Stage Direction: *[Here he ascendeth the throne]*: This direction is from the First Quarto; the First Folio reads only "*Sound*". Although the direction for Richard to go up to the throne comes only from the First Quarto, on the early stages it would not have been possible for Richard to get into the throne in any other way unless he were to be found already in it in the discovery space in the center of the stage. However, this would not have been a very practical way to play the scene unless the throne were then to be thrust out. So complicated an action surely would have warranted a fuller direction in one or the other of the early texts. Given the way these two lines are structured, it seems clear that what Shakespeare intended was for Richard to ascend the throne with Buckingham's assistance, to echo the assistance he has provided Richard in his quest in the previous three acts. Burbage was almost certainly assisted into the throne by whoever played Buckingham.

After 1660 it became ever more practical to either have Richard enter and ascend the throne or to be already seated in it when the scene opened. Cibber began this latter method with his production and many have followed it since, notably Alexander (1984) who, by putting the interval just before it, allowed Sher and the others to take their places before the lights went up. Of those who have him ascend, with or without Buckingham's assistance, some were notable: Emlyn Williams (Old Vic, 1937) delayed sitting down much in the manner of someone who was saving the best bit until last; Olivier (1955) sank into the throne which was too big so that his feet did not reach the floor, at which point Anne, now Queen Anne, fainted; Alan Bates (Festival Theatre, Stratford, Ontario, 1967) tripped as he ascended the throne; John Wood (Morahan/Koltai, 1979) sat with a great sigh of relief.

8: **touch:** touchstone, used for testing the purity of gold
13: **thrice-renownèd:** very great; perhaps also a reference to the English monarch's title as King of England, Ireland, and France

Act 4, Scene 2]

Sound a sennet. Enter RICHARD [III,] in pomp,
[crowned,] BUCKINGHAM, CATESBY,
RATCLIFF, LOVELL [A PAGE, and others]

RICHARD III
  Stand all apart. Cousin of Buckingham.

BUCKINGHAM
  My gracious sovereign.

RICHARD III
  Give me thy hand.
                            Sound [trumpets. Here he ascendeth the throne]
  Thus high, by thy advice
  And thy assistance, is King Richard seated.
  But shall we wear these glories for a day,   5
  Or shall they last, and we rejoice in them?

BUCKINGHAM
  Still live they, and for ever let them last.

RICHARD III
  Ah, Buckingham, now do I play the touch,
  To try if thou be current gold indeed.
  Young Edward lives, think now what I would speak.   10

BUCKINGHAM
  Say on, my loving lord.

RICHARD III
  Why, Buckingham, I say, I would be king,

BUCKINGHAM
  Why so you are, my thrice-renownèd lord.

14: "Ha! Am I King?": Wallace Acton as Richard and the Ensemble in the 2003 Shakespeare Theatre Company production directed by Gale Edwards
Photo: Carol Rosegg

15: **consequence:** conclusion
19, 20: **suddenly:** immediately
24: **breath:** breathing space
26: **resolve you:** give you my answer
28: **iron-witted:** dull
29: **unrespective:** heedless; **for me:** on my side
30: **considerate:** considering, thoughtful

32: Scene: **Boy:** Since the Page is called "boy" by Richard, it has generally been assumed that he is a youth or child. Some directors have not been able to deal with the idea of having a child about the court who can so readily name a potential murderer, so they have cut the Page and given his lines and function to Catesby. Olivier did this in his film (1955). Bogdanov (1989) has Richard ask the question of Ratcliff; no Page was present. In the Alexander production (1984), the Page was an adult, not a child; in Howell's BBC production (1983) the Page was not only a boy, but an angelic one with an angelic voice.

32-41: **Boy...the man:** Since he merged Ratcliff and Tyrrel, Loncraine (1995) cut these lines, along with 4.2.66-68.

RICHARD III

    Ha! Am I King? 'Tis so. But Edward lives.

BUCKINGHAM

    True, noble prince.

RICHARD III

                O bitter consequence,   15
    That Edward still should live "true noble prince"!
    Cousin, thou wert not wont to be so dull.
    Shall I be plain? I wish the bastards dead;
    And I would have it suddenly performed.
    What sayst thou now? Speak suddenly. Be brief.   20

BUCKINGHAM

    Your Grace may do your pleasure.

RICHARD III

    Tut, tut, thou art all ice, thy kindness freezes.
    Say, have I thy consent that they shall die?

BUCKINGHAM

    Give me some breath, some little pause, dear lord,
    Before I positively speak in this.   25
    I will resolve you herein presently.

                               Exit BUCKINGHAM

CATESBY

    [*Aside to another*] The King is angry. See he gnaws the lip.

RICHARD III

    I will converse with iron-witted fools
    And unrespective boys. None are for me
    That look into me with considerate eyes.   30
    High-reaching Buckingham grows circumspect.
    Boy!

PAGE

    My lord?

35: **close:** secret

Set design by William Bloodgood for the 1993 Oregon Shakespeare Festival
production directed by James Edmondson
Courtesy of Oregon Shakespeare Festival

42: **deep-revolving:** deeply thinking or pondering; **witty:** clever

52: **close:** secluded

53: **Inquire me out:** find me; **mean poor:** impoverished

55: **foolish:** simple-minded

RICHARD III
　Know'st thou not any whom corrupting gold
　Will tempt unto a close exploit of death?　　　　　　　　35

PAGE
　I know a discontented gentleman
　Whose humble means match not his haughty spirit.
　Gold were as good as twenty orators,
　And will, no doubt, tempt him to anything.

RICHARD III
　What is his name?

PAGE
　　　　　　　His name, my lord, is Tyrrel.　　　　　　40

RICHARD III
　I partly know the man. Go, call him hither, boy.

　　　　　　　　　　　　　　　　　　Exit [PAGE]

　[*Aside*] The deep-revolving, witty Buckingham
　No more shall be the neighbor to my counsels.
　Hath he so long held out with me untired,
　And stops he now for breath? Well, be it so.　　　　45
　　　　　　　　　　　　　　　　　　Enter STANLEY

　How now, Lord Stanley, what's the news?

STANLEY
　Know, my loving lord,
　The Marquess Dorset, as I hear, is fled
　To Richmond, in the parts where he abides.

　　　　　　　　　　　　　　　　　　[Stands aside]

RICHARD III
　Come hither, Catesby. Rumor it abroad　　　　　　50
　That Anne, my wife, is very grievous sick.
　I will take order for her keeping close.
　Inquire me out some mean poor gentleman,
　Whom I will marry straight to Clarence' daughter.
　The boy is foolish, and I fear not him.　　　　　　55

56: dream'st: daydream

56-59: Scene: I say...damage me: Bogdanov (1989) had Catesby grab Anne (present on stage) by the arm and lead her off stage with the look of a man who was going to perform the deed Richard had described.

58: stands me much upon: is very important to me

59: stop: prevent

60: brother's daughter: i.e., Elizabeth, daughter of Edward IV

64: pluck on: attract more

65: Stage Direction: *Enter TYRREL:* Cibber cut Tyrel and went straight to Buckingham's re-entry (line 82); Edmund Kean restored most of the cut, and the lines gradually crept back into performance. Olivier (1955) reversed the Tyrrel and final Buckingham incidents.

66-68: Is thy...lord: Since he has merged Ratcliff and Tyrrel, Loncraine (1995) cut these lines, along with 4.2.32-41.

68: Prove: test

70: Please you: if it pleases you

73: upon: with

75: open means: free access

Look how thou dream'st! I say again, give out
That Anne my queen is sick, and like to die.
About it; for it stands me much upon
To stop all hopes whose growth may damage me.

[Exit CATESBY]

[Aside] I must be married to my brother's daughter,   60
Or else my kingdom stands on brittle glass.
Murder her brothers, and then marry her,
Uncertain way of gain. But I am in
So far in blood that sin will pluck on sin.
Tear-falling pity dwells not in this eye.   65

Enter TYRREL

Is thy name Tyrrel?

TYRREL
James Tyrrel, and your most obedient subject.

RICHARD III
Art thou, indeed?

TYRREL
                    Prove me, my gracious lord.

RICHARD III
Dar'st thou resolve to kill a friend of mine?

TYRREL
Please you. But I had rather kill two enemies.   70

RICHARD III
Why then thou hast it. Two deep enemies,
Foes to my rest and my sweet sleep's disturbers
Are they that I would have thee deal upon.
Tyrrel, I mean those bastards in the Tower.

TYRREL
Let me have open means to come to them,   75
And soon I'll rid you from the fear of them.

78: **token:** an object, in performance often a ring, which will be recognized as giving royal authority

80: **prefer:** advance you in rank or possessions

82-119: Scene: **My lord...in the vein:** Cibber's alteration of this section produces a text very like that found in the First Folio, and Nicholas Rowe, the first editor of Shakespeare, prints that version in his 1709 edition. The lines from the First Quarto are not restored to a reading edition until Alexander Pope's of 1728; in this particular instance, our edition follows Pope. Note that lines 98-118 are found only in the quartos, indicating that there may have been a tradition of playing the scene dating back to the First Quarto.

The most common method of playing this passage, in either version, is for Richard to ignore or look through Buckingham as he makes his requests. This was certainly the way Olivier (stage and film, 1955) played it, using his scepter to push Buckingham aside when he spoke to Stanley (lines 85, 91-92). John Wood (Morahan/Koltai, 1979) rather obviously fell asleep during Buckingham's request for the earldom. Ian Holm (Hall/Barton, 1963) gave Buckingham the finger and pushed him aside. Through the nineteenth century, there was a tradition of Buckingham kneeling and clutching Richard's robes as he made his request. The First Quarto permits Richard to display more violence toward Buckingham than does the First Folio: "A king perhaps— / *BUCKINGHAM* Why then, resolve me whether you will or no. / *RICHARD III* Thou troublest me; I am not in the vein."

88: **pawned:** pledged

89: **Hereford:** from the First Quarto, the First Folio reads "Hertford"

RICHARD III
Thou sing'st sweet music. Hark, come hither, Tyrrel
Go, by this token. Rise, and lend thine ear.

Whispers

There is no more but so. Say it is done,
And I will love thee and prefer thee for it.   80

TYRREL
I will dispatch it straight.

Exit
Enter BUCKINGHAM

BUCKINGHAM
My lord, I have considered in my mind
The late request that you did sound me in.

RICHARD III
Well, let that rest. Dorset is fled to Richmond.

BUCKINGHAM
I hear that news, my lord.   85

RICHARD III
Stanley, he is your wife's son. Well, look unto it.

BUCKINGHAM
My lord, I claim the gift, my due by promise,
For which your honor and your faith is pawned;
Th' earldom of Hereford and the moveables,
Which you have promisèd I shall possess.   90

RICHARD III
Stanley, look to your wife. If she convey
Letters to Richmond, you shall answer it.

BUCKINGHAM
What says your Highness to my just request?

96: peevish: childishly irritating

98-118: BUCKINGHAM...no.: from the First Quarto, this passage is not in the First Folio

101: "My lord, your promise for the earldom——": Peter Dinklage as Richard and Ty Burrell as Buckingham in the 2004 Public Theater production directed by Peter DuBois
Photo: Michal Daniel

102-106: When...Richmond: This incident can be found in the contemporary chronicle histories.

102: Exeter: county town of Devonshire, in the west of England

104: Rougemont: literally, red hill. It was a Norman castle at Exeter and site of a famous siege in the twelfth century. It could have been pronounced at the time to sound like "Richmond."

RICHARD III
  I do remember me, Henry the Sixth
  Did prophesy that Richmond should be king,   95
  When Richmond was a little peevish boy.
  A king perhaps—

BUCKINGHAM
  My lord—

RICHARD III
  How chance the prophet could not at that time
  Have told me, I being by, that I should kill him?   100

BUCKINGHAM
  My lord, your promise for the earldom—

RICHARD III
  Richmond! When last I was at Exeter,
  The Mayor in courtesy showed me the castle
  And called it Rougemont, at which name I started,
  Because a bard of Ireland told me once   105
  I should not live long after I saw Richmond.

BUCKINGHAM
  My lord—

RICHARD III
  Ay, what's o'clock?

BUCKINGHAM
  I am thus bold to put your Grace in mind
  Of what you promised me.   110

RICHARD III
  Well, but what's o'clock?

BUCKINGHAM
  Upon the stroke of ten.

115: **jack:** figure on a clock that tricks the bell; also a lowborn person (see note 1.3.53)

117: "I am not in the giving vein today": Henry Goodman as Richard and Malcolm Sinclair as Buckingham in the 2003 Royal Shakespeare Company production directed by Sean Holmes
Photo: Donald Cooper

119: Stage Direction: *[Exeunt, manet BUCKINGHAM]*: The First Folio and the First Quarto provide only the bare "*Exit*" as a direction here.

120: **deep:** important

123: **Brecknock:** Buckingham's family seat in southeast Wales; **fearful:** full of fears

RICHARD III
  Well, let it strike.

BUCKINGHAM
  Why let it strike?

RICHARD III
  Because that, like a jack, thou keep'st the stroke   115
  Betwixt thy begging and my meditation.
  I am not in the giving vein today.

BUCKINGHAM
  Why then, resolve me whether you will or no.

RICHARD III
  Thou troublest me; I am not in the vein.
                    [Exeunt, manet BUCKINGHAM]

BUCKINGHAM
  And is it thus? Repays he my deep service   120
  With such contempt? Made I him King for this?
  O, let me think on Hastings and be gone
  To Brecknock, while my fearful head is on.
                                        Exit

0: Scene: Following the convention of a new scene beginning when the stage is cleared, editors since Alexander Pope (1725) have marked a scene division at this point, as we do here, but neither the First Folio nor quartos 1-8 do so.

tracks 16-18

1–27:
Brian Spink as Tyrrel and Peter Finch as Richard III
Steve Hodson as Tyrrel and David Troughton as Richard III

1-22: Scene: **The tyrannous...bloody King:** Since at least 1700, there has been a tendency to play the events Tyrrel describes rather than to let him merely report them. In Olivier's film (1955), Tyrrel's soliloquy was a voiceover while Forrest and Dighton commit the murders.

1: **tyrannous:** cruel
2: **most arch:** chiefest
4: **Dighton and Forrest:** mentioned in Sir Thomas More's *History of Richard III*; **suborn:** procure someone by unlawful means to commit a crime.
5: **ruthless:** from the First Quarto, the First Folio reads "ruthful," which has the reverse meaning from that intended
6: **fleshed villains:** criminals used to murder
8: **their deaths':** i.e., the deaths of the two princes
10: **girdling:** surrounding, i.e., embracing
15: **once:** from the First Quarto, the First Folio reads "one"
18: **replenishèd:** perfect
19: **prime:** first; **she framed:** nature created

22: Scene: *Enter RICHARD III:* When Sher (Alexander, 1984) entered, he was once again on crutches.
23: Scene: Loncraine cut the first twenty-two lines of the scene, instead showing Tyrrel smothering one of the princes, and then had Tyrrel coming to Richard, rather than the reverse.

23: **hail:** from the First Quarto, the First Folio reads "health"
25: **gave in charge:** ordered

Act 4, Scene 3

Enter TYRREL

TYRREL
The tyrannous and bloody act is done.
The most arch deed of piteous massacre
That ever yet this land was guilty of.
Dighton and Forrest, whom I did suborn
To do this piece of ruthless butchery,   5
Albeit they were fleshed villains, bloody dogs,
Melted with tenderness and mild compassion
Wept like two children in their deaths' sad story.
"O, thus," quoth Dighton, "lay the gentle babes."
"Thus, thus," quoth Forrest, "girdling one another   10
Within their alabaster innocent arms.
Their lips were four red roses on a stalk,
And in their summer beauty kissed each other.
A book of prayers on their pillow lay,
Which once," quoth Forrest, "almost changed my mind.   15
But, O, the devil—" there the villain stopped;
When Dighton thus told on: "We smotherèd
The most replenishèd sweet work of nature,
That from the prime creation e'er she framed."
Hence both are gone with conscience and remorse;   20
They could not speak; and so I left them both
To bring this tidings to the bloody King.

Enter RICHARD III

And here he comes.—All hail, my sovereign lord.

RICHARD III
Kind Tyrrel, am I happy in thy news?

TYRREL
If to have done the thing you gave in charge   25
Beget your happiness, be happy then,
For it is done.

28: Scene: **And buried, gentle Tyrrel:** In Cibber's version, Tyrrel asks Richard how they are to be buried and Richard responds, "Get me a coffin / Full of holes, let 'em be cram'd into't. / And, hark thee, in the night-tide throw 'em down / The Thames; once in they'll find the way to th' bottom."

31: **at:** from the First Quarto, the First Folio reads "and"; **after-supper:** probably dessert, or the last course
32: **process:** method
34: **inheritor:** possessor

35: Scene: **[*Exit TYRREL*]:** Richard Mansfield (London, Globe, 1889) had an off-stage scuffle and cry from Tyrrel to imply that he has been killed as he exited; Hands (1970, 1980) had Tyrrel followed off by two of Richard's thugs who clearly intend to kill him. Whatever historical circumstances may tell us, this is certainly his last appearance in this play.

Costume rendering for Tyrrel from the 1953 production at the Shakespeare Memorial Theatre in Stratford-upon-Avon directed by Glen Byam Shaw
Rare Book and Special Collection Library, University of Illinois at Urbana-Champaign

36: **pent up close:** securely shut up, imprisoned
37: **meanly:** basely
42: **knot:** union, in marriage
45: **bluntly:** suddenly, and without proper address

RICHARD III
        But did'st thou see them dead?

TYRREL
  I did, my lord.

RICHARD III
        And buried, gentle Tyrrel?

TYRREL
  The chaplain of the Tower hath buried them,
  But where, to say the truth, I do not know.   30

RICHARD III
  Come to me Tyrrel soon, at after-supper
  When thou shalt tell the process of their death.
  Meantime, but think how I may do thee good,
  And be inheritor of thy desire.
  Farewell till then.

TYRREL
        I humbly take my leave.   35
                      [Exit TYRREL]

RICHARD III
  The son of Clarence have I pent up close,
  His daughter meanly have I matched in marriage,
  The sons of Edward sleep in Abraham's bosom,
  And Anne my wife hath bid this world goodnight.
  Now, for I know the Breton Richmond aims   40
  At young Elizabeth, my brother's daughter,
  And by that knot, looks proudly on the crown,
  To her go I, a jolly thriving wooer.

                      Enter RATCLIFF

RATCLIFF
  My lord.

RICHARD III
  Good or bad news, that thou com'st in so bluntly?   45

Costume rendering for Ratcliff from the 1953 production at the Shakespeare
Memorial Theatre in Stratford-upon-Avon directed by Glen Byam Shaw
Rare Book and Special Collection Library, University of Illinois at Urbana-Champaign

46: **Morton:** i.e., John Morton, Bishop of Ely, see 3.4

50: **rash-levied strength:** hastily raised army

52: **servitor:** servant

53: **leads:** leads to

55: **Jove's Mercury:** Mercury was the messenger of the gods, particularly Jove

57: **brief:** speedy, not delaying

RATCLIFF
    Bad news, my lord. Morton is fled to Richmond;
    And Buckingham, backed with the hardy Welshmen,
    Is in the field, and still his power increaseth.

RICHARD III
    Ely with Richmond troubles me more near
    Than Buckingham and his rash-levied strength.   50
    Come, I have learned that fearful commenting
    Is leaden servitor to dull delay;
    Delay leads impotent and snail-paced beggary;
    Then fiery expedition be my wing,
    Jove's Mercury, and herald for a king.   55
    Go, muster men. My counsel is my shield.
    We must be brief when traitors brave the field.

Exeunt

0: Scene: the First Folio does have a scene division here, but because of its earlier lack of one at 4.3, this is labeled "*Scena Tertia*" (scene three). Throughout the eighteenth and nineteenth centuries there was a tradition of setting this scene at the gateway to The Tower or near it. In Shakespeare's time, Margaret would have merely entered from one of the stage doors onto the stage. Morahan (National Theatre, 1979), who had placed Margaret behind the throne in 4.2, has her come from behind it as the scene opens. Bogdanov (1989) had a very large throne (possibly a replica of the real English coronation chair) center stage and Margaret entered stage left of it and sat. Alexander (1984) did not have Margaret aside at any point but rather front and center, with the Duchess of York and Queen Elizabeth flanking her and slightly behind, near the walls. Instead of coming forward at line 35, she stood and moved around to each of the other women.

1-431: Scene: **So...woman:** Olivier (1955) cut this entire segment.

1: **mellow:** ripen

5: **induction:** introduction, also opening of a play

6: **will to:** will go to; **consequence:** result, also conclusion of the play

10: **unblown:** unopened, still in the bud; from the First Quarto, the First Folio reads "unblowed"; **sweets:** flowers

12: **doom perpetual:** everlasting damnation

17: **crazed:** cracked

19: **Edward Plantagenet:** either Edward IV, her son, or Edward V, her grandson; perhaps both. Plantagenet is the family name, whether Yorkist or Lancastrian.

20: **quit:** pay for

21: **Edward for Edward:** i.e., Edward V for Margaret's son, Edward, Prince of Wales (see *Henry VI, Part 3*); **a dying debt:** a debt the payment for which is death

Act 4, Scene 4]

Enter old QUEEN MARGARET

QUEEN MARGARET
So, now prosperity begins to mellow,
And drop into the rotten mouth of death.
Here in these confines slyly have I lurked,
To watch the waning of mine adversaries.
A dire induction am I witness to,   5
And will to France, hoping the consequence
Will prove as bitter, black, and tragical.
Withdraw thee, wretched Margaret, who comes here?

[Stands aside]
Enter DUCHESS [OF YORK] and QUEEN [ELIZABETH]

QUEEN ELIZABETH
Ah, my young princes! Ah, my tender babes,
My unblown flowers, new-appearing sweets,   10
If yet your gentle souls fly in the air
And be not fixed in doom perpetual,
Hover about me with your airy wings
And hear your mother's lamentation.

QUEEN MARGARET
[Aside] Hover about her; say that right for right   15
Hath dimmed your infant morn to agèd night.

DUCHESS OF YORK
So many miseries have crazed my voice,
That my woe-wearied tongue is still and mute.
Edward Plantagenet, why art thou dead?

QUEEN MARGARET
[Aside] Plantagenet doth quit Plantagenet;   20
Edward for Edward pays a dying debt.

24: **When:** whenever

25: **holy Harry:** i.e., Henry VI; **sweet son:** i.e., Edward, Prince of Wales

34–77:
Celia Imrie as Queen Elizabeth, Geraldine McEwan as Queen Margaret,
and Auriol Smith as Duchess of York
Sonia Ritter as Queen Elizabeth, Margaret Robertson as Queen Margaret,
and Mary Wimbush as Duchess of York

36: **seigniory:** sovereignty or lordship, perhaps with the secondary meaning of seniority

38: **society:** companions

39: **Tell over:** count; **Tell...mine:** from the First Quarto, not in the First Folio

39-114: Scene: **Tell over...France:** This competition in sorrow was generally cut until the middle of the twentieth century, and even now, it is usually much shortened. When it has been played uncut, it has usually attracted negative critical reaction. It is a hard passage to sustain on stage, requiring considerable skill and stamina on the part of the three actors.

43: **Thou hadst a Richard:** i.e., Queen Elizabeth's younger son, the little prince, Richard, Duke of York

44: **Richard:** i.e., the Duchess of York's husband, Richard, Duke of York

45: **Rutland:** see notes for 1.2.158-60 and 1.3.182; **holp'st:** helped; from Q3-Q6 and F2, Q1-Q2 and F1 read "hop'st"

QUEEN ELIZABETH
Wilt thou, O God, fly from such gentle lambs,
And throw them in the entrails of the wolf?
When didst thou sleep when such a deed was done?

QUEEN MARGARET
[*Aside*] When holy Harry died, and my sweet son.   25

DUCHESS OF YORK
Dead life, blind sight, poor mortal living ghost,
Woe's scene, world's shame, grave's due by life usurped,
Brief abstract and record of tedious days,
Rest thy unrest on England's lawful earth,
Unlawfully made drunk with innocent blood.   30

QUEEN ELIZABETH
Ah, that thou wouldst as soon afford a grave
As thou canst yield a melancholy seat,
Then would I hide my bones, not rest them here.
Ah, who hath any cause to mourn but we?

QUEEN MARGARET
[*Coming forward to them*] If ancient sorrow be most reverend,   35
Give mine the benefit of seigniory,
And let my griefs frown on the upper hand.
If sorrow can admit society,
Tell over your woes again by viewing mine.
I had an Edward, till a Richard killed him;   40
I had a husband, till a Richard killed him.
Thou hadst an Edward, till a Richard killed him;
Thou hadst a Richard, till a Richard killed him.

DUCHESS OF YORK
I had a Richard too, and thou didst kill him;
I had a Rutland too, thou holp'st to kill him.   45

QUEEN MARGARET
Thou hadst a Clarence too, and Richard killed him.
From forth the kennel of thy womb hath crept

tracks 19-21

34–77:
Celia Imrie as Queen Elizabeth, Geraldine McEwan as Queen Margaret, and
Auriol Smith as Duchess of York
Sonia Ritter as Queen Elizabeth, Margaret Robertson as Queen Margaret,
and Mary Wimbush as Duchess of York

52: **excellent:** supreme
55: **carnal:** bloody, murderous, also flesh-eating
62: **Thy Edward:** i.e., Edward IV
63: **Thy:** from the First Quarto, the First Folio reads "The"; **other Edward:** i.e.,
Edward V; **quit:** pay for
64: **boot:** an extra addition
68: **adulterate Hastings:** Hastings committed adultery with Mistress Shore.
70: **intelligencer:** informer or spy
71: **factor:** agent
75: **from hence:** away
76: **bond:** lease

77: "That I may live to say, 'The dog is dead.'": Ann Penfold as Elizabeth and June
Watson as Margaret in the 1989 English Shakespeare Company production
directed by Michael Bogdanov
Photo: Donald Cooper

80: **bottled...toad:** see 1.3.241 and 1.3.245

A hell-hound that doth hunt us all to death.
That dog, that had his teeth before his eyes,
To worry lambs and lap their gentle blood,   50
That foul defacer of God's handiwork,
That excellent grand tyrant of the earth,
Thy womb let loose, to chase us to our graves.
O upright, just, and true-disposing God,
How do I thank thee, that this carnal cur   55
Preys on the issue of his mother's body,
And makes her pew-fellow with others' moan.

DUCHESS OF YORK
O Harry's wife, triumph not in my woes.
God witness with me, I have wept for thine.

QUEEN MARGARET
Bear with me. I am hungry for revenge,   60
And now I cloy me with beholding it.
Thy Edward he is dead, that killed my Edward,
Thy other Edward dead, to quit my Edward;
Young York, he is but boot, because both they
Matched not the high perfection of my loss.   65
Thy Clarence he is dead that stabbed my Edward;
And the beholders of this frantic play,
Th' adulterate Hastings, Rivers, Vaughan, Grey,
Untimely smothered in their dusky graves.
Richard yet lives, hell's black intelligencer,   70
Only reserved their factor to buy souls
And send them thither. But at hand, at hand
Ensues his piteous and unpitied end.
Earth gapes, hell burns, fiends roar, saints pray,
To have him suddenly conveyed from hence.   75
Cancel his bond of life, dear God I pray,
That I may live to say, "The dog is dead."

QUEEN ELIZABETH
O, thou didst prophesy the time would come
That I should wish for thee to help me curse
That bottled spider, that foul bunch-backed toad!   80

82: **I called:** see line 1.3.240
83: **presentation:** representation
84: **index:** prologue; **pageant:** play
85: **heaved a-high:** lifted high in rank
87-88: **garish flag...shot:** brightly colored flag or pennant, like a guidon, carried into battle by a standard bearer to draw the opposition's fire
94: **bending:** bowing
96: **Decline:** run through in order
100: **very caitiff:** true wretch
101: **scorned at:** mocked
106: **thought:** memory
109: **just:** fit, proper

115-116: "O thou well skilled in curses, stay awhile, / And teach me how to curse mine enemies": Jennifer Harmon as Queen Margaret and Diana LaMar as Queen Elizabeth in the 2003 Shakespeare Theatre Company production directed by Gale Edwards
Photo: Carol Rosegg

QUEEN MARGARET
   I called thee then "vain flourish of my fortune."
   I called thee then poor shadow, "painted queen,"
   The presentation of but what I was,
   The flattering index of a direful pageant,
   One heaved a-high, to be hurled down below,   85
   A mother only mocked with two fair babes,
   A dream of what thou wast, a garish flag
   To be the aim of every dangerous shot,
   A sign of dignity, a breath, a bubble,
   A queen in jest, only to fill the scene.   90
   Where is thy husband now? Where be thy brothers?
   Where be thy two sons? Wherein dost thou joy?
   Who sues and kneels and says "God save the Queen?"
   Where be the bending peers that flattered thee?
   Where be the thronging troops that followed thee?   95
   Decline all this, and see what now thou art:
   For happy wife, a most distressèd widow;
   For joyful mother, one that wails the name;
   For one being sued to, one that humbly sues;
   For queen, a very caitiff crowned with care;   100
   For she that scorned at me, now scorned of me;
   For she being feared of all, now fearing one;
   For she commanding all, obeyed of none.
   Thus hath the course of justice whirled about,
   And left thee but a very prey to time,   105
   Having no more but thought of what thou wast,
   To torture thee the more, being what thou art.
   Thou didst usurp my place, and dost thou not
   Usurp the just proportion of my sorrow?
   Now thy proud neck bears half my burdened yoke,   110
   From which even here I slip my wearied head,
   And leave the burden of it all on thee.
   Farewell, York's wife, and queen of sad mischance,
   These English woes shall make me smile in France.

QUEEN ELIZABETH
   O thou well skilled in curses, stay awhile,   115
   And teach me how to curse mine enemies.

122: **Revolving:** thinking upon, pondering
123: **quicken:** enliven
127: **intestate:** from the First Quarto, the First Folio reads "intestine"; "intestate" means not having made a will, not properly disposed of in law
134: **exclaims:** outcries
134: Stage Direction: *[marching, with drums and trumpets]:* from the First Quarto

134: Scene: ***Enter King RICHARD III, and his train [marching, with drums and trumpets]:*** On Shakespeare's stage, Richard would have entered with some (five or six) soldiers. Trumpets and drums would sound but remain off stage. The eighteenth and nineteenth centuries made this a grand procession with music and much marching about. In the case of Charles Kean and others, the set included a working drawbridge. John Wood and his companions (Morahan/Koltai, 1979) came on with a map and toy soldiers, which they placed on the floor and played war with. Sher (Alexander, 1984) was borne in on his throne/chair without his crutches.

134: Stage Direction: *Enter King Richard III, and his train [marching, with drums and trumpets]:* Scene rendering from the 1953 production at the Shakespeare Memorial Theatre in Stratford-upon-Avon directed by Glen Byam Shaw

135: **expedition:** military movement, and perhaps also haste (from "expedite")
136: **intercepted:** prevented, stopped

QUEEN MARGARET
> Forbear to sleep the night, and fast the day;
> Compare dead happiness with living woe;
> Think that thy babes were sweeter than they were,
> And he that slew them fouler than he is.   120
> Bettering thy loss makes the bad causer worse.
> Revolving this will teach thee how to curse.

QUEEN ELIZABETH
> My words are dull; O quicken them with thine.

QUEEN MARGARET
> Thy woes will make them sharp, and pierce like mine.

> *Exit MARGARET*

DUCHESS OF YORK
> Why should calamity be full of words?   125

QUEEN ELIZABETH
> Windy attorneys to their client woes,
> Airy succeeders of intestate joys,
> Poor breathing orators of miseries,
> Let them have scope, though what they will impart
> Help nothing else, yet do they ease the heart.   130

DUCHESS OF YORK
> If so, then be not tongue-tied. Go with me,
> And in the breath of bitter words let's smother
> My damnèd son, that thy two sweet sons smothered.

> *[Trumpet sounds]*

> The trumpet sounds, be copious in exclaims.
> *Enter King RICHARD III, and his train*
> *[marching, with drums and trumpets]*

RICHARD III
> Who intercepts my expedition?   135

DUCHESS OF YORK
> O, she that might have intercepted thee,
> By strangling thee in her accursèd womb,
> From all the slaughters, wretch, that thou hast done.

141: **owed:** owned, or was owed
148: **alarum:** call to arms

148-150: Scene: **A flourish...I say:** From Shakespeare's time onward, this has been a blast of loud horn calls and other noises to silence the women. However, there have been some exceptions. John Wood's command (Morahan/Koltai, 1979) produced a blast on toy trumpets and whistles.

149-150: "Let not the heavens hear these telltale women / Rail on the Lord's anointed": Kevin Kline as Richard and Madeleine Potter as Anne in the 1983 Public Theater production directed by Jane Howell

Photo: George E. Joseph

151: **patient:** calm; **fair:** politely
152: **report:** loud noise
158: **brook:** endure; **accent:** tone

QUEEN ELIZABETH
Hid'st thou that forehead with a golden crown,
Where't should be branded, if that right were right,   140
The slaughter of the prince that owed that crown,
And the dire death of my poor sons and brothers?
Tell me, thou villain-slave, where are my children?

DUCHESS OF YORK
Thou toad, thou toad, where is thy brother Clarence?
And little Ned Plantagenet, his son?   145

QUEEN ELIZABETH
Where is the gentle Rivers, Vaughan, Grey?

DUCHESS OF YORK
Where is kind Hastings?

RICHARD III
A flourish, trumpets! Strike alarum, drums!
Let not the heavens hear these telltale women
Rail on the Lord's anointed. Strike, I say!   150
Flourish. Alarums

Either be patient, and entreat me fair,
Or with the clamorous report of war
Thus will I drown your exclamations.

DUCHESS OF YORK
Art thou my son?

RICHARD III
Ay, I thank God, my father, and yourself.   155

DUCHESS OF YORK
Then patiently hear my impatience.

RICHARD III
Madam, I have a touch of your condition,
That cannot brook the accent of reproof.

163: **stayed:** waited

166: **holy rood:** holy cross

169: **Tetchy:** peevish, irritable; **wayward:** disobedient

171: **prime of manhood:** young adulthood; **venturous:** risky, daring

172: **age confirmed:** maturity

176: **Humphrey Hower:** This reference and pun has never been satisfactorily explained. In the First Quarto, it is printed as "Humphrey houre", sounding like some proverbial event rather than a person. In any case, it is a further example of Richard bantering with his mother.

178: **disgracious:** displeasing

DUCHESS OF YORK
    O, let me speak!

RICHARD III
    Do then, but I'll not hear.   160

DUCHESS OF YORK
    I will be mild and gentle in my words.

RICHARD III
    And brief, good mother, for I am in haste.

DUCHESS OF YORK
    Art thou so hasty? I have stayed for thee,
    God knows, in torment and in agony.

RICHARD III
    And came I not at last to comfort you?   165

DUCHESS OF YORK
    No, by the holy rood, thou know'st it well,
    Thou cam'st on earth to make the earth my hell.
    A grievous burden was thy birth to me;
    Tetchy and wayward was thy infancy;
    Thy school days frightful, desp'rate, wild, and furious;   170
    Thy prime of manhood daring, bold, and venturous;
    Thy age confirmed, proud, subtle, sly, and bloody,
    More mild, but yet more harmful, kind in hatred.
    What comfortable hour canst thou name,
    That ever graced me with thy company?   175

RICHARD III
    Faith, none, but Humphrey Hower, that called your Grace
    To breakfast once, forth of my company.
    If I be so disgracious in your eye,
    Let me march on, and not offend you madam.
    Strike up the drum.

DUCHESS OF YORK
                    I prithee, hear me speak.   180

185: **turn:** return

188: Scene: **Therefore:** In Alexander's production (1984), Yvonne Coulet (Duchess of York) pulled Sher from his throne and he crawled on the floor until she left, when he then regained his seat. When he left his seat in line 250, he used his scepter has a cane.

188: "Therefore take with thee my most grievous curse": Sir Derek Jacobi as Richard and Barbara Jefford as the Duchess of York in the 1989 Phoenix Theatre production directed by Clifford Williams

Photo: Donald Cooper

190: **complete:** full

193: **Whisper:** whisper to

199-431: Scene: **Stay, madam...so, farewell:** This "wooing" scene was cut from 232 lines to 71 lines by Cibber and 50 by Irving. When it was played in full in 1936 (directed by Henry Cass, Old Vic) critical commentary implied that this had not been done before, or at least not in living memory. Starting at least with Ian Holm (Hall/Barton, 1963) and John Wood (Morahan/Koltai, 1979), the scene has been played as perverse eroticism in which Richard appeals to Elizabeth's sexuality (e.g., Elizabeth kissed Richard passionately on the mouth and he drew away at line 428 in the Hall/Barton production).

203: **level:** aim

RICHARD III
You speak too bitterly.

DUCHESS OF YORK
                    Hear me a word;
For I shall never speak to thee again.

RICHARD III
So.

DUCHESS OF YORK
Either thou wilt die, by God's just ordinance,
Ere from this war thou turn a conqueror,   185
Or I with grief and extreme age shall perish
And never more behold thy face again.
Therefore take with thee my most grievous curse,
Which in the day of battle tire thee more
Than all the complete armor that thou wear'st.   190
My prayers on the adverse party fight,
And there the little souls of Edward's children
Whisper the spirits of thine enemies
And promise them success and victory.
Bloody thou art, bloody will be thy end.   195
Shame serves thy life and doth thy death attend.
                                                      Exit

QUEEN ELIZABETH
Though far more cause, yet much less spirit to curse
Abides in me. I say amen to her.

RICHARD III
Stay, madam. I must speak a word with you.

QUEEN ELIZABETH
I have no more sons of the royal blood   200
For thee to murder. For my daughters, Richard,
They shall be praying nuns, not weeping queens,
And therefore level not to hit their lives.

207: **manners:** morals

210: **So:** so that

216: **opposite:** adverse, hostile

217: **ill:** evil

218: **unavoided:** unavoidable

219: **avoided:** rejected, or devoid of

RICHARD III
  You have a daughter called Elizabeth,
  Virtuous and fair, royal and gracious?   205

QUEEN ELIZABETH
  And must she die for this? O, let her live,
  And I'll corrupt her manners, stain her beauty,
  Slander myself as false to Edward's bed,
  Throw over her the veil of infamy.
  So she may live unscarred of bleeding slaughter,   210
  I will confess she was not Edward's daughter.

RICHARD III
  Wrong not her birth, she is a royal princess.

QUEEN ELIZABETH
  To save her life, I'll say she is not so.

RICHARD III
  Her life is safest only in her birth.

QUEEN ELIZABETH
  And only in that safety died her brothers.   215

RICHARD III
  Lo, at their birth good stars were opposite.

QUEEN ELIZABETH
  No, to their lives ill friends were contrary.

RICHARD III
  All unavoided is the doom of destiny.

QUEEN ELIZABETH
  True, when avoided grace makes destiny.
  My babes were destined to a fairer death,   220
  If grace had blessed thee with a fairer life.

RICHARD III
  You speak as if that I had slain my cousins?

223: **cozened:** tricked, cheated

226: **all indirectly:** not explicitly ordered but suggested

230: **still:** constant

233: **bay:** inlet, or the hunting term, "to be at bay"

234: **bark:** boat; **tackling:** masts, spars, ropes, and the like; **reft:** bereft, deprived of

240: **covered with:** hidden by

245: **type:** symbol

248: **demise:** give or transfer

QUEEN ELIZABETH
Cousins indeed, and by their uncle cozened
Of comfort, kingdom, kindred, freedom, life.
Whose hand soever lanced their tender hearts,   225
Thy head, all indirectly, gave direction.
No doubt the murderous knife was dull and blunt
Till it was whetted on thy stone-hard heart,
To revel in the entrails of my lambs.
But that still use of grief makes wild grief tame,   230
My tongue should to thy ears not name my boys
Till that my nails were anchored in thine eyes,
And I, in such a desp'rate bay of death,
Like a poor bark of sails and tackling reft,
Rush all to pieces on thy rocky bosom.   235

RICHARD III
Madam, so thrive I in my enterprise
And dangerous success of bloody wars
As I intend more good to you and yours
Than ever you and yours by me were harmed.

QUEEN ELIZABETH
What good is covered with the face of heaven,   240
To be discovered, that can do me good?

RICHARD III
Th' advancement of your children, gentle lady.

QUEEN ELIZABETH
Up to some scaffold, there to lose their heads.

RICHARD III
Unto the dignity and height of fortune,
The high imperial type of this earth's glory.   245

QUEEN ELIZABETH
Flatter my sorrow with report of it.
Tell me what state, what dignity, what honor,
Canst thou demise to any child of mine?

250: **withal:** moreover

251: **Lethe:** river of forgetfulness in classical mythology

254: **process:** narrative

255: **kindness' date:** length of your kindness

256: "Then know, that from my soul I love thy daughter": Stacy Keach as Richard and Franchelle Stewart Dorn as Queen Elizabeth in the 1990 production by the Shakespeare Theatre Company directed by Michael Kahn
Photo: Joan Marcus

262: **confound:** confuse

RICHARD III
    Even all I have—ay, and myself and all—
    Will I withal endow a child of thine;   250
    So in the Lethe of thy angry soul
    Thou drown the sad remembrance of those wrongs
    Which thou supposest I have done to thee.

QUEEN ELIZABETH
    Be brief, lest that be process of thy kindness
    Last longer telling than thy kindness' date.   255

RICHARD III
    Then know, that from my soul I love thy daughter.

QUEEN ELIZABETH
    My daughter's mother thinks it with her soul.

RICHARD III
    What do you think?

QUEEN ELIZABETH
    That thou dost love my daughter from thy soul.
    So from thy soul's love didst thou love her brothers,   260
    And from my heart's love I do thank thee for it.

RICHARD III
    Be not so hasty to confound my meaning.
    I mean that with my soul I love thy daughter,
    And do intend to make her Queen of England.

QUEEN ELIZABETH
    Well then, who dost thou mean shall be her king?   265

RICHARD III
    Even he that makes her queen. Who else should be?

QUEEN ELIZABETH
    What, thou?

268: **would I:** from the First Quarto, the First Folio reads "I would". The emendation is made for metrical reasons.

269: **humor:** disposition

274: **haply:** perhaps

278: **sap:** blood

282: **mad'st away:** killed

284: **Mad'st quick conveyance with:** killed

285: **is:** from the First Quarto, the First Folio omits the verb

RICHARD III
                    Even so. How think you of it?

QUEEN ELIZABETH
    How canst thou woo her?

RICHARD III
                        That would I learn of you,
    As one being best acquainted with her humor.

QUEEN ELIZABETH
    And wilt thou learn of me?   270

RICHARD III
    Madam, with all my heart.

QUEEN ELIZABETH
    Send to her, by the man that slew her brothers,
    A pair of bleeding hearts; thereon engrave
    "Edward" and "York." Then haply will she weep.
    Therefore present to her—as sometime Margaret   275
    Did to thy father, steeped in Rutland's blood—
    A handkerchief, which say to her did drain
    The purple sap from her sweet brother's body,
    And bid her dry her weeping eyes withal.
    If this inducement move her not to love,   280
    Send her a letter of thy noble deeds;
    Tell her thou mad'st away her uncle Clarence,
    Her uncle Rivers, ay, and for her sake,
    Mad'st quick conveyance with her good aunt Anne.

RICHARD III
    You mock me, madam, this is not the way   285
    To win your daughter.

QUEEN ELIZABETH
                        There is no other way
    Unless thou couldst put on some other shape,
    And not be Richard, that hath done all this.

291: **spoil:** slaughter

293: **unadvisedly:** unwisely

294: **after-hours:** later

298: **quicken your increase:** bring life to your offspring

300: **grandam's:** grandmother's

303: **mettle:** character

304-305: **Of all...sorrow:** i.e., the pain you endured giving birth to your daughter will be endured by her while giving birth to your grandchild

306: **vexation to your youth:** caused you trouble when you were young

308: **son:** i.e., son-in-law

321: **What:** interjection introducing an exclamation

RICHARD III
  Say that I did all this for love of her?

QUEEN ELIZABETH
  Nay, then indeed she cannot choose but hate thee,   290
  Having bought love with such a bloody spoil.

RICHARD III
  Look what is done cannot be now amended.
  Men shall deal unadvisedly sometimes,
  Which after-hours gives leisure to repent.
  If I did take the kingdom from your sons,   295
  To make amends, I'll give it to your daughter.
  If I have killed the issue of your womb,
  To quicken your increase, I will beget
  Mine issue of your blood upon your daughter.
  A grandam's name is little less in love   300
  Than is the doting title of a mother;
  They are as children but one step below,
  Even of your mettle, of your very blood,
  Of all one pain, save for a night of groans
  Endured of her, for whom you bid like sorrow.   305
  Your children were vexation to your youth,
  But mine shall be a comfort to your age.
  The loss you have is but a son being king,
  And by that loss your daughter is made queen.
  I cannot make you what amends I would,   310
  Therefore accept such kindness as I can.
  Dorset your son, that with a fearful soul
  Leads discontented steps in foreign soil,
  This fair alliance quickly shall call home
  To high promotions and great dignity.   315
  The king that calls your beauteous daughter wife
  Familiarly shall call thy Dorset brother.
  Again shall you be mother to a king,
  And all the ruins of distressful times
  Repaired with double riches of content.   320
  What, we have many goodly days to see!
  The liquid drops of tears that you have shed

324: **Advantaging:** increasing

336: **retail:** recount

344: **Infer:** mention

347: **That:** that thing; **King's King:** God

Shall come again, transformed to orient pearl,
Advantaging their love with interest
Of ten times double gain of happiness.   325
Go then, my mother, to thy daughter go.
Make bold her bashful years with your experience;
Prepare her ears to hear a wooer's tale.
Put in her tender heart th' aspiring flame
Of golden sovereignty; acquaint the princess   330
With the sweet silent hours of marriage joys;
And when this arm of mine hath chastisèd
The petty rebel, dull-brained Buckingham,
Bound with triumphant garlands will I come,
And lead thy daughter to a conqueror's bed,   335
To whom I will retail my conquest won,
And she shall be sole victoress, Caesar's Caesar.

QUEEN ELIZABETH
What were I best to say? Her father's brother
Would be her lord? Or shall I say her uncle?
Or he that slew her brothers and her uncles?   340
Under what title shall I woo for thee,
That God, the law, my honor and her love,
Can make seem pleasing to her tender years?

RICHARD III
Infer fair England's peace by this alliance.

QUEEN ELIZABETH
Which she shall purchase with still lasting war.   345

RICHARD III
Tell her the King, that may command, entreats.

QUEEN ELIZABETH
That at her hands which the King's King forbids.

RICHARD III
Say, she shall be a high and mighty queen.

349: **vail:** abase

352: **in force:** in effect

359: **speeds:** succeeds

QUEEN ELIZABETH
To vail the title, as her mother doth.

RICHARD III
Say I will love her everlastingly.   350

QUEEN ELIZABETH
But how long shall that title "ever" last?

RICHARD III
Sweetly in force unto her fair life's end.

QUEEN ELIZABETH
But how long fairly shall her sweet life last?

RICHARD III
As long as heaven and nature lengthens it.

QUEEN ELIZABETH
As long as hell and Richard likes of it.   355

RICHARD III
Say I, her sovereign, am her subject low.

QUEEN ELIZABETH
But she, your subject, loathes such sovereignty.

RICHARD III
Be eloquent in my behalf to her.

QUEEN ELIZABETH
An honest tale speeds best being plainly told.

RICHARD III
Then plainly to her tell my loving tale.   360

QUEEN ELIZABETH
Plain and not honest is too harsh a style.

362: **quick:** hasty

363-367: **O no...my crown:** In the First Folio, the order of the lines are different. 4.4.366 appears after 4.4.364 as the last line of that speech by Queen Elizabeth, and 4.4.365 appears immediately before 4.4.367 as part of that speech by Richard:

QUEEN ELIZABETH
> O no, my reasons are too deep and dead;
> Too deep and dead, poor infants, in their graves.
> Harp on it still shall I till heart-strings break.

RICHARD III
> Harp not on that string, madam, that is past.
> Now by my George, my Garter, and my crown –

The order of the lines here are from the First Quarto.

367: **my George, my Garter:** emblems of the knightly Order of the Garter, founded around 1348 by Edward III

RICHARD III
  Your reasons are too shallow and too quick.

QUEEN ELIZABETH
  O no, my reasons are too deep and dead;
  Too deep and dead, poor infants, in their graves.

RICHARD III
  Harp not on that string, madam, that is past.   365

QUEEN ELIZABETH
  Harp on it still shall I till heart-strings break.

RICHARD III
  Now by my George, my Garter, and my crown—

QUEEN ELIZABETH
  Profaned, dishonored, and the third usurped.

RICHARD III
  I swear—

QUEEN ELIZABETH
                    By nothing, for this is no oath.
  Thy George, profaned, hath lost his lordly honor;   370
  Thy Garter, blemished, pawned his knightly virtue;
  Thy crown, usurped, disgraced his kingly glory.
  If something thou wouldst swear to be believed,
  Swear then by something that thou hast not wronged.

RICHARD III
  Then, by myself—

QUEEN ELIZABETH
                    Thy self is self-misused.   375

RICHARD III
  Now, by the world—

378: God: from the First Quarto, the First Folio reads "Heaven"; **God's:** from the First Quarto, the First Folio reads "Heavens" (removed under the "Act to Restrain the Abuses of Players")

389: o'erpast: already passed

391: Hereafter time: in the future

393: Ungoverned: without parental supervision; **in:** from the First Quarto, the First Folio reads "with"

394: parents: Although this is plural, the only living parent whose children Richard has had killed is Queen Elizabeth.

397: o'erpast: from the First Quarto, the First Folio reads "repast"

QUEEN ELIZABETH
> 'Tis full of thy foul wrongs.

RICHARD III
My father's death—

QUEEN ELIZABETH
> Thy life hath it dishonored.

RICHARD III
Why then, by God—

QUEEN ELIZABETH
> God's wrong is most of all.
If thou didst fear to break an oath with Him,
The unity the King my husband made   380
Thou hadst not broken, nor my brothers died.
If thou hadst feared to break an oath by Him,
Th' imperial metal, circling now thy head,
Had graced the tender temples of my child,
And both the princes had been breathing here,   385
Which now, two tender bedfellows to dust,
Thy broken faith hath made a prey for worms.
What canst thou swear by now?

RICHARD III
> The time to come.

QUEEN ELIZABETH
That thou hast wrongèd in the time o'erpast;
For I myself have many tears to wash   390
Hereafter time, for time past wronged by thee.
The children live whose fathers thou hast slaughtered,
Ungoverned youth, to wail it in their age;
The parents live, whose children thou hast butchered,
Old barren plants, to wail it with their age.   395
Swear not by time to come; for that thou hast
Misused ere used, by time ill-used o'erpast.

400: **confound:** overthrow

403: **opposite:** opposed, adverse

406: **tender:** regard

414: Scene: **Be the attorney:** Having regained his seat, Sher (Alexander, 1984) pulled Tomelty (Elizabeth) onto his lap.

414: "Be the attorney of my love to her": Antony Sher as Richard and Frances Tomelty as Queen Elizabeth in the 1984 Royal Shakespeare Company production directed by Bill Alexander

Photo: Donald Cooper

414: **attorney:** advocate

418: **peevish:** foolish

RICHARD III

   As I intend to prosper and repent,
   So thrive I in my dangerous affairs
   Of hostile arms. Myself myself confound,   400
   Heaven and fortune bar me happy hours,
   Day, yield me not thy light; nor night thy rest,
   Be opposite all planets of good luck
   To my proceeding if, with dear heart's love,
   Immaculate devotion, holy thoughts,   405
   I tender not thy beauteous princely daughter.
   In her consists my happiness and thine.
   Without her follows to myself and thee,
   Herself, the land, and many a Christian soul,
   Death, desolation, ruin and decay.   410
   It cannot be avoided but by this;
   It will not be avoided but by this.
   Therefore, dear mother (I must call you so)
   Be the attorney of my love to her.
   Plead what I will be, not what I have been;   415
   Not my deserts, but what I will deserve.
   Urge the necessity and state of times,
   And be not peevish found in great designs.

QUEEN ELIZABETH

   Shall I be tempted of the devil thus?

RICHARD III

   Ay, if the devil tempt you to do good.   420

QUEEN ELIZABETH

   Shall I forget myself to be myself?

RICHARD III

   Ay, if your self's remembrance wrong yourself.

QUEEN ELIZABETH

   Yet thou didst kill my children.

425: **spicery:** fragrant spices

425-426: **they...themselves:** like the Phoenix, they will breed new selves from their old dead selves

426: **recomforture:** consolation, comfort; this is the only recorded use of this word

429: **shortly:** soon

430: Stage Direction: ***Exit QUEEN ELIZABETH:*** This stage direction is placed here in the First Folio although quartos 1-6 and almost all modern editions place it one line later. For performance reasons, we chose the First Folio placement: given the ambiguity of Elizabeth's situation, it might have been dramatically more effective to have Richard's line 430 said to her departing back, particularly given the extreme cynicism of his next line.

432: Stage Direction: ***Enter RATCLIFF; [CATESBY following]:*** This is the placement from the First Quarto; the First Folio places this stage direction one line later.

435: **Rideth:** lies anchored; **puissant:** powerful

437: **unresolved:** undetermined or unwilling

439: **hull:** drift, with sails furled

441: **light-foot:** quick-footed, swift; **post:** go at speed

RICHARD III
> But in your daughter's womb I bury them.
> Where in that nest of spicery they will breed   425
> Selves of themselves, to your recomforture.

QUEEN ELIZABETH
> Shall I go win my daughter to thy will?

RICHARD III
> And be a happy mother by the deed.

QUEEN ELIZABETH
> I go. Write to me very shortly.
> And you shall understand from me her mind.   430

> *Exit QUEEN ELIZABETH*

RICHARD III
> Bear her my true love's kiss; and so, farewell.
> Relenting fool, and shallow, changing woman!

> *Enter RATCLIFF; [CATESBY following]*

> How now, what news?

RATCLIFF
> My mighty sovereign, on the western coast
> Rideth a puissant navy. To our shores   435
> Throng many doubtful hollow-hearted friends,
> Unarmed and unresolved to beat them back.
> 'Tis thought that Richmond is their admiral;
> And there they hull, expecting but the aid
> Of Buckingham to welcome them ashore.   440

RICHARD III
> Some light-foot friend post to the Duke of Norfolk.
> Ratcliff, thyself, or Catesby—where is he?

CATESBY
> Here, my good lord.

RICHARD III
> Catesby, fly to the duke.

445: **Ratcliff:** The First Folio has this addressed, in error, to Catesby, who has already been given another command. The First Quarto combines it with the previous line. Nicholas Rowe (1709) was the first editor to make this emendation. **Salisbury:** town in southwest England on the edge of Salisbury Plain; county seat of Wiltshire

449: **deliver:** say

449, 450: **him:** Duke of Norfolk

450: **straight:** immediately

452: **suddenly:** at once

459-460: Scene: **None good...reported:** Sher (Alexander, 1984) treated Stanley's statement as a riddle and made a parlor game of answering it.

CATESBY
  I will, my lord, with all convenient haste.

RICHARD III
  Ratcliff, come hither. Post thou to Salisbury.   445
  When thou com'st thither—[*To CATESBY*] Dull, unmindful villain,
  Why stay'st thou here and go'st not to the duke?

CATESBY
  First, mighty liege, tell me your Highness' pleasure,
  What from your Grace I shall deliver to him.

RICHARD III
  O, true, good Catesby. Bid him levy straight   450
  The greatest strength and power that he can make
  And meet me suddenly at Salisbury.

CATESBY
  I go.

                                                          Exit

RATCLIFF
  What, may it please you, shall I do at Salisbury?

RICHARD III
  Why, what wouldst thou do there before I go?   455

RATCLIFF
  Your Highness told me I should post before.

RICHARD III
  My mind is changed.

                                          Enter LORD STANLEY
  Stanley, what news with you?

STANLEY
  None good, my liege, to please you with the hearing,
  Nor none so bad but well may be reported.   460

461: Hoyday: exclamation of playfulness, surprise, or wonder

463: nearest way: directly

466: White-livered runagate: cowardly renegade

478: Welshman: Henry, Earl of Richmond and later Henry VII, was from a Welsh family, the Tudors. His father was Edmund Tudor and his mother was Margaret Beaufort. She was the only daughter of John Beaufort, Duke of Somerset, and great-great-granddaughter of Edward III through the liaison of John of Gaunt, Duke of Lancaster, with Katherine Swynford. Margaret Beaufort's last marriage (she was twice widowed) was to Thomas Stanley, Earl of Derby.

RICHARD III
    Hoyday, a riddle! Neither good nor bad.
    What need'st thou run so many miles about
    When thou mayst tell thy tale the nearest way?
    Once more, what news?

STANLEY
                         Richmond is on the seas.

RICHARD III
    There let him sink, and be the seas on him.   465
    White-livered runagate, what doth he there?

STANLEY
    I know not, mighty sovereign, but by guess.

RICHARD III
    Well, as you guess?

STANLEY
    Stirred up by Dorset, Buckingham, and Morton,
    He makes for England, here to claim the crown.   470

RICHARD III
    Is the chair empty? Is the sword unswayed?
    Is the King dead? The empire unpossessed?
    What heir of York is there alive but we?
    And who is England's king but great York's heir?
    Then tell me, what makes he upon the seas?   475

STANLEY
    Unless for that, my liege, I cannot guess.

RICHARD III
    Unless for that he comes to be your liege,
    You cannot guess wherefore the Welshman comes.
    Thou wilt revolt, and fly to him, I fear.

STANLEY
    No, my good lord, therefore mistrust me not.   480

481: **power:** army

497: **Look:** make sure

RICHARD III

    Where is thy power then, to beat him back?
    Where be thy tenants and thy followers?
    Are they not now upon the western shore,
    Safe-conducting the rebels from their ships?

STANLEY

    No, my good lord, my friends are in the north.   485

RICHARD III

    Cold friends to me. What do they in the north,
    When they should serve their sovereign in the west?

STANLEY

    They have not been commanded, mighty king.
    Pleaseth your Majesty to give me leave,
    I'll muster up my friends, and meet your Grace   490
    Where and what time your Majesty shall please.

RICHARD III

    Ay, thou wouldst be gone to join with Richmond.
    But I'll not trust thee.

STANLEY

                 Most mighty sovereign,
    You have no cause to hold my friendship doubtful.
    I never was nor never will be false.   495

RICHARD III

    Go then, and muster men; but leave behind
    Your son, George Stanley. Look your heart be firm,
    Or else his head's assurance is but frail.

STANLEY

    So deal with him as I prove true to you.

                           Exit STANLEY
                        Enter MESSENGER

500: Speech Prefix: **FIRST MESSENGER:** In both the First Folio and the First Quarto, he is merely called "*a Messenger*" and the later ones are both called "*another Messenger*". Here, the numbering of them is conventional.

501: advertisèd: informed

502-503: Scene: **Sir Edward...brother:** There is considerable confusion here because although Shakespeare is following his source accurately (Edward Hall, *The Union of the Two Noble and Illustre Families of Lancaster and York*, 1548; the First Quarto erroneously names Sir Edward as Sir William), Peter Courtenay, the Bishop of Exeter, actually participated in the rising in the west against Richard. However, a near cousin, Edward Courtney, the future Earl of Devon, also participated in this rising.

509: Stage Direction: *He striketh him*: Sir Laurence Olivier as Richard in the 1955 production directed by Sir Laurence Olivier

Photo: Courtesy of Douglas Lanier

505: Guilfords: magnates in the county of Kent, just south of London

509: Scene: *He striketh him*: In trying to strike the messengers, Sher (Alexander, 1984) falls from his chair.

509: Out on ye: an exclamation of impatience; **owls:** owls were birds of ill omen

515: I cry thee mercy: I beg your pardon

517: well-advisèd: careful

FIRST MESSENGER
  My gracious sovereign, now in Devonshire,   500
  As I by friends am well advertisèd,
  Sir Edward Courtney, and the haughty prelate,
  Bishop of Exeter, his elder brother,
  With many more confederates, are in arms.

                              Enter another MESSENGER

SECOND MESSENGER
  In Kent, my liege, the Guilfords are in arms,   505
  And every hour more competitors
  Flock to the rebels, and their power grows strong.

                              Enter another MESSENGER

THIRD MESSENGER
  My lord, the army of the Duke of Buckingham—

RICHARD III
  Out on ye, owls! Nothing but songs of death?

                                              He striketh him
  There, take thou that, till thou bring better news.   510

THIRD MESSENGER
  The news I have to tell your Majesty
  Is, that by sudden floods and fall of waters,
  Buckingham's army is dispersed and scattered,
  And he himself wandered away alone,
  No man knows whither.

RICHARD III
                        I cry thee mercy.   515
  There is my purse to cure that blow of thine.
  Hath any well-advisèd friend proclaimed
  Reward to him that brings the traitor in?

THIRD MESSENGER
  Such proclamation hath been made, my lord.

                              Enter another MESSENGER

520: **Sir Thomas Lovell:** of the Norfolk gentry and not to be confused with Lord Francis Lovel, Richard's chamberlain

521: **Yorkshire:** county in the north of England

523: **Breton:** from Brittany

524: **Dorsetshire:** in the far southwest of England

526: **assistants:** supporters

528: **Upon his party:** on his behalf

529: **Hoised:** hoisted

533: Scene: **the Duke of Buckingham is taken:** At this line, Cibber inserted probably his most famous piece of showmanship in the play, giving Richard the line, "Off with his head! So much for Buckingham." This became one of the critical moments on which performances were judged, and this addition was generally on stage into the 1930s; Olivier said the line in his film (1955).

535: **Milford:** Milford Haven on the coast of Wales

536: **tidings:** from the First Quarto, the First Folio reads "Newes"

537: **reason:** debate, discuss

FOURTH MESSENGER

    Sir Thomas Lovell, and Lord Marquess Dorset,   520
    'Tis said, my liege, in Yorkshire are in arms.
    But this good comfort bring I to your Highness,
    The Breton navy is dispersed by tempest.
    Richmond, in Dorsetshire, sent out a boat
    Unto the shore to ask those on the banks   525
    If they were his assistants, yea or no?
    Who answered him, they came from Buckingham
    Upon his party. He, mistrusting them,
    Hoised sail and made away for Brittany.

RICHARD III

    March on, march on, since we are up in arms,   530
    If not to fight with foreign enemies,
    Yet to beat down these rebels here at home.

Enter CATESBY

CATESBY

    My liege, the Duke of Buckingham is taken.
    That is the best news. That the Earl of Richmond
    Is with a mighty power landed at Milford   535
    Is colder tidings, but yet they must be told.

RICHARD III

    Away towards Salisbury. While we reason here,
    A royal battle might be won and lost.
    Someone take order Buckingham be brought
    To Salisbury, the rest march on with me.   540

Flourish. Exeunt.

0: Scene: This is marked scene four in the First Folio; see note 3.5.0 on act and scene divisions. This scene was cut by almost every production from Cibber onward.

1: Stage Direction: *SIR CHRISTOPHER [URSWICK]*: a priest (the title "Sir" was typical for clergy at the time) who was chaplain to Margaret Beaufort, Stanley's wife and Richmond's mother. He served as a messenger between Richmond in France and the anti-Richard faction in England, and landed at Milford Haven with Richmond. He eventually became Henry VII's private chaplain.

3: **franked:** penned
5: **present:** immediate
7: **Withal:** in addition; **Queen:** Elizabeth
10: **Pembroke:** coastal town in southwest Wales across an estuary from Milford Haven; **Ha'rfordwest:** Haverfordwest is to the north of Pembroke
11: **men of name:** titled men
12: **Sir Walter Herbert:** a kinsman of Buckingham
13: **Sir Gilbert Talbot:** kinsman to the earls of Shrewsbury; **Sir William Stanley:** i.e., brother to Stanley, the Earl of Derby
14: **Oxford:** John de Vere, Earl of Oxford. He had been held captive by Richard but escaped with the help of his jailer, Sir James Blount, to join Richmond; **Pembroke:** Jasper Tudor, Earl of Pembroke and half-brother of Richmond. Milford Haven was part of Jasper Tudor's holdings; **Sir James Blunt:** Sir James Blount, jailer of John de Vere, Earl of Oxford. In November 1484 Blount freed his prisoner and went with him to join Richmond in France. He accompanied Richmond's invasion of England in 1485 and was knighted by him at his landing at Milford Haven.
15: **Rice ap Thomas:** Sir Rhys ap Thomas, a powerful magnate in Wales second only to Jasper Tudor, Earl of Pembroke
19: **withal:** with
20: **resolve:** explain

Act 4, Scene 5]

Enter [STANLEY, EARL OF] DERBY and
SIR CHRISTOPHER [URSWICK]

STANLEY
Sir Christopher, tell Richmond this from me:
That in the sty of this most deadly boar
My son, George Stanley, is franked up in hold;
If I revolt, off goes young George's head.
The fear of that holds off my present aid.   5
So get thee gone. Commend me to thy lord.
Withal say, that the Queen hath heartily consented
He should espouse Elizabeth her daughter.
But, tell me, where is princely Richmond now?

CHRISTOPHER
At Pembroke, or at Ha'rfordwest, in Wales.   10

STANLEY
What men of name resort to him?

CHRISTOPHER
Sir Walter Herbert, a renownèd soldier;
Sir Gilbert Talbot, Sir William Stanley;
Oxford, redoubted Pembroke, Sir James Blunt,
And Rice ap Thomas, with a valiant crew,   15
And many other of great name and worth.
And towards London they do bend their power,
If by the way they be not fought withal.

STANLEY
Well, hie thee to thy lord. I kiss his hand.
My letter will resolve him of my mind.   20
Farewell.

Exeunt

[Richard III

Act 5

0: **Scene:** This scene was cut by Cibber and almost all nineteenth-century productions, even ones purporting to be restoring the text; modern productions usually include it. It is, after all, Buckingham's one chance to make a moralizing speech. On the modern stage, the Sheriff is usually replaced by either Ratcliff or Catesby.

tracks 22-24

1–29:
Philip Voss as Duke of Buckingham
Nicholas Farrell as Duke of Buckingham

10: **All Soul's Day:** commemoration of the souls of all the dead on November 2, following All Saint's Day on November 1; the mass for All Soul's Day contains the sequence "Dies Irae" (Day of Wrath). Shakespeare has compressed historical events so that the execution of Buckingham (November, 1483) seems to happen just before the Battle of Bosworth in August, 1485, twenty-one months after Buckingham'sactual execution.

19: **determined respite of my wrongs:** appointed time to pay for my wrongs

Act 5, Scene 1]

BUCKINGHAM
Will not King Richard let me speak with him?

SHERIFF
No, my good lord, therefore be patient.

BUCKINGHAM
Hastings, and Edward's children, Grey and Rivers,
Holy King Henry, and thy fair son Edward,
Vaughan, and all that have miscarried   5
By underhand corrupted foul injustice,
If that your moody discontented souls
Do through the clouds behold this present hour,
Even for revenge mock my destruction
This is All Souls' Day, fellow, is it not?   10

SHERIFF
It is.

BUCKINGHAM
Why, then, All Souls' Day is my body's doomsday.
This is the day which, in King Edward's time,
I wished might fall on me, when I was found
False to his children and his wife's allies.   15
This is the day wherein I wished to fall
By the false faith of him whom most I trusted.
This, this All Souls' Day to my fearful soul
Is the determined respite of my wrongs.
That high All-Seer which I dallied with   20
Hath turned my feignèd prayer on my head
And given in earnest what I begged in jest.

tracks 22-24

1–29:
Philip Voss as Duke of Buckingham
Nicholas Farrell as Duke of Buckingham

25: "Margaret's curse falls heavy on my neck": John Nettles as Buckingham and the Ensemble in the 1996 Royal Shakespeare Company production directed by Steven Pimlott

Photo: Donald Cooper

Thus doth he force the swords of wicked men
To turn their own points on their masters' bosoms.
Thus Margaret's curse falls heavy on my neck: 25
"When he," quoth she, "shall split thy heart with sorrow,
Remember Margaret was a prophetess."
Come, lead me, officers, to the block of shame.
Wrong hath but wrong, and blame the due of blame.

Exeunt BUCKINGHAM with officers

0: **Scene:** Although this scene was played more or less normally well into the nine-teenth century, with productions again taking the opportunity to stage grand proces-sions (e.g., Charles Kean marched Richmond's troops on and off through the wings so that the end of the procession was never seen), there has been a tendency, starting with Irving, to move most of this scene to Richmond's entry at 5.3.19. Loncraine (1995), going outside the text, had the marriage between Richmond and Elizabeth open this scene, including Richmond's prayer (5.3.109-19) as part of the ceremony.

3: **bowels:** interior

5: **father:** i.e., stepfather

9: **wash:** pig swill

10: **embowelled bosoms:** disemboweled stomachs

11: **center:** from the First Quarto, the First Folio reads "Centry"

12, 13: **Leicester, Tamworth:** towns in central England near Bosworth where Richard and Richmond will meet in battle

14: **cheerly:** heartily

21: **dearest:** greatest

22: **vantage:** advantage

24: **meaner creatures:** men of lesser rank

Costume rendering for Richmond from the 1953 production at the Shakespeare Memorial Theatre in Stratford-upon-Avon directed by Glen Byam Shaw

Rare Book and Special Collection Library, University of Illinois at Urbana-Champaign

Act 5, Scene 2]

Enter RICHMOND, OXFORD, BLUNT, HERBERT,
and others, with drum and colors

RICHMOND
Fellows in arms, and my most loving friends,
Bruised underneath the yoke of tyranny,
Thus far into the bowels of the land
Have we marched on without impediment;
And here receive we from our father Stanley   5
Lines of fair comfort and encouragement.
The wretched, bloody, and usurping boar,
That spoiled your summer fields and fruitful vines,
Swills your warm blood like wash, and makes his trough
In your embowelled bosoms. This foul swine   10
Is now even in the center of this isle,
Near to the town of Leicester, as we learn.
From Tamworth thither is but one day's march.
In God's name, cheerly on, courageous friends,
To reap the harvest of perpetual peace   15
By this one bloody trial of sharp war.

OXFORD
Every man's conscience is a thousand men,
To fight against this guilty homicide.

HERBERT
I doubt not but his friends will turn to us.

BLUNT
He hath no friends, but who are friends for fear,   20
Which in his dearest need will fly from him.

RICHMOND
All for our vantage. Then in God's name march.
True hope is swift, and flies with swallow's wings;
Kings it makes gods, and meaner creatures kings.

Exeunt

0: Scene: the First Folio does not provide a scene division here even though the stage has been cleared. Alexander Pope (1725) is the first editor to insert this scene division.

0: Stage Direction: **SURREY:** the Earl of Surrey, Thomas Howard, was the son of the Duke of Norfolk, John Howard

1: Scene: **Here pitch our tent:** Much ink has been spilled in trying to explain the tents of Richard and Richmond and their use in the performance of this scene. Approximating the size of the Globe stage to be about the same size as that of The Theatre (from whose timbers it was built) we can assume dimensions of 45 feet in width, a depth of 30 feet, and two massive stage pillars toward the front at either side to support the Heavens. Onto this space, and perhaps using the pillars as part of the support for the tents, it should have been possible to erect the tents of Richard and Richmond on either side of the stage. Note that Richard directs them to erect his tent at lines 1, 7, and 14 and mentions it in lines 51 and 78; Richmond refers to his tent three times, the latter time directing his associates into it (lines 23, 32, and 46); and the stage directions specifically mention a tent at line 46, telling us Stanley enters a tent at line 79. Such a weight of evidence from the early texts, as authoritative a set of witnesses as we are ever likely to have, would seem to silence all debate about what happened on English stages before 1660, but it has not. The issue is that after 1660 (really after Cibber in 1700), there were considerable problems with having both tents on stage simultaneously; in Cibber's case, it was largely due to the way he had the ghosts enter and exit. Thus, Cibber's text did not mention tents of any kind until line 48 and, in the printed editions of his acting text, not until line 79. In the middle of the nineteenth century, the productions of Phelps and Calvert restored the tents to the stage, and by Guthrie's 1937 production (Old Vic), the tents were represented by pieces of painted canvas. Most productions since then have attempted, in some way, to place something representing both camps on the stage.

1: **Bosworth field:** site of Richard's final battle and the last battle of the Wars of the Roses on 22 August 1485. It is ten miles west of Leicester and near the villages of Market Bosworth and Sutton Cheney.
5: **knocks:** blows
8: **all's one for that:** that does not matter
9: **descried:** seen, discovered
11: **battalia:** main body of troops in battle order
13: **want:** lack

Act 5, Scene 3

Enter RICHARD III in arms, with NORFOLK,
RATCLIFF, EARL OF SURREY, [and others]

RICHARD III
Here pitch our tent, even here in Bosworth field.
My Lord of Surrey, why look you so sad?

SURREY
My heart is ten times lighter than my looks.

RICHARD III
My Lord of Norfolk—

NORFOLK
Here, most gracious liege.

RICHARD III
Norfolk, we must have knocks, ha, must we not?   5

NORFOLK
We must both give and take, my loving lord.

RICHARD III
Up with my tent. Here will I lie tonight,
But where tomorrow? Well, all's one for that.
Who hath descried the number of the traitors?

NORFOLK
Six or seven thousand is their utmost power.   10

RICHARD III
Why, our battalia trebles that account.
Besides, the King's name is a tower of strength,
Which they upon the adverse faction want.

18: Stage Direction: *Exeunt*: The reason there is no scene division at this point is that the stage is not actually cleared, with Richard, his tent, and his troops having set up camp on the extreme edge of the stage or in some similar withdrawn place. This was probably the case in Shakespeare's theater and has regularly been the case in the theater since 1660.

20: **track:** from the First Quarto, the First Folio reads "Tract"; **fiery car:** the sun god's chariot

21: **token:** promise

22: **Sir William Brandon:** He died at Bosworth carrying Richmond's standard; he was the father of Charles Brandon, Duke of Suffolk.

24: **battle:** disposition of forces

25: **Limit:** appoint; **charge:** assignment

26: **part in just:** divide exactly; **power:** army

28: **you:** from the Second Folio. The First Folio reads "your", and the word does not appear in quartos 1-8. **Sir Walter Herbert:** kinsman of Duke of Buckingham

29: **keeps:** stays with

31: **by the second hour:** the first hour after sunrise, which, in August in England, would be between 5 and 6 a.m.

35: **colors:** battle flags and ensigns

40: **make:** find

41: **needful:** necessary

Up with my tent! Come, noble gentlemen,
Let us survey the vantage of the ground.   15
Call for some men of sound direction;
Let's lack no discipline, make no delay,
For lords, tomorrow is a busy day.

Exeunt

Enter RICHMOND, SIR WILLIAM BRANDON, OXFORD, DORSET,
[HERBERT, BLUNT, and others who put up Richmond's tent]

RICHMOND
The weary sun hath made a golden set,
And by the bright track of his fiery car,   20
Gives token of a goodly day tomorrow.
Sir William Brandon, you shall bear my standard.
Give me some ink and paper in my tent,
I'll draw the form and model of our battle,
Limit each leader to his several charge,   25
And part in just proportion our small power.
My Lord of Oxford, you, Sir William Brandon,
And you, Sir Walter Herbert, stay with me.
The Earl of Pembroke keeps his regiment;
Good Captain Blunt, bear my goodnight to him   30
And by the second hour in the morning
Desire the earl to see me in my tent.
Yet one thing more, good captain, do for me.
Where is Lord Stanley quartered, do you know?

BLUNT
Unless I have mista'en his colors much,   35
Which well I am assured I have not done,
His regiment lies half a mile at least
South from the mighty power of the King.

RICHMOND
If without peril it be possible,
Sweet Blunt, make some good means to speak with him   40
And give him from me this most needful note.

46: Stage Direction: ***They withdraw into the tent***: We assume that Richmond's tent has been set up on the other side of the stage or in some other withdrawn part. See note 5.3.18. Thus, when Richard enters at the next stage direction, he is merely returning to the main part of the stage, not entering from off stage.

49-end of play: **I will not sup tonight...God say amen:** From here to the end of the play (5.4.54) the copy-text is the First Quarto rather than the First Folio (see "About the Text").

50: **beaver:** visor on a helmet

54: **Use careful watch:** choose reliable watchmen; **sentinels:** from the First Folio, the First Quarto uses the singular form of the word

BLUNT
>Upon my life, my lord, I'll undertake it,
>And so, God give you quiet rest tonight.

RICHMOND
>Goodnight, good Captain Blunt.

[Exit BLUNT]
>Come gentlemen,
>Let us consult upon tomorrow's business.   45
>Into my tent. The dew is raw and cold.

They withdraw into the tent
Enter RICHARD III, NORFOLK, RATCLIFF,
CATESBY, [and others]

RICHARD III
>What is't o'clock?

CATESBY
>It's suppertime, my lord. It's nine o'clock.

RICHARD III
>I will not sup tonight. Give me some ink and paper.
>What, is my beaver easier than it was,   50
>And all my armor laid into my tent?

CATESBY
>It is, my liege, and all things are in readiness.

RICHARD III
>Good Norfolk, hie thee to thy charge.
>Use careful watch, choose trusty sentinels.

NORFOLK
>I go, my lord.   55

RICHARD III
>Stir with the lark tomorrow, gentle Norfolk.

57: Stage Direction: *[Exit]:* from the First Folio, the First Quarto does not provide an exit for Norfolk

59: Speech Prefix: **CATESBY:** All early editions assign this response to Ratcliff, and the First Folio even has Richard call for Ratcliff in the previous line, though the First Quarto reads "Catesby." Since Ratcliff is called to in line 67, the speech prefix is changed. Alexander Pope (1725) is the first editor to make this emendation.

60: **pursuivant-at-arms:** junior officer who attends a herald

64: **watch:** either a guard for his tent or a watch light, a candle marked to record the passage of time

65: **white Surrey:** Richard is reported by Hall to have entered Leicester on "a great white courser" but this name may be Shakespeare's invention

66: **staves:** shafts of his lances

69: **Northumberland:** i.e., Henry Percy, Earl of Northumberland. Although he brought significant forces from the north supposedly to support Richard, he withheld them from the Battle of Bosworth field and did not participate in the fight.

71: **cockshut time:** twilight

75: **wont:** accustomed

NORFOLK
I warrant you, my lord.

[Exit]

RICHARD III
Catesby.

CATESBY
My lord.

RICHARD III
Send out a pursuivant-at-arms   60
To Stanley's regiment. Bid him bring his power
Before sunrising, lest his son George fall
Into the blind cave of eternal night.

[Exit CATESBY]

Fill me a bowl of wine. Give me a watch.
Saddle white Surrey for the field tomorrow.   65
Look that my staves be sound, and not too heavy.
Ratcliff!

RATCLIFF
My lord.

RICHARD III
Sawst thou the melancholy Lord Northumberland?

RATCLIFF
Thomas the Earl of Surrey and himself,   70
Much about cockshut time, from troop to troop
Went through the army cheering up the soldiers.

RICHARD III
So, I am satisfied. Give me a bowl of wine.
I have not that alacrity of spirit
Nor cheer of mind that I was wont to have.   75
Set it down. Is ink and paper ready?

78: "Ratcliff, about the mid of night come to my tent": Ian McKellen as Richard in the 1990 National Theatre production directed by Richard Eyre
Photo: Donald Cooper

79: Stage Direction: *[and...RICHARD sleeps]*: again, the tents of both Richard and Richmond must be assumed to be on stage. See notes on 5.3.18 and 5.3.46 above. Richard must fall asleep, as does Richmond at 5.3.118.

82: **father-in-law:** i.e., stepfather
84: **by attorney:** as deputy
87: **flaky darkness breaks:** flakes (streaks) of light show darkness breaking
88: **season:** time
89: **battle:** disposition of troops
90: **arbitrament:** direction or control
91: **mortal-staring:** deadly
92: **would:** would do
93: **deceive the time:** take my time to act
94: **doubtful shock of arms:** uncertain outcome of battle
96: **brother:** half-brother
98: **leisure:** lack of leisure
99: **ceremonious:** formal
100: **ample:** large

RATCLIFF
    It is, my lord.

RICHARD III
                    Bid my guard watch. Leave me.
    Ratcliff, about the mid of night come to my tent
    And help to arm me. Leave me, I say.
              Exeunt RATCLIFF [and the other attendants. RICHARD sleeps.]
                    Enter [STANLEY, EARL OF] DERBY to RICHMOND
                        in his tent, [lords and others attending]

STANLEY
    Fortune and victory sit on thy helm.   80

RICHMOND
    All comfort that the dark night can afford
    Be to thy person, noble father-in-law.
    Tell me, how fares our noble mother?

STANLEY
    I, by attorney, bless thee from thy mother,
    Who prays continually for Richmond's good.   85
    So much for that. The silent hours steal on,
    And flaky darkness breaks within the east.
    In brief—for so the season bids us be—
    Prepare thy battle early in the morning,
    And put thy fortune to the arbitrament   90
    Of bloody strokes and mortal-staring war.
    I, as I may—that which I would I cannot—
    With best advantage will deceive the time,
    And aid thee in this doubtful shock of arms.
    But on thy side I may not be too forward,   95
    Lest being seen, thy brother, tender George,
    Be executed in his father's sight.
    Farewell. The leisure and the fearful time
    Cuts off the ceremonious vows of love
    And ample interchange of sweet discourse,   100
    Which so long sundered friends should dwell upon.
    God give us leisure for these rites of love.
    Once more, adieu. Be valiant and speed well.

106: **peise:** weigh

108: Stage Direction: *[manet RICHMOND]:* from the First Folio, the First Quarto provides only *"Exeunt"*

117: **Ere:** from the First Folio, the First Quarto reads "Eare"

118: Stage Direction: *[Sleeps]:* from the First Folio, the First Quarto provides no direction

118-177: Scene: ***Enter...pride. [Exit]:*** On the Early English stages ghosts traditionally entered by rising through the trap in the center of the stage and sinking down through it when they exited. Editorial tradition stretching from the early eighteenth century until the middle of the twentieth century provides no exit direction until after all the ghosts speak, and then they all exit, or vanish, as a group after line 177. Although this may be dramatically effective it has several practical arguments against it: for example, in the stage practices of Shakespeare's time, eleven actor-ghosts would have been on stage along with Richard, Richmond, their tents, and perhaps other actors and props. During the two centuries when Cibber's reduced company of ghosts held the stage, this would have been less of a problem, but when all eleven were restored to performance in the twentieth century, concerns of crowding again arise. The present edition has provided exits for each ghost after the ghost or ghosts' speech, but readers should be aware of the alternative tradition in performance; these exits have been editorial added and are in no way authoritative textually.

We must assume that with the tents and sleeping figures of Richard and Richmond at either side of the stage, the intention was for the ghosts to stand somewhere in the middle and direct their lines first to one side and then to the other. This is certainly how they entered throughout the eighteenth century (the frontispiece to Rowe's edition of 1709 shows one of them doing this) until Edmund Kean ended the practice by bringing them on stage in gauze. Cibber reduced Shakespeare's eleven ghosts to only four (Henry VI, Lady Anne, and the two little Princes) and expanded their speeches; they probably no longer entered and exited through the trap. Until nearly the end of the nineteenth century, there continued to be only four of them. Once the ghosts began entering from the wings in the twentieth century and all eleven were restored to the text, it became usual for them to exit after delivering their speeches.

118: Speech Prefix: **Ghost [of Prince Edward] to RICHARD III:** here, and at lines 122, 125, 129, 137, 145, 147, 151, 158, 165, and 174 the direction concerning who is addressed is embedded in the speech prefixes or in the text in both the First Quarto and the First Folio. Where they did not exist, they have been added.

127: **Tower and me:** where Richard killed Henry VI; see *Henry VI, Part 3* (5.6)

RICHMOND
    Good lords, conduct him to his regiment.
    I'll strive, with troubled thoughts, to take a nap,   105
    Lest leaden slumber peise me down tomorrow,
    When I should mount with wings of victory.
    Once more, good night, kind lords and gentlemen.

                           Exeunt, [manet RICHMOND]
    O Thou, whose captain I account myself,
    Look on my forces with a gracious eye.   110
    Put in their hands Thy bruising irons of wrath,
    That they may crush down with a heavy fall
    The usurping helmets of our adversaries.
    Make us Thy ministers of chastisement,
    That we may praise Thee in the victory.   115
    To Thee I do commend my watchful soul,
    Ere I let fall the windows of mine eyes:
    Sleeping and waking, O, defend me still!

                              [Sleeps]
    Enter the ghost of young PRINCE EDWARD, son
        of KING HENRY THE SIXTH, to RICHARD

Ghost [of PRINCE EDWARD] to RICHARD III
    Let me sit heavy on thy soul tomorrow.
    Think how thou stab'st me in my prime of youth   120
    At Tewkesbury. Despair therefore, and die.
    [To RICHMOND] Be cheerful, Richmond, for the wrongèd souls
    Of butchered princes fight in thy behalf.
    King Henry's issue, Richmond, comforts thee.

                              [Exit]
    Enter the ghost of KING HENRY THE SIXTH

Ghost [of KING HENRY VI] to RICHARD III
    When I was mortal, my anointed body   125
    By thee was punched full of deadly holes.
    Think on the Tower and me. Despair, and die.
    Harry the Sixth bids thee despair, and die.
    [To RICHMOND] Virtuous and holy, be thou conqueror.
    Harry, that prophesied thou shouldst be king,   130
    Doth comfort thee in thy sleep. Live and flourish.

                              [Exit]
    Enter the ghost of CLARENCE

Anton Lesser and the Ensemble in the 1989 Royal Shakespeare Company
production directed by Adrian Noble

Photo: Donald Cooper

140: Speech Prefix: **RIVERS:** from the First Folio, the First Quarto reads *"King"*

146: Stage Direction: *[Exeunt]:* The Third Quarto (Q3) moved the Princes' entrance and
speeches to follow Hastings (line 159), and the remaining five quartos and the First
Folio follow Q3 in this arrangement. Many modern editors also follow Q3, since all the
other ghosts appear in the order in which they died. However, Q3 has no textual
authority; the arrangement of the remaining quartos and the First Folio is a consequence of one being copied from the printing preceding it. Therefore, the arrangement of Q1 and Q2, the two early printings with the clearest authority, is followed.

152: **annoy:** harm

Ghost of CLARENCE [to RICHARD III]
    Let me sit heavy on thy soul tomorrow.
    I, that was washed to death with fulsome wine,
    Poor Clarence, by thy guile betrayed to death.
    Tomorrow in the battle think on me,   135
    And fall thy edgeless sword. Despair and die.
    [*To RICHMOND*] Thou offspring of the House of Lancaster,
    The wrongèd heirs of York do pray for thee,
    Good angels gu ard thy battle. Live and flourish.

                                                 [Exit]
          Enter the ghosts of RIVERS, GREY, [and] VAUGHAN

[Ghost of RIVERS to RICHARD III]
    Let me sit heavy on thy soul tomorrow,   140
    Rivers. that died at Pomfret. Despair and die.

[Ghost of] GREY [to RICHARD III]
    Think upon Grey, and let thy soul despair.

[Ghost of] VAUGHAN [to RICHARD III]
    Think upon Vaughan, and with guilty fear
    Let fall thy lance. Despair and die.

All to RICHMOND
    Awake, and think our wrongs in Richard's bosom   145
    Will conquer him. Awake, and win the day.

                                          [Exeunt]
           Enter the ghosts of the two young princes

Ghosts [to RICHARD]
    Dream on thy cousins smothered in the Tower.
    Let us be lead within thy bosom, Richard,
    And weigh thee down to ruin, shame, and death.
    Thy nephews's souls bid thee despair and die.   150
    [*To RICHMOND*] Sleep, Richmond, sleep in peace and wake in joy.
    Good angels guard thee from the boar's annoy.
    Live, and beget a happy race of kings.
    Edward's unhappy sons do bid thee flourish.

                                        [Exeunt]
               Enter the ghost of HASTINGS

177: Stage Direction: ***RICHARD III starteth up out of a dream***: This was Garrick's most famous moment (see illustration below), and most actors since have put a good deal of effort into this moment. Whether this would have been a more arresting moment if all the ghosts have just exited or if only the last one has is a matter of critical judgment.

177: Stage Direction: *Richard III starteth up out of a dream*: "David Garrick as Richard III," by William Hogarth (1745)

Courtesy of the Library of Congress

tracks 25–27

178–207:
Kenneth Branagh as Richard III
David Troughton as Richard III

178-207: **Give me...head of Richard:** Cibber cut this to nine lines; nineteenth century attempts to restore the text still cut lines 186-93 and 203-04.

179: **Soft:** wait

Ghost [of HASTINGS to RICHARD III]
    Bloody and guilty, guiltily awake,   155
    And in a bloody battle end thy days.
    Think on Lord Hastings. Despair and die.
    [*To RICHMOND*] Quiet untroubled soul, awake, awake.
    Arm, fight, and conquer for fair England's sake.

                                   [Exit]
                Enter the ghost of LADY ANNE, his wife

[Ghost of LADY ANNE to RICHARD III]
    Richard, thy wife, that wretched Anne thy wife,   160
    That never slept a quiet hour with thee,
    Now fills thy sleep with perturbations.
    Tomorrow in the battle think on me,
    And fall thy edgeless sword. Despair and die.
    [*To RICHMOND*] Thou quiet soul, sleep thou a quiet sleep.   165
    Dream of success and happy victory.
    Thy adversary's wife doth pray for thee.

                                     [Exit]
                   Enter the ghost of BUCKINGHAM

[Ghost of BUCKINGHAM to RICHARD III]
    The first was I that helped thee to the crown;
    The last was I that felt thy tyranny.
    O, in the battle think on Buckingham,   170
    And die in terror of thy guiltiness.
    Dream on, dream on, of bloody deeds and death.
    Fainting, despair; despairing, yield thy breath.
    [*To RICHMOND*] I died for hope ere I could lend thee aid,
    But cheer thy heart, and be thou not dismayed.   175
    God and good angels fight on Richmond's side,
    And Richard falls in height of all his pride.

                                     [Exit]
             RICHARD III starteth up out of a dream

RICHARD III
    Give me another horse, bind up my wounds,
    Have mercy, Jesu!—Soft, I did but dream.
    O coward conscience, how dost thou afflict me?   180

178–207:
Kenneth Branagh as Richard III
David Troughton as Richard III

Ghosts of Richard's victims haunt him in the 1953 production at the Shakespeare Memorial Theatre in Stratford-upon-Avon directed by Glen Byam Shaw
Rare Book and Special Collection Library, University of Illinois at Urbana-Champaign

181: **burn blue:** burn badly; a traditional sign of ghostly presence; see *Julius Caesar*, 4.2.327

184: **am:** from the First Folio, the First Quarto reads "and"

194: **several:** different

200: **bar:** bar of justice

205: **Methought:** it seemed to me

206: **threat:** threaten

The lights burn blue. It is now dead midnight.
Cold fearful drops stand on my trembling flesh.
What do I fear? Myself? There's none else by.
Richard loves Richard, that is, I am I.
Is there a murderer here? No. Yes, I am.   185
Then fly. What, from myself? Great reason why;
Lest I revenge. What, myself upon myself?
Alack. I love myself. Wherefore? For any good
That I myself have done unto myself?
O, no. Alas, I rather hate myself   190
For hateful deeds committed by myself.
I am a villain. Yet I lie; I am not.
Fool, of thyself speak well. Fool, do not flatter.
My conscience hath a thousand several tongues,
And every tongue brings in a several tale,   195
And every tale condemns me for a villain.
Perjury, perjury, in the highest degree;
Murder, stern murder, in the direst degree;
All several sins, all used in each degree,
Throng to the bar, crying all "Guilty, guilty!"   200
I shall despair. There is no creature loves me,
And if I die no soul shall pity me.
And wherefore should they, since that I myself
Find in myself no pity to myself?
Methought the souls of all that I had murdered   205
Came to my tent, and every one did threat
Tomorrow's vengeance on the head of Richard.

Enter RATCLIFF

RATCLIFF
  My lord.

RICHARD III
  'Zounds, who is there?

RATCLIFF
  Ratcliff, my lord, 'tis I. The early village cock   210
  Hath twice done salutation to the morn.
  Your friends are up and buckle on their armor.

216: **shadows:** illusions or dreams

220: **proof:** impenetrable armor

223: Stage Direction: ***Enter the LORDS to RICHMOND, [sitting in his tent]:*** If tents are actually used on stage (see note 5.3.1), then there must be some provision for removing them. Clearly at least Richmond's is still in place at this point. Richmond's might be removed during the exchanges in lines 226-37 and Richard's at line 291, for Richard's "Come, bustle, bustle" has the characteristics of an order. There are several other opportunities for their removal that might also be appropriate. The stage direction "sitting in his tent" comes from the First Folio; the First Quarto lacks it.

224, 227, 236: Speech Prefixes: All early texts call for the entry of "LORDS" and we assume that they speak line 224 in unison. However, lines 227 and 236 are not lines spoken by a group, so we assume each is spoken by only one of the lords.

228: **fairest-boding:** most promising

228–271:
Charles Simpson as Earl of Richmond
Jamie Glover as Earl of Richmond

RICHARD III
    O Ratcliff, I have dreamed a fearful dream.
    What think'st thou, will our friends prove all true?

RATCLIFF
    No doubt, my lord.

RICHARD III
                 O Ratcliff, I fear, I fear.   215

RATCLIFF
    Nay, good my lord, be not afraid of shadows.

RICHARD III
    By the apostle Paul, shadows tonight
    Have struck more terror to the soul of Richard
    Than can the substance of ten thousand soldiers
    Armed in proof and led by shallow Richmond.   220
    'Tis not yet near day. Come, go with me.
    Under our tents I'll play the eavesdropper
    To see if any mean to shrink from me.
                                     Exeunt
        Enter the LORDS to RICHMOND, [sitting in his tent]

LORDS
    Good morrow, Richmond.

RICHMOND
    Cry mercy, lords and watchful gentlemen,   225
    That you have ta'en a tardy sluggard here.

A LORD
    How have you slept, my lord?

RICHMOND
    The sweetest sleep, and fairest-boding dreams
    That ever entered in a drowsy head,
    Have I since your departure had, my lords.   230
    Methought their souls, whose bodies Richard murdered,

tracks 28-30

228–271:
Charles Simpson as Earl of Richmond
Jamie Glover as Earl of Richmond

232: **cried on:** invoked
233: **jocund:** cheerful
236: **How far into the morning is it, lords:** see note 5.3.224
237: **give direction:** to give orders to his soldiers, though he probably also means this as an introduction to the oration which now follows

237, 315: Stage Directions: *His oration to his soldiers, His oration to his Army*: As their titles imply, these are formal addresses to their respective troops and we must assume that such a direction indicates that the actors broke off from their conversations with particular followers and addressed all in their companies in a formal fashion. We must remember that in Shakespeare's theater the whole of Richard and Richmond's armies were those actors on the stage at this moment.

Scene: Olivier (1955) cut both the orations. In Hirsch's 1976 production at Stratford, Ontario, Richmond's and Richard's orations were intercut and delivered almost simultaneously. In Alexander's 1984 production Richard and Richmond each address the audience with their forces beside them. Loncraine (1995) cut Richmond's oration and only has a part of Richard's.

251-252: **base foul stone...set:** image from jewelry. Richard is the common stone made valuable by the backing (foil) of the throne (chair) of England but is a fake jewel in a valuable setting.
255: **ward:** protect
259: **fat:** wealth
263: **quits:** repays

Came to my tent, and cried on victory.
I promise you, my soul is very jocund
In the remembrance of so fair a dream.
How far into the morning is it, lords?   235

A LORD
Upon the stroke of four.

RICHMOND
Why, then 'tis time to arm and give direction.

His oration to his soldiers

More than I have said, loving countrymen,
The leisure and enforcement of the time
Forbids to dwell upon. Yet remember this,   240
God and our good cause fight upon our side.
The prayers of holy saints and wrongèd souls,
Like high-reared bulwarks, stand before our faces.
Richard except, those whom we fight against
Had rather have us win than him they follow.   245
For what is he they follow? Truly, gentlemen,
A bloody tyrant and a homicide;
One raised in blood, and one in blood established;
One that made means to come by what he hath,
And slaughtered those that were the means to help him;   250
A base foul stone, made precious by the foil
Of England's chair, where he is falsely set;
One that hath ever been God's enemy.
Then if you fight against God's enemy,
God will in justice ward you as His soldiers.   255
If you do sweat to put a tyrant down,
You sleep in peace, the tyrant being slain.
If you do fight against your country's foes,
Your country's fat shall pay your pains the hire.
If you do fight in safeguard of your wives,   260
Your wives shall welcome home the conquerors.
If you do free your children from the sword,
Your children's children quits it in your age.

228–271:
Charles Simpson as Earl of Richmond
Jamie Glover as Earl of Richmond

266-269: For me...thereof: Richmond says he will not be ransomed if he is captured and will die first, but if he wins, his followers will share in the spoils of war.
271: Scene: **God, and Saint George, Richmond, and victory:** In Charles Kean's 1846 production in New York, Richmond's troops charged across the stage at this point.

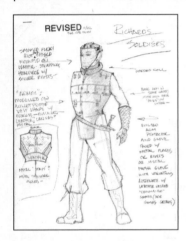

Costume rendering for Richard's soldiers by Deborah M. Dryden from the 1993 Oregon Shakespeare Festival production directed by James Edmondson
Courtesy of Oregon Shakespeare Festival

273: he: i.e., Richmond
276: Stage Direction: *The clock striketh:* This stage direction is placed one line later in the First Quarto and the First Folio.
277: Tell: count the strokes; **calendar:** Richard means an almanac.
278: Who...today: who saw the sun come up
280: braved: adorned
282: Ratcliff: In the First Quarto the reading is "some bodie Rat.", in the First Folio "somebody. *Ratcliffe*." The editorial tradition since the edition of Dr. Samuel Johnson (1765) has been to place "Ratcliff" on a separate line, primarily because 281 is already a metrically regular line, and partly because lines 279-281 are usually treated as a generalized line. Also, in line 282, Richard turns to address Ratcliff.

Then, in the name of God and all these rights,
Advance your standards, draw your willing swords.   265
For me, the ransom of my bold attempt
Shall be this cold corpse on the earth's cold face.
But if I thrive, the gain of my attempt
The least of you shall share his part thereof.
Sound drums and trumpets boldly and cheerfully.   270
God, and Saint George, Richmond, and victory!

[Exeunt]
Enter RICHARD III, RATCLIFF, [attendants and soldiers]

RICHARD III
What said Northumberland as touching Richmond?

RATCLIFF
That he was never trainèd up in arms.

RICHARD III
He said the truth. And what said Surrey then?

RATCLIFF
He smiled and said "The better for our purpose."   275

RICHARD III
He was in the right, and so indeed it is.

The clock striketh

Tell the clock there. Give me a calendar.
Who saw the sun today?

RATCLIFF
                    Not I, my lord.

RICHARD III
Then he disdains to shine, for by the book
He should have braved the east an hour ago.   280
A black day will it be to somebody.
Ratcliff!

RATCLIFF
My lord.

284: **not:** from the First Folio, the First Quarto reads "nor"

285: **lour:** scowl

286: **would:** wish; **dewy...ground:** the dew would dry up

290: **vaunts:** displays themselves proudly

291: **Caparison:** the elaborate coverings for a warhorse

295: **foreward:** vanguard; **drawn:** extended

301: **puissance:** power

302: **wingèd:** flanked; **chiefest horse:** best cavalry

303: **boot:** from the First Folio, the First Quarto reads "bootes"

306: Speech Prefix: **RICHARD III:** There is no speech prefix in any of the early editions, making it appear that Norfolk is reading the letter aloud since it seems to be a continuation of his speech. However, since he has already found and presumably, read, the note, it is not him but Richard who is the logical reader. Edward Capell (1768) was the first editor to make this emendation.

306: **Jockey:** a contemptuous name for John Howard, Duke of Norfolk, playing on a nickname for John, Jock

307: *Dickon:* a contemptuous name for Richard playing on the normal nickname, Dick

308: Scene: **A thing...enemy:** Perhaps one of Cibber's most lasting inventions – one should not be surprised to hear it uttered even today – is his replacement of this line with, "A weak invention of the enemy." No matter which line is uttered in performance, the way Richard treats the paper (whether scornfully, or with foreboding, or with mirth) is important, showing his state of mind just before the battle.

310: **babbling:** foolish

RICHARD III
>The sun will not be seen today,
>The sky doth frown and lour upon our army.   285
>I would these dewy tears were from the ground.
>Not shine today? Why, what is that to me
>More than to Richmond, for the selfsame heaven
>That frowns on me looks sadly upon him.

>>>>*Enter NORFOLK*

NORFOLK
>Arm, arm, my lord, the foe vaunts in the field.   290

RICHARD III
>Come, bustle, bustle. Caparison my horse.
>Call up Lord Stanley, bid him bring his power.
>I will lead forth my soldiers to the plain,
>And thus my battle shall be orderèd:
>My foreward shall be drawn out all in length,   295
>Consisting equally of horse and foot;
>Our archers shall be placèd in the midst.
>John Duke of Norfolk, Thomas Earl of Surrey,
>Shall have the leading of this foot and horse.
>They thus directed, we will follow   300
>In the main battle, whose puissance on either side
>Shall be well wingèd with our chiefest horse.
>This, and Saint George to boot. What think'st thou, Norfolk?

NORFOLK
>A good direction, warlike sovereign.

>>>>*He sheweth him a paper*
>This found I on my tent this morning.   305

RICHARD III
>[*Reads*]
>*"Jockey of Norfolk, be not so bold,*
>*For Dickon thy master is bought and sold."*
>A thing devised by the enemy.
>Go, gentleman, every man unto his charge.
>Let not our babbling dreams affright our souls;   310

315: Stage Direction: *His oration to his Army*: see note 5.3.237

315: Stage Direction: *His oration to his Army*: Ramaz Chkhikvadze as Richard in the 1980 (Georgia/USSR) Rustaveli Theatre Company production directed by Robert Sturua

Photo: Donald Cooper

316: **inferred:** reported or said

319: **lackey:** hanger-on

320: **o'ercloyèd:** over full

324: **distain:** stain

326: **mother's cost:** Shakespeare, by using the 1587 edition of Holinshed's *Chronicles* as a primary source for this play, is led into error by a misprint in that edition, where "mother" is wrongly printed for "brother," that is, brother-in-law (the Duke of Burgundy, who was contributing to Richmond's upkeep while he was in France). Some modern editors feel so strongly about this, seeing it as an affront to the Duchess of York, that they emend the text to "brother's cost." Others, including this one, merely note the problem.

328: **overshoes in snow:** snow deeper than the tops of shoes

330: **overweening:** arrogant

332: **fond:** foolish

333: **means:** wherewithal to live

336: **bobbed:** pummeled

339: Stage Direction: *[Drum afar off]*: from the First Folio, the First Quarto has no direction

343: **welkin:** sky

343: Stage Direction: *[Enter a MESSENGER]*: from the First Folio, the First Quarto has no direction

Conscience is but a word that cowards use,
Devised at first to keep the strong in awe.
Our strong arms be our conscience, swords our law.
March on, join bravely, let us to it pell mell,
If not to heaven, then hand in hand to hell.   315

His oration to his Army

What shall I say more than I have inferred?
Remember whom you are to cope withal,
A sort of vagabonds, rascals, and runaways,
A scum of Bretons, and base lackey peasants,
Whom their o'ercloyèd country vomits forth   320
To desperate ventures and assured destruction.
You sleeping safe, they bring to you unrest;
You having lands and blessed with beauteous wives,
They would restrain the one, distain the other.
And who doth lead them but a paltry fellow,   325
Long kept in Brittany at our mother's cost,
A milksop, one that never in his life
Felt so much cold as overshoes in snow?
Let's whip these stragglers o'er the seas again,
Lash hence these overweening rags of France,   330
These famished beggars weary of their lives,
Who, but for dreaming on this fond exploit,
For want of means, poor rats, had hanged themselves.
If we be conquered, let men conquer us,
And not these bastard Bretons, whom our fathers   335
Have in their own land beaten, bobbed, and thumped,
And in record, left them the heirs of shame.
Shall these enjoy our lands, lie with our wives,
Ravish our daughters?
                                                            [Drum afar off]
                        Hark, I hear their drum.
Fight, gentlemen of England. Fight, bold yeomen.   340
Draw, archers, draw your arrows to the head.
Spur your proud horses hard, and ride in blood;
Amaze the welkin with your broken staves.
                                            [Enter a MESSENGER]
What says Lord Stanley, will he bring his power?

345: **deny:** refuse

352: **spleen:** anger. The spleen was thought to be the organ of anger.

MESSENGER
My lord, he doth deny to come.   345

RICHARD III
Off with his son George's head!

NORFOLK
My lord, the enemy is past the marsh,
After the battle let George Stanley die.

RICHARD III
A thousand hearts are great within my bosom.
Advance our standards, set upon our foes,   350
Our ancient word of courage, fair Saint George,
Inspire us with the spleen of fiery dragons.
Upon them! Victory sits on our helms.

Exeunt

0: Scene: Although no early editions mark a scene division here, the stage action conforms to the convention for starting a new scene since the stage has been cleared. Edward Capell (1768) is the first editor to make such a division.

0: Stage Direction: *Alarum, excursions:* "Alarum, excursions" is, firstly, a call, probably by a wind instrument, to battle, and secondly, the act of rushing out or making a sortie. In other words, one is sound effect and the other is a direction to actors to undertake specific actions. On the early stages through the eighteenth century, the "excursions" would probably have been no more than a dozen extras rushing in and out. The nineteenth century treated this much more realistically, and Kean's production not only had a sizeable body of troops but also the shooting of arrows on stage. However, in 1819, the troop of extras were so numerous that they inflicted injuries on each other. By the end of the century, things became so chaotic that productions reacted against the whole business by reducing the numbers and making the fighting more stylized. Guthrie's soldiers (Old Vic, 1937) threw themselves into various "attitudes," and in Morahan's (1979) they fought in slow motion. In modern productions, the "excursions" may be merely the sound effects of fighting off stage.

tracks 31-33

1–13:
Jonathan Keeble as Catesby and Kenneth Branagh as Richard III
Richard Gale as Catesby and Peter Finch as Richard III

7: Scene: **A horse, a horse, my kingdom for a horse:** Today this line is an actor's curse since it is perhaps the only line from the play that every member of the audience will know. Indeed, as Al Pacino demonstrated in his film *Looking for Richard*, it is a line that even the proverbial man on the street knows. Bogdanov (1989) kept it but had it shouted by Richard from off stage; Loncraine/McKellen (1995) kept it in theirs, having Richard utter it while in an immobilized jeep.

9: **cast:** cast of the dice
10: **hazard:** risk

13: Stage Direction: *[Exeunt]:* No early edition provides an exit direction at this point; Lewis Theobald (1733) is the first editor to do so. To treat this exit and re-entry as a full scene division violates the convention that states that a character who has just exited should not immediately enter at the beginning of the next scene. Since there appears to be no distinction between these directions and those found at line 6, no scene division is made, though that has been the case since Alexander Dyce's edition of 1857. The action is continuous, accompanied by trumpet calls.

Act 5, Scene 4]

Alarum, excursions. Enter CATESBY

CATESBY
  Rescue, my Lord of Norfolk, rescue, rescue!
  The King enacts more wonders than a man,
  Daring an opposite to every danger.
  His horse is slain, and all on foot he fights,
  Seeking for Richmond in the throat of death   5
  Rescue, fair lord, or else the day is lost!

[Alarums.] Enter RICHARD III

RICHARD III
  A horse, a horse, my kingdom for a horse!

CATESBY
  Withdraw, my lord, I'll help you to a horse.

RICHARD III
  Slave, I have set my life upon a cast,
  And I will stand the hazard of the die.   10
  I think there be six Richmonds in the field;
  Five have I slain today instead of him.
  A horse, a horse, my kingdom for a horse!

[Exeunt]
Alarum. Enter RICHARD III and RICHMOND, they fight,
RICHARD III is slain. Then retreat being sounded,
[exit RICHMOND removing RICHARD'S body. Retreat
still sounding,] Enter RICHMOND, [LORD STANLEY, EARL OF]
DERBY bearing the crown, with other lords and [others]

RICHMOND
  God and your arms be praised, victorious friends,
  The day is ours, the bloody dog is dead.   15

Stacy Keach as Richard in the 1990 Shakespeare Theatre Company
production directed by Michael Kahn

Photo: Joan Marcus

Anton Lesser as Richard and Simon Dormandy in the 1989 Royal Shakespeare
Company production directed by Adrian Noble

Photo: Donald Cooper

Antony Sher as Richard in the 1984 Royal Shakespeare Company production
directed by Bill Alexander

Photo: Donald Cooper

Geraint Wyn Davies as Richard and David Gross as Richmond in the 2007
Shakespeare Theatre Company production directed by Michael Kahn

Photo: Carol Rosegg

17: **this long-usurpèd royalty:** the crown

19: **withal:** with

25: **name:** title

26: Speech Prefix: **STANLEY:** from the First Folio, the First Quarto has no speech prefix and prints the list of the dead in italic and indented; **Walter:** from the First Folio, the First Quarto reads "Water"; **Ferrers:** Walter Devereux, first Baron Ferrers of Chartley. All early editions read "Ferris"; this emendation was first made by Edward Capell (1768).

27: **Sir Robert Brakenbury:** the lieutenant of The Tower

31: **as we:** when I; Richmond is already using the royal plural; **ta'en the sacrament:** Richmond is referring to the oath taken at Rheims cathedral on the Eucharist that he would marry Elizabeth, daughter of Edward IV.

32: **white rose and the red:** the symbols of the Yorkist and Lancastrian branches of the Plantagenet family

STANLEY

Courageous Richmond, well hast thou acquit thee.
Lo, here this long-usurpèd royalty
From the dead temples of this bloody wretch
Have I plucked off, to grace thy brows withal.
Wear it, enjoy it, and make much of it.   20

RICHMOND

Great God of heaven, say amen to all!
But tell me, is young George Stanley living?

STANLEY

He is, my lord, and safe in Leicester town,
Whither, if it please you, we may now withdraw us.

RICHMOND

What men of name are slain on either side?   25

STANLEY

John, Duke of Norfolk, Walter, Lord Ferrers,
Sir Robert Brakenbury, and Sir William Brandon.

RICHMOND

Inter their bodies as become their births.
Proclaim a pardon to the soldiers fled,
That in submission will return to us.   30
And then, as we have ta'en the sacrament,
We will unite the white rose and the red;
Smile heaven upon this fair conjunction,
That long have frowned upon their enmity.
What traitor hears me, and says not amen?   35
England hath long been mad, and scarred herself;
The brother blindly shed the brother's blood,
The father rashly slaughtered his own son,
The son, compelled, been butcher to the sire.
All this divided York and Lancaster,   40
Divided in their dire division.
O, now let Richmond and Elizabeth,
The true succeeders of each royal house,

54: Stage Direction: *[Exeunt]*: from the First Folio, the First Quarto provides no final
exit

Scene: Jane Howell (1983) produced one of the most moving effects in the performance history of this play. The camera slowly panned over a large pile of dead,
wounded bodies (male and female, children and adults), and then there came the
sound of manic laughter. As the camera panned upward, we saw that the laughter
was coming from Margaret, now with her hair down and without her hat and
scarves. She was seated and holding the dead body of Richard, now stripped of its
armor. She continues to laugh and rock him until the scene fades. The dead, either
from Bosworth, but more likely from all the civil wars which have consumed eight
plays (*Richard II* through *Richard III*), or forty acts, are gathered in death with their
last king and his triumphing tormentor. This effect draws a painful and firm line
under the English Civil Wars.

By God's fair ordinance conjoin together,
And let their heirs, God, if Thy will be so,   45
Enrich the time to come with smooth-faced peace,
With smiling plenty and fair prosperous days.
Abate the edge of traitors, gracious Lord,
That would reduce these bloody days again,
And make poor England weep in streams of blood.   50
Let them not live to taste this land's increase,
That would with treason wound this fair land's peace.
Now civil wounds are stopped, peace lives again.
That she may long live here, God say amen.

[Exeunt]

Actor Speaks:
Antony Sher on his Richard III

FROM HIS AUTOBIOGRAPHY, *Beside Myself*, BY KIND PERMISSION
OF THE AUTHOR AND HIS PUBLISHERS, HUTCHINSON

Olivier. It all came down to Olivier. It often does when you're playing Shake-speare. Of the five main ones I've done – Richard, Macbeth, Shylock, Titus, Leontes – he created memorable portraits of four. (He never played Leontes, a loss for the world if a relief to me.) But nowhere does his giant shadow, his defining silhouettes, fall more completely than over Richard; so completely that you can barely see the role underneath. This lies in dense shade. Richard's dark soul and the master's black magic have become one. The page-boy haircut, the long nose, the muscular hump, the broken-wing arm, the elegantly lame leg – these things were surely requested by Shakespeare personally, in some lost manuscript (probably shredded and eaten by Olivier). You're left scurrying round the perimeter of this indelible shape, trying to find some break, some little peephole.

"Now is the winter of our discontent." You don't even like to say it. Don't like to hold it in your mouth. It's been in someone else's. His. You can taste his spit. Feel his bite marks round the edges. His poised, staccato delivery is imprinted on the line: "Now. Is the wintah. Of our. Discon-tent."

Once I'd agreed to do the part, an image haunted me: my Richard, still in its infancy, lying there in a cradle, while a huge black figure, fully formed, famously deformed, an infamous child killer, slowly limps towards it.

The RSC invited me to attend the press conference for the new season. Beforehand, I met Ken Branagh for the first time. I confided my fear to him, thinking I'd have a soulmate. After all, his role, Henry V, had the same warning sign hanging over it: *This is the property of Laurence Olivier – trespassers will be prosecuted.* But Branagh just replied cheerfully, "Oh look, Olivier's performances exist, there's nothing we can do about them, may as well just get on with the job." *Just get on with the job?* The fearlessness, the folly of youth, I thought, staring at the cherubic face topped with red-gold hair – he'll find out!

Or not. As far as I know Branagh wasn't born with a cowl round his head– he just arrived with a written guarantee in his hand. It was from God and it said, "You're gonna make it, kid."

The nonchalance, the certainty with which he'd spoken to me that day were the same qualities which graced his performance as Henry a few weeks later. It was his first time on the Stratford main stage, yet he appeared to be strolling round his backyard. Which proved to be the case, in a way. He left the RSC soon afterwards, formed his own company, did plays, then movies, filmed *Henry*, was nominated for several Oscars and took off into the far blue yonder.

Meanwhile, back on earth, I found myself in a familiar dilemma as I began pre-rehearsal preparations for *Richard III*. How to find a way in? How to see it as a new play? I wanted to picture Shakespeare turning up on my doorstep one day, looking remarkably like Rob Knights and handing over a stack of paper: "Here – this is for you if you want it." Research was the answer. Research wakes you up. Right then, let's start with the historical Richard, the real king. No – wrong – dead end. The real king bears no relation to Shakespeare's version, as letters from the Richard III Society will continue to remind me long into the run ("You are yet another actor to ignore truth and integrity in order to launch yourself on an ego-trip enabled by the monstrous lie perpetrated by Shakespeare about a most valiant, honourable and excelling King"). All right, where next? Discussing it with Monty, he reckons that Shakespeare's Richard is probably psychopathic. Let's have a look at these guys, then. The timing's good. The papers are full of a sensational murder trial. The Muswell Hill Monster, Dennis Nilsen. Mad or bad? Sick or evil? No one seems able to say for sure, but there's certainly something about Nilsen that carries a whiff of Richard III. They share intelligence, cunning, and sick humour – Nilsen complains about running out of neckties as the strangulations increase, and when the police find human flesh in his drains he suggests it's Kentucky Fried Chicken. Mind you, I'm wary of playing too funny a Richard III; that seems like the most obvious and least interesting choice. It's called *The Tragedy of King Richard III* (maybe I've got Gambon echoing in my head – "It is *The Tragedy of King Lear!*") and the man has to possess real danger. Which comes from him being an outsider, the Crookback. With Charlotte Arnold, my merrily bullying physio from the

Achilles injury, I visit homes for the disabled. Many of the people I meet, observe and sketch are on crutches. Hey, I remember crutches. I lived on them for about six weeks after the operation. Crutches...they're quite interesting...like extra limbs...

I say it to Charlotte first: 'What about playing him on crutches?'

She laughs. Maybe I am joking. Maybe the idea is ludicrous. But discussing it further, she says that because crutches are designed to take the body weight they would at least be *safe*. Richard III is notorious for crippling actors who play him. Sustaining a twisted position in this huge role leaves people with bad backs and knees for years to come. (In 1992, Simon Russell Beale played a gloriously poison-toad Richard, but had to leave halfway through with a slipped disc.) Having already encountered these problems as the Fool, I'm determined to find a risk-free solution this time.

"I'm half thinking of playing him on crutches."

Bill Alexander is on the receiving end of the idea now. We've worked together happily on *Molière* and *Tartuffe*. Something about our different styles fits together well: his patient Englishness alongside my impulsive Jewish Africanness; his perceptive, text-based approach with my more physical, theatrical excesses. We pull in opposite directions, yet stretch rather than hurt one another; we both grow. An attractive, kindly, rather scruffy man, Bill is greatly liked by his companies and that's a help too.

He answers: "But Richard's a soldier. How would he go into battle on crutches?"

I back off immediately – "Well, absolutely, what a dumb idea."

But it won't go away. I decide to test out the crutches privately. Charlotte sends two pairs to the Barbican stage door while *Maydays* is on:

14/2/84. After the show, I'm struggling into the car park with the four crutches when Alison Steadman drives out. She stops in horror. "Richard III," I offer in explanation. She nods knowingly. "Mike Leigh will be proud of you." Back at home I experiment nervously. The elbow crutches are much better than the armpit variety because you can let go and use your hands. Swinging along on them, stretching like an animal, pawing the ground, rearing up on hind legs, I find they have possibilities.

My fascination with the crutches and Bill's caution about them both become irrelevant when we go into rehearsals. As soon as I get stuck into the text (speaking rather than discussing it), and into the psychology of Richard and into his relationships with the other characters (cooking especially well with Penny Downie's Lady Anne and Mal Storry's Buckingham), the physicality of the character suddenly seems less important. It's a trap for me anyway. There's an element of truth in jousting between Roger Allam (Clarence) and myself; I call him the Voice Beautiful, he calls me the Body Busy. But then just when I'm ready to ditch the crutches, a curious reversal occurs and Bill starts arguing for them. Actually, it's two Bills by now. Bill Dudley, the designer, has joined the debate. He likes the four-legged idea, reminding us that whenever people curse Richard they use bestial imagery – "a hell hound", "this carnal cur", "that foul bunch-back'd toad" – and says that by addling long, hanging sleeves to the costume (our setting is medieval) he can even make it six-legged – Queen Margaret's special curse is "bottled spider!". We do another test, adding the hump:

14/2/84. Conference Hall. Evening Solus Call. The Bills chat among themselves, pretending not to watch as I begin moving round the room. There's a large mirror at one end so I can observe as well. Charging head on, the massive back rolls heavily like a bison's. Spreading the crutches sideways, I look like some weird bird or giant insect. The wing span (Richard's reach) is enormous and threatening. The range of movement is endless: dancing backward like a spider, sideways like a crab. And you can cover distances very swiftly with a sweeping, scooping action, almost like rowing, the polio-afflicted legs dragging along underneath. We try "Now is the winter". For the section about his deformity, I deliberately, slowly exhibit it. Bill A. likes this: "It becomes a poem of self-hatred, a mannequin parade of the latest deformities." At the end of the session everyone is smiling. "Looks promising," we all say to one another cautiously, but excited. It does seem to contribute to, not hinder, our early work on the text. I drive home to Chipping Campden. It's just gone dark, the sky is still glowing blue, the countryside looks like weird grey cutouts as the headlamps of the car swing round the narrow lanes. It makes a crazy theatrical effect. I'm trying to contain the excitement, the jubilation. Tchaikovsky's First Piano Concerto is playing on Radio 2. Glorious slush.

But what of Bill's initial point – how does Richard go into battle with crutches? Well, yes, he *is* vulnerable. Play his deformity any way you choose and he *is* vulnerable. He's a disabled man going to war. Our solution is to transfer him from the crutches on to a horse (a huge armour-coated horse-structure which is then carried by his soldiers – like they've carried him on the bier-throne). When this horse is shot from under him in battle, he's definitely in trouble. And Shakespeare has provided the appropriate reaction:

"A horse, a horse, my kingdom for a horse!"

We will certainly earn the right to say that line.

So – the crutches are in. A lot of other early ideas aren't. Like the Quasimo-do-type facial prosthetics I've been sketching. Or my resistence to the comedy in the play. Later I will see someone achieve a real heavyweight, non-comic reading of Richard – Ian McKellen in Richard Eyre's revelatory National Theatre production – but for now it seems impossible. For now it seems like an exuberant, even vulgar, young man's play (Shakespeare was about twenty-eight when he wrote it), and I'm an exuberant, even vulgar, youngish actor (aged thirty-five), and though Bill Alexander (thirty-seven) isn't vulgar at all, he oversees this particular union between role and actor with relish.

We're a hit. Beyond wildest dreams. Every time I start a new project my two Geminian halves go to war. One promises disaster, the other fantasy land. For *Richard III* the fantasy was people saying it was the best since Olivier's. Well, they did. Audiences flocked, queued overnight, bartered for black market tickets. Big names traveled to Stratford to see us: Peter Brook, Michael Caine, Donald Sutherland, Charlton Heston. Mom and Dad happened to be at the same matinee as Heston and shared the VIP room at the interval. This made more impact on Dad than the show (through which he'd slept soundly) and he went round for days afterwards shamelessly name-dropping – "I had tea with Moses."

A Voice Coach's Perspective on Speaking Shakespeare

KEEPING SHAKESPEARE PRACTICAL

Andrew Wade

track 34-35

Introduction to Speaking Shakespeare: Sir Derek Jacobi
Speaking Shakespeare: Andrew Wade with Nathaniel Shaw

Why, you might be wondering, is it so important to keep Shakespeare practical? What do I mean by practical? Why is this the way to discover how to speak the text and understand it?

Plays themselves are not simply literary events—they demand interpreters in the deepest sense of the word, and the language of Shakespeare requires, therefore, not a vocal demonstration of writing techniques but an imaginative response to that writing. The key word here is imagination. The task of the voice coach is to offer relevant choices to the actor so that the actor's imagination is titillated, excited by the language, which he or she can then share with an audience, playing on that audience's imagination. Take the word "IF" – it is only composed of two letters when written, but if you say it aloud and listen to what it implies, then your reaction, the way the word plays through you, can change the perception of meaning. "Iffffffff"… you might hear and feel it implying "possibilities," "choices," "questioning," "trying to work something out." The saying of this word provokes active investigation of thought. What an apt word to launch a play: "If music be the food of love, play on" (Act 1, Scene 1 in *Twelfth Night, Or What You Will*). How this word engages the listener and immediately sets up an involvement is about more than audibility. How we verbalize sounds has a direct link to meaning and understanding. In the words of Touchstone in *As You Like It*, "Much value in if."

I was working with a company in Vancouver on *Macbeth* and at the end of the first week's rehearsal – after having explored our voices and opening out different pieces of text to hear the possibilities of the rhythm, feeling how the meter affects the thinking and feeling, looking at structure and form— one of the actors admitted he was also a writer of soap operas and that I had completely changed his way of writing. Specifically, in saying a line like "The multitudinous seas incarnadine/ Making the green one red" he heard the complexity of meaning revealed in the use of polysyllabic words becoming monosyllabic, layered upon the words' individual dictionary definitions. The writer was reminded that merely reproducing the speech of everyday life was nowhere near as powerful and effective as language that is shaped.

Do you think soap operas would benefit from rhyming couplets? Somehow this is difficult to imagine! But, the writer's comments set me thinking. As I am constantly trying to find ways of exploring the acting process, of opening out actors' connection with language that isn't their own, I thought it would be a good idea to involve writers and actors in some practical work on language. After talking to Cicely Berry (Voice Director, Royal Shakespeare Company) and Colin Chambers (then RSC Production Adviser), we put together a group of writers and actors who were interested in taking part. It was a fascinating experience all round, and it broke down barriers and misconceptions.

The actors discovered, for instance, that a writer is not coming from a very different place as they in their creative search; that an idea or an image may result from a struggle to define a gut feeling and not from some crafted, well-formed idea in the head. The physical connection of language to the body was reaffirmed. After working with a group on Yeats' poem "Easter 1916," Ann Devlin changed the title of the play she was writing for the Royal Shakespeare Company to *After Easter*. She had experienced the poem read aloud by a circle of participants, each voice becoming a realization of the shape of the writing. Thus it made a much fuller impact on her and caused her thinking to shift. Such practical exchanges, through language work and voice, feed and stimulate my work to go beyond making sure the actors' voices are technically sound.

It is, of course, no different when we work on a Shakespeare play. A similar connection with the language is crucial. Playing Shakespeare, in many ways, is crafted instinct. The task is thus to find the best way to tap into someone's imagination. As Peter Brook put it: "People forget that a text is dumb. To make it speak, one must create a communication machine. A living network, like a nervous system, must be made if a text which comes from far away is to touch the sensibility of the present."

This journey is never to be taken for granted. It is the process that every text must undergo every time it is staged. There is no definitive rehearsal that would solve problems or indicate ways of staging a given play. Again, this is where creative, practical work on voice can help forge new meaning by offering areas of exploration and challenge. The central idea behind my work comes back to posing the question, "How does meaning change by speaking out aloud?" It would be unwise to jump hastily to the end process for, as Peter Brook says, "Shakespeare's words are records of the words that he wanted spoken, words issuing from people's mouths, with pitch, pause and rhythm and gesture as part of their meaning. A word does not start as a word – it is the end product which begins as an impulse, stimulated by attitude and behavior which dictates the need for expression." [1]

PRACTICALLY SPEAKING

Something happens when we vocalize, when we isolate sounds, when we start to speak words aloud, when we put them to the test of our physicality, of our anatomy. We expose ourselves in a way that makes taking the language back more difficult. Our body begins a debate with itself, becomes alive with the vibrations of sound produced in the mouth or rooted deep in the muscles that aim at defining sound. In fact, the spoken words bring into play all the senses, before sense and another level of meaning are reached.

"How do I know what I think, until I hear what I say," Oscar Wilde once said. A concrete illustration of this phrase was reported to me when I was leading a workshop recently. A grandmother said the work we had done that day reminded her of what her six-year-old grandson had said to his mother while they were driving through Wales: "Look, mummy, sheep! Sheep! Sheep!!" "You don't have to keep telling us," the mother replied, but the boy said, "How do I know they're there, if I don't tell you?!"

Therefore, when we speak of ideas, of sense, we slightly take for granted those physical processes that affect and change their meaning. We tend to separate something that is an organic whole. In doing so, we become blind to the fact that it is precisely this physical connection to the words that enables the actors to make the language theirs.

The struggle for meaning is not just impressionistic theatre mystique; it is an indispensable aspect of the rehearsal process and carries on during the life of every production. In this struggle, practical work on Shakespeare is vital and may help spark creativity and shed some light on the way meaning is born into language. After a performance of *More Words*, a show devised and directed by Cicely Berry and myself, Katie Mitchell (a former Artistic Director of The Other Place in Stratford-upon-Avon) gave me an essay by Ted Hughes that echoes with the piece. In it, Ted Hughes compares the writing of a poem – the coming into existence of words – to the capture of a wild animal. You will notice that in the following passage Hughes talks of "spirit" or "living parts" but never of "thought" or "sense." With great care and precaution, he advises, "It is better to call [the poem] an assembly of living parts moved by a single spirit. The living parts are the words, the images, the rhythms. The spirit is the life which inhabits them when they all work together. It is impossible to say which comes first, parts or spirit."

This is also true of life in words, as many are connected directly to one or several of our senses. Here Hughes talks revealingly of "the five senses," of "word," "action," and "muscle," all things which a practical approach to language is more likely to allow one to perceive and do justice to.

Words that live are those which we hear, like "click" or "chuckle," or which we see, like "freckled" or "veined," or which we taste, like "vinegar" or "sugar," or touch, like "prickle" or "oily," or smell, like "tar" or "onion," words which belong to one of the five senses. Or words that act and seem to use their muscles, like "flick" or "balance." [2]

In this way, practically working on Shakespeare to arrive at understanding lends itself rather well, I think, to what Adrian Noble (former Artistic Director of the RSC) calls "a theatre of poetry," a form of art that, rooted deeply in its classical origins, would seek to awaken the imagination of its audiences through love and respect for words while satisfying our eternal craving for myths and twice-told tales.

This can only be achieved at some cost. There is indeed a difficult battle to fight and hopefully win "the battle of the word to survive." This phrase was coined by Michael Redgrave at the beginning of the 1950s, a period when theatre began to be deeply influenced by more physical forms, such as mime.[3] Although the context is obviously different, the fight today is of the same nature.

LISTENING TO SHAKESPEARE

Because of the influence of television, our way of speaking as well as listening has changed. It is crucial to be aware of this. We can get fairly close to the way *Henry V* or *Hamlet* was staged in Shakespeare's time; we can try also to reconstruct the way English was spoken. But somehow, all these fall short of the real and most important goal: the Elizabethan ear. How did one "hear" a Shakespeare play? This is hardest to know. My personal view is that we will probably never know for sure. We are, even when we hear a Shakespeare play or a recording from the past, bound irrevocably to modernity. The Elizabethan ear was no doubt different from our own, as people were not spoken to or entertained, in the same way. A modern voice has to engage us in a different way in order to make us truly listen in a society that seems to rely solely on the belief that image is truth, that it is more important to show rather than to tell.

Sometimes, we say that a speech in Shakespeare, or even an entire production, is not well-spoken, not up to standard. What do we mean by that? Evidently, there are a certain number of "guidelines" that any actor now has to know when working on a classical text. Yet, even when these are known, actors still have to make choices when they speak. A sound is not a sound without somebody to lend an ear to it: rhetoric is nothing without an audience.

There are a certain number of factors that affect the receiver's ear. These can be cultural factors such as the transition between different acting styles or the level of training that our contemporary ear has had. There are also personal and emotional factors. Often we feel the performance was not well-spoken because, somehow, it did not live up to our expectations of how we think it should have been performed. Is it that many of us have a self-conscious model, perhaps our own first experience of Shakespeare, that meant something to us and became our reference point for the future (some treasured performance kept under glass)? Nothing from then on can quite compare with that experience.

Most of the time, however, it is more complex than nostalgia. Take, for example, the thorny area of accent. I remind myself constantly that audibility is not embedded in Received Pronunciation or Standard American. The familiarity that those in power have with speech and the articulate confidence gained from coming from the right quarters can lead us all to hear certain types of voices as outshining others. But, to my mind, the role of theatre is at least to question these assumptions so that we do not perpetuate those givens but work towards a broader tolerance.

In Canada on a production of *Twelfth Night*, I was working with an actor who was from Newfoundland. His own natural rhythms in speaking seemed completely at home with Shakespeare's. Is this because his root voice has direct links back to the voice of Shakespeare's time? It does seem that compared to British dialects, which are predominantly about pitch, many North American dialects have a wonderful respect and vibrancy in their use of vowels. Shakespeare's language seems to me very vowel-aware. How useful it is for an actor to isolate the vowels in the spoken words to hear the music they produce, the rich patterns, their direct connection to feelings. North Americans more easily respond to this and allow it to feed their speaking. I can only assume it is closer to how the Elizabethans spoke.

In *Othello* the very names of the characters have a direct connection to one vowel in particular. All the male names, except the Duke, end in the sound OH: Othello, Cassio, Iago, Brabantio, etc. Furthermore, the sound OH ripples through the play both consciously and unconsciously. "Oh" occurs repeatedly and, more interestingly, is contained within other words: "so," "soul," and "know." These words resonate throughout the play, reinforcing another level of meaning. The repeating of the same sounds affects us beyond what we can quite say.

Vowels come from deep within us, from our very core. We speak vowels before we speak consonants. They seem to reveal the feelings that require the consonants to give the shape to what we perceive as making sense.

Working with actors who are bilingual (or ones for whom English is not the native language) is fascinating because of the way it allows the actor to have an awareness of the cadence in Shakespeare. There seems to be an objective perception to the musical patterns in the text, and the use of alliteration and assonance are often more easily heard not just as literary devices, but also as means by which meaning is formed and revealed to an audience.

Every speech pattern (i.e., accent, rhythm) is capable of audibility. Each has its own music, each can become an accent when juxtaposed against another. The point at which a speech pattern becomes audible is in the dynamic of the physical making of those sounds. The speaker must have the desire to get through to a listener and must be confident that every speech pattern has a right to be heard.

SPEAKING SHAKESPEARE

So—the way to speak Shakespeare is not intrinsically tied to a particular sound; rather, it is how a speaker energetically connects to that language. Central to this is how we relate to the form of Shakespeare. Shakespeare employs verse, prose, and rhetorical devices to communicate meaning. For example, in *Romeo and Juliet*, the use of contrasts helps us to quantify Juliet's feelings: "And learn me how to lose a winning match," "Whiter than new snow upon a raven's back." These extreme opposites, "lose" and "winning," "new snow" and "raven's back," are her means to express and make sense of her feelings.

On a more personal note, I am often reminded how much, as an individual, I owe to Shakespeare's spoken word. The rather quiet and inarticulate schoolboy I once was found in the speaking and the acting of those words a means to quench his thirst for expression.

NOTES:

(1) Peter Brook, *The Empty Space* (Harmondsworth: Penguin, 1972).

(2) Ted Hughes, *Winter Pollen* (London: Faber and Faber, 1995).

(3) Michael Redgrave, *The Actor's Ways and Means* (London: Heinemann, 1951).

In the Age of Shakespeare

Thomas Garvey

One of the earliest published pictures of Shakespeare's birthplace, from an original watercolor by Phoebe Dighton (1834)

The works of William Shakespeare have won the love of millions since he first set pen to paper some four hundred years ago, but at first blush, his plays can seem difficult to understand, even willfully obscure. There are so many strange words: not fancy, exactly, but often only half-familiar. And the very fabric of the language seems to spring from a world of forgotten assumptions, a vast network of beliefs and superstitions that have long been dispelled from the modern mind.

In fact, when "Gulielmus filius Johannes Shakespeare" (Latin for "William, son of John Shakespeare") was baptized in Stratford-on-Avon in 1564, English itself was only just settling into its current form; no dictionary had yet been written, and Shakespeare coined hundreds of words himself. Astronomy and medicine were entangled with astrology and the occult arts; democracy was waiting to be reborn; and even educated people believed in witches and fairies, and that the sun revolved around the Earth. Yet somehow Shakespeare still speaks to us today, in a voice as fresh and direct as the day his lines were first spoken, and to better understand both their artistic depth and enduring power, we must first understand something of his age.

REVOLUTION AND RELIGION

Shakespeare was born into a nation on the verge of global power, yet torn by religious strife. Henry VIII, the much-married father of Elizabeth I, had

From *The Book of Martyrs* (1563), this woodcut shows the Archbishop of Canterbury being burned at the stake in March 1556

Map of London ca. 1625

defied the pope by proclaiming a new national church, with himself as its head. After Henry's death, however, his daughter Mary reinstituted Catholicism via a murderous nationwide campaign, going so far as to burn the Archbishop of Canterbury at the stake. But after a mere five years, the childless Mary also died, and when her half-sister Elizabeth was crowned, she declared the Church of England again triumphant.

In the wake of so many religious reversals, it is impossible to know which form of faith lay closest to the English heart, and at first, Elizabeth was content with mere outward deference to the Anglican Church. Once the pope hinted her assassination would not be a mortal sin, however, the suppression of Catholicism grew more savage, and many Catholics—including some known in Stratford—were hunted down and executed, which meant being hanged, disemboweled, and carved into quarters. Many scholars suspect that Shakespeare himself was raised a Catholic (his father's testament of faith was found hidden in his childhood home). We can speculate about the impact this religious tumult may have had on his plays. Indeed, while explicit Catholic themes, such as the description of purgatory in *Hamlet*, are rare, the larger themes of disguise and double allegiance are prominent across the canon. Prince Hal offers false friendship to Falstaff in the histories, the heroines of the comedies are forced to disguise themselves as men, and the action of the tragedies is driven by double-dealing villains. "I am not what I am," Iago tells us (and himself) in *Othello*, summing up in a single stroke what may have been Shakespeare's formative social and spiritual experience.

If religious conflict rippled beneath the body politic like some ominous undertow, on its surface the tide of English power was clearly on the rise. The defeat of the Spanish Armada in 1588 had established Britain as a global power; by 1595 Sir Walter Raleigh had founded the colony of Virginia (named for the Virgin Queen), and discovered a new crop, tobacco, which would inspire a burgeoning international trade. After decades of strife and the threat of invasion, England enjoyed a welcome stability. As the national coffers grew, so did London; over the course of Elizabeth's reign, the city would nearly double in size to a population of some two hundred thousand.

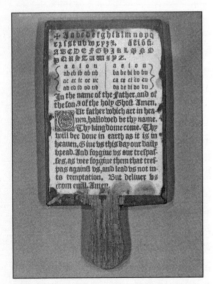

Hornbook from Shakespeare's lifetime

A 1639 engraving of a scene from a royal state visit of Marie de Medici depicts London's packed, closely crowded half-timbered houses.

FROM COUNTRY TO COURT

The urban boom brought a new dimension to British life—the mentality of the metropolis. By contrast, in Stratford-upon-Avon, the rhythms of the rural world still held sway. Educated in the local grammar school, Shakespeare was taught to read and write by a schoolmaster called an "abecedarian," and as he grew older, he was introduced to logic, rhetoric, and Latin. Like most schoolboys of his time, he was familiar with Roman mythology and may have learned a little Greek, perhaps by translating passages of the New Testament. Thus while he never attended a university, Shakespeare could confidently refer in his plays to myths and legends that today we associate with the highly educated.

Beyond the classroom, however, he was immersed in the life of the countryside, and his writing all but revels in its flora and fauna, from the wounded deer of *As You Like It* to the herbs and flowers which Ophelia scatters in *Hamlet*. Pagan rituals abounded in the rural villages of Shakespeare's day, where residents danced around maypoles in spring, performed "mummers' plays" in winter, and recited rhymes year-round to ward off witches and fairies.

The custom most pertinent to Shakespeare's art was the medieval "mystery play," in which moral allegories were enacted in country homes and village squares by troupes of traveling actors. These strolling players—usually four men and two boys who played the women's roles—often lightened the moralizing with bawdy interludes in a mix of high and low feeling, which would become a defining feature of Shakespeare's art. Occasionally even a professional troupe, such as Lord Strange's Men, or the Queen's Men, would arrive in town, perhaps coming straight to Shakespeare's door (his father was the town's bailiff) for permission to perform.

Rarely, however, did such troupes stray far from their base in London, the nation's rapidly expanding capital and cultural center. The city itself had existed since the time of the Romans (who built the original London Bridge), but it was not until the Renaissance that its population spilled beyond its ancient walls and began to grow along (and across) the Thames, by whose banks the Tudors had built their glorious palaces. It was these two contradictory worlds—a modern metropolis cheek-by-jowl with a medieval court—that provided the two very different audiences who applauded Shakespeare's plays.

Londoners both high and low craved distraction. Elizabeth's court constantly celebrated her reign with dazzling pageants and performances that required a local pool of professional actors and musicians. Beyond the graceful landscape of the royal parks, however, the general populace was packed into little more than a square mile of cramped and crooked streets where theatrical entertainment was frowned upon as compromising public morals.

Just outside the jurisdiction of the city fathers, however, across the twenty arches of London Bridge on the south bank of the Thames, lay the wilder district of "Southwark." A grim reminder of royal power lay at the end of the bridge—the decapitated heads of traitors stared down from pikes at passersby. Once beyond their baleful gaze, people found the amusements they desired, and their growing numbers meant a market suddenly existed for daily entertainment. Bear-baiting and cockfighting flourished, along with taverns, brothels, and even the new institution of the theater.

Southwark, as depicted in Hollar's long view of London (1647). Blackfriars is on the top right and the labels of bear-baiting and the Globe were inadvertently reversed.

THE ADVENT OF THE THEATRE

The first building in England designed for the performance of plays—called, straightforwardly enough, "The Theatre"—was built in London when Shakespeare was still a boy. It was owned by James Burbage, father of Richard Burbage, who would become Shakespeare's lead actor in the acting company, the Lord Chamberlain's Men. "The Theatre," consciously or unconsciously, resembled the yards in which traveling players had long plied their trade—it was an open-air polygon, with three tiers of galleries surrounding a canopied stage in a flat central yard, which was ideal for the athletic competitions the building also hosted. The innovative arena must have found an appreciative audience, for it was soon joined by the Curtain, and then the Rose, which was the first theater to rise in Southwark among the brothels, bars, and bear-baiting pits.

Even as these new venues were being built, a revolution in the drama itself was taking place. Just as Renaissance artists turned to classical models for inspiration, so English writers looked to Roman verse as a prototype for the new national drama. "Blank verse," or iambic pentameter (that is, a poetic line with five alternating stressed and unstressed syllables), was an adaptation of Latin forms, and first appeared in England in a translation of Virgil's *Aeneid*. Blank verse was first spoken on stage in 1561, in the now-forgotten *Gorboduc*, but it was not until the brilliant Christopher Marlowe (born the same year as Shakespeare) transformed it into the "mighty line" of such plays as *Tamburlaine* (1587) that the power and flexibility of the form made it the baseline of English drama.

Marlowe—who, unlike Shakespeare, had attended college—led the "university wits," a clique of hard-living free thinkers who in between all manner of exploits managed to define a new form of theater. The dates of Shakespeare's arrival in London are unknown—we have no record of him in Stratford after 1585—but by the early 1590s he had already absorbed the essence of Marlowe's invention, and begun producing astonishing innovations of his own.

While the "university wits" had worked with myth and fantasy, however, Shakespeare turned to a grand new theme, English history—penning the three-part saga of *Henry VI* in or around 1590. The trilogy was such a success that Shakespeare became the envy of his circle—one unhappy competitor, Robert Greene, even complained in 1592 of "an upstart crow...beautified with our feathers...[who is] in his own conceit the only Shake-scene in a country."

Such jibes perhaps only confirmed Shakespeare's estimation of himself, for he began to apply his mastery of blank verse in all directions, succeeding at tragedy (*Titus Andronicus*), farce (*The Comedy of Errors*), and romantic comedy (*The Two Gentlemen of Verona*). He drew his plots from everywhere: existing poems, romances, folk tales, even other plays. In fact a number of Shakespeare's dramas (*Hamlet* included) may be revisions of earlier texts owned by his troupe. Since copyright laws did not exist, acting companies usually kept their texts close to their chests, only allowing publication when a play was no longer popular, or, conversely, when a play was *so* popular (as with *Romeo and Juliet*) that unauthorized versions had already been printed.

Demand for new plays and performance venues steadily increased. Soon, new theaters (the Hope and the Swan) joined the Rose in Southwark, followed shortly by the legendary Globe, which opened in 1600. (After some trouble with their lease, Shakespeare's acting troupe, the Lord

pendeſt on ſo meane a ſtay . Baſe minded men all thꝛee
of you,if by my miſerie you be not warnd:foꝛ vnto none
of you (like mee) ſought thoſe burres to cleaue : thoſe
Puppets (J meane) that ſpake from our mouths, thoſe
Anticks garniſht in our colours. Js it not ſtrange,that
J,to whom they all haue beene beholding: is it not like
that you,to whome they all haue beene beholding, ſhall
(were yee in that caſe as J am now) bee both at once of
them foꝛſaken '? Yes truſt them not : foꝛ there is an vp=
ſtart Crow, beautified with our feathers, that with his
Tygers hart wrapt in a Players hyde, ſuppoſes he is as
well able to bombaſt out a blanke verſe as the beſt of
you : and beeing an abſolute Iohannes fac totum, is in
his owne conceit the onely Shake-ſcene in a countrey.
O that J might intreat your rare wits to be imploied in
moꝛe pꝛofitable courſes : & let thoſe Apes imitate your
paſt excellence, and neuer moꝛe acquaint them with
your admired inuentions . J knowe the beſt huſband of

Greene's insult, lines 9–14

Chamberlain's Men, had disassembled "The Theatre" and transported its timbers across the Thames, using them as the structure for the Globe.) Shakespeare was a shareholder in this new venture, with its motto "All the world's a stage," and continued to write and perform for it as well. Full-length plays were now being presented every afternoon but Sunday, and the public appetite for new material seemed endless.

The only curb on the public's hunger for theater was its fear of the plague—for popular belief held the disease was easily spread in crowds. Even worse, the infection was completely beyond the powers of Elizabethan medicine, which held that health derived from four "humors" or internal fluids identified as bile, phlegm, blood, and choler. Such articles of faith, however, were utterly ineffective against a genuine health crisis, and in times of plague, the authorities' panicked response was to shut down any venue where large crowds might congregate. The theaters would be closed for lengthy periods in 1593, 1597, and 1603, during which times Shakespeare was forced to play at court, tour the provinces, or, as many scholars believe, write what would become his famous cycle of sonnets.

The Next Stage

Between these catastrophic closings, the theater thrived as the great medium of its day; it functioned as film, television, and radio combined as well as a venue for music and dance (all performances, even tragedies, ended with a dance). Moreover, the theater was the place to see and be seen; for a

Famous scale model of the Globe completed by Dr. John Cranford Adams in 1954. Collectively, 25,000 pieces were used in constructing the replica. Dr. Adams used walnut to imitate the timber of the Globe, plaster was placed with a spoon and medicine dropper, and 6,500 tiny "bricks" measured by pencil eraser strips were individually placed on the model.

penny you could stand through a performance in the yard, a penny more bought you a seat in the galleries, while yet another purchased you a cushion. The wealthy, the poor, the royal, and the common all gathered at the Globe, and Shakespeare designed his plays—with their action, humor, and highly refined poetry—not only to satisfy their divergent tastes but also to respond to their differing points of view. In the crucible of Elizabethan theater, the various classes could briefly see themselves as others saw them, and drama could genuinely show "the age and body of the time his form and pressure," to quote Hamlet himself.

In order to accommodate his expanding art, the simplicity of the Elizabethan stage had developed a startling flexibility. The canopied platform of the Globe had a trap in its floor for sudden disappearances, while an alcove at the rear, between the pillars supporting its roof, allowed for "discoveries" and interior space. Above, a balcony made possible the love scene in *Romeo and Juliet,* while still higher, the thatched roof could double as a tower or rampart. And though the stage was largely free of scenery, the costumes were sumptuous—a theater troupe's clothing was its greatest asset. Patrons were used to real drums banging in battle scenes and real cannons firing overhead (in fact, a misfire would one day set the Globe aflame).

With the death of Elizabeth, and the accession of James I to the throne in 1603, Shakespeare only saw his power and influence grow. James, who considered himself an intellectual and something of a scholar, took over the patronage of the Lord Chamberlain's Men, renaming them the King's Men; the troupe even marched in his celebratory entrance to London. At this pinnacle of both artistic power and prestige, Shakespeare composed *Othello*, *King Lear*, and *Macbeth* in quick succession, and soon the King's Men acquired a new, indoor theater in London, which allowed the integration of more music and spectacle into his work. At this wildly popular venue, Shakespeare developed a new form of drama that scholars have dubbed "the romance," which combined elements of comedy and tragedy in a magnificent vision that would culminate in the playwright's last masterpiece, *The Tempest*. Not long after this final innovation, Shakespeare retired to Stratford a wealthy and prominent gentleman.

Beyond the Elizabethan Universe

This is how Shakespeare fit into his age. But how did he transcend it? The answer lies in the plays themselves. For even as we see in the surface of his drama the belief system of England in the sixteenth century, Shakespeare himself is always questioning his own culture, holding its ideas up to the light and shaking them, sometimes hard. In the case of the Elizabethan faith in astrology, Shakespeare had his villain Edmund sneer, "We make guilty of our disasters the sun, the moon, and stars; as if we were villains on necessity." When pondering the medieval code of chivalry, Falstaff decides, "The better part of valor is discretion." The divine right of kings is questioned in *Richard II*, and the inferior status of women—a belief that survived even the crowning of Elizabeth—appears ridiculous before the brilliant examples of Portia (*The Merchant of Venice*) and Rosalind (*As You Like It*). Perhaps it is through this constant shifting of perspective, this relentless sense of exploration, that the playwright somehow outlived the limits of his own period, and became, in the words of his rival Ben Jonson, "not just for an age, but for all time."

track 36

Conclusion of the Sourcebooks Shakespeare
Richard III: *Sir Derek Jacobi*

About the Online Teaching Resources

The Sourcebooks Shakespeare is committed to supporting students and educators in the study of Shakespeare. A web site with additional articles and essays, extended audio, a forum for discussions, as well as other resources can be found at www.sourcebooksshakespeare.com. To illustrate how the Sourcebooks Shakespeare may be used in your class, Jeremy Ehrlich, the head of education at the Folger Shakespeare Library, contributed an essay called "Working with Audio in the Classroom." The following is an excerpt:

One possible way of approaching basic audio work in the classroom is shown in the handout [on the site]. It is meant to give some guidance for the first-time user of audio in the classroom. I would urge you to adapt this to the particular circumstances and interests of your own students.

To use it, divide the students into four groups. Assign each group one of the four technical elements of audio – volume, pitch, pace, and pause – to follow as you play them an audio clip or clips. In the first section, have them record what they hear: the range they encounter in the clip and the places where their element changes. In the second section, have them suggest words for the tone of the passage based in part on their answers to the first. Sections three and four deal with tools of the actor. Modern acting theory finds the actor's objective is his single most important acting choice; an actor may then choose from a variety of tactics in order to achieve that objective. Thus, if a character's objective on stage is to get sympathy from his scene partner, he may start out by complaining, then shift to another tactic (asking for sympathy directly? throwing a tantrum?) if the first tactic fails. Asking your students to try to explain what they think a character is trying to get, and how she is trying to do it, is a way for them to follow this process through closely. Finally, the handout asks students to think about the meaning (theme) of the passage, concluding with a traditional and important tool of text analysis.

As you can see, this activity is more interesting and, probably, easier for students when it's used with multiple versions of the same piece of text. While defining an actor's motivation is difficult in a vacuum, doing so in relation to another performance may be easier: one Othello may be more concerned with gaining respect, while another Othello may be more concerned with obtaining love, for instance. This activity may be done outside of a group setting, although for students doing this work for the first time I suggest group work so they will be able to share answers on some potentially thought-provoking questions...

For the complete essay, please visit www.sourcebooksshakespeare.com.

Acknowledgments

The series editors wish to give heartfelt thanks to the advisory editors of the series, David Bevington and Peter Holland, for their ongoing support, timely advice, and keen brilliance.

We are incredibly grateful to the community of Shakespeare scholars for their generosity in sharing their talents, collections, and even their address books. We would not have been able to put together such an august list of contributors without their help. Our sincere thanks go to our text editor, William Proctor Williams, for his brilliant work and his continuing guidance, and to Lois Potter, Tom Garvey, Doug Lanier, and Andrew Wade for their marvelous essays. We are also very grateful to Sir Antony Sher, his agent, Mic Cheetham, his assistant, Sue, and his publishers, Hutchinson, for his essay on his portrayal of Richard.

Our research was aided immensely by the wonderful staff at Shakespeare archives and libraries around the world: Susan Brock, Helen Hargest, and the staff at The Shakespeare Birthplace Trust; Jeremy Ehrlich, Bettina Smith, and everyone at the Folger Shakespeare Library; and Gene Rinkel, Bruce Swann, and Tim Cole from the Rare Books and Special Collections Library at the University of Illinois. These individuals were instrumental in helping us gather audio: Justyn Baker, Janet Benson, Barbara Brown, Liz Cooper for the Olivier audio, and Helen Robson of the RSC for the Sher audio. The following are the talented photographers who shared their work with us: Donald Cooper, George Joseph, Michal Daniel, and Carol Rosegg. Thank you to Jessica Talmage at the Mary Evans Picture Library and to Tracey Tomaso at Corbis. We appreciate all your help. Extra appreciation goes to Doug Lanier for all his guidance and the use of his personal Shakespeare collection.

From the world of drama, the following shared their passion with us and helped us develop the series into a true partnership between the artistic and academic communities. We are indebted to: Liza Holtmeier, Lauren Beyea, and the team from the Shakespeare Theatre Company; Nancy Becker of The Shakespeare Society; and Nathaniel Shaw.

With respect to the audio, we extend our heartfelt thanks to our narrating team: our director, John Tydeman, our esteemed narrator, Sir Derek

Jacobi, and the staff of Motivation Studios. John has been a wonderful, generous resource to us and we look forward to future collaborations. We owe a debt of gratitude to Nicolas Soames for introducing us and for being unfailingly helpful. Thanks also to the "Speaking Shakespeare" team: Andrew Wade and Nathaniel Shaw for that wonderful recording, and Joe Plummer for his excellent work on the audio analysis.

Thank you to Tanya Gough, the proprietor of The Poor Yorick Shakespeare Catalog, for all her efforts on behalf of the series. Our personal thanks for their kindness and unstinting support go to our friends and our extended families.

Finally, thanks to everyone at Sourcebooks who contributed their talents in realizing The Sourcebooks Shakespeare–in particular: Todd Green, Todd Stocke, Megan Dempster, and Melanie Thompson. Special mention to Nikki Braziel and Elizabeth Lhost, assistants extraordinaire for the Sourcebooks Shakespeare.

So, thanks to all at once and to each one (*Macbeth,* 5.7.104)

Audio Credits

In all cases, we have attempted to provide archival audio in its original form. While we have tried to achieve the best possible quality on the archival audio, some audio quality is the result of source limitations. Archival audio research by Marie Macaisa. Narration script by Joe Plummer and Marie Macaisa. Audio editing by Motivation Sound Studios, Marie Macaisa, and Todd Stocke. Narration recording and audio engineering by Motivation Sound Studios, London, UK. Mastering by Paul Estby. Recording for "Speaking Shakespeare" by Dubway Studios, New York City, USA.

Narrated by Sir Derek Jacobi
Directed by John Tydeman
Produced by Marie Macaisa

Photo Credits

Every effort has been made to correctly attribute all the materials reproduced in this book. If any errors have been made, we will be happy to correct them in future editions. Photos are credited on the pages in which they appear.

Images from the 1953 production at the Shakespeare Memorial Theatre directed by Glen Byam Shaw are courtesy of the Rare Book and Special Collections Library, University of Illinois at Urbana-Champaign.

Photos from the Shakespeare Theatre Company's 1990 production directed by Michael Kahn are © 1990 Joan Marcus; from its 2003 production directed by Gale Edwards are © 2003 Carol Rosegg; from its 2007 production directed by Michael Kahn are © 2007 Carol Rosegg.

Photos from *Richard III* (1955) directed by Laurence Olivier are courtesy of Douglas Lanier.

Photos from *Richard III* (1995) directed by Richard Loncraine are courtesy of MGM and Douglas Lanier.

Photos from the Public Theater's 1957 production directed by Stuart Vaughan are © 1957 George E. Joseph; from its 1983 production directed by Jane Howell are © 1983 George E. Joseph; from its 1990 production directed by Robin Phillips are © 1990 George E. Joseph; from its 2004 production directed by Peter DuBois are © 2004 Michal Daniel.

Photos from the Royal Shakespeare Company's 1980 production directed by Terry Hands are © 1980 Donald Cooper; from its 1984 production directed by Bill Alexander are © 1984 Donald Cooper; from its 1989 production directed by Adrian Noble are © 1989 Donald Cooper; from its 1992 production directed by Sam Mendes are © 1992 Donald Cooper; from its 1996 production directed by Steven Pimlott are © 1996 Donald Cooper; from its 2001 production directed by Michael Boyd are © 2001 Donald Cooper; from its 2003 production directed by Sean Holmes are © 2003 Donald Cooper.

Photos from the Oregon Shakespeare Festival's 1993 production directed by James Edmondson and its 2005 production directed by Libby Appel are courtesy of the Oregon Shakespeare Festival.

Photos from the English Shakespeare Company's 1989 production directed by Michael Bogdanov are © 1989 Donald Cooper.

Photos from the Phoenix Theatre's 1989 production directed by Clifford Williams are © 1989 Donald Cooper.

Photos from the Rustaveli Theatre Company's 1980 production directed by Robert Sturva are © 1980 Donald Cooper.

The "Theatrical Atlas" image is courtesy of the Library of Congress, Prints & Photographs Division, British Cartoon Prints Collection.

Photos from the 1990 National Theatre's production directed by Richard Eyre are © 1990 Donald Cooper.

Photos from the 2002 Sheffield Crucible's production directed by Michael Grandage are © 2002 Donald Cooper.

Photos from the 2003 Shakespeare's Globe production directed by Barry Kyle are © 2003 Donald Cooper.

Photos from the 2004 Acting Company's production directed by Eve Shapiro are © 2004 Richard Termine.

William Shakespeare's signature (on the title page) courtesy of Mary Evans Picture Library. Other images from the Mary Evans Picture Library used in the text are credited on the pages in which they appear.

Images from "In the Age of Shakespeare" courtesy of The Folger Shakespeare Library.

About the Contributors

TEXT EDITOR
William Proctor Williams is professor of English emeritus at Northern Illinois University and senior lecturer in English at the University of Akron. He has received numerous grants and awards including a National Endowment for the Humanities research grant and a Senior Fulbright Research Fellowship; and in 2003–04, he was the Myra and Charlton Hinman Fellow at the Folger Shakespeare Library. He is currently at work on the New Variorum Edition of *Titus Andronicus*, a critical edition of the works of Cosmo Manuche, and a study of Dr. Zachariah Pasfield, who licensed books for the press from 1600 until 1610.

SERIES EDITORS
Marie Macaisa spent twenty years in her first career: high tech. She has a bachelor's degree in computer science from the Massachusetts Institute of Technology and a master's degree in artificial intelligence from the University of Pennsylvania. She became the series editor of The Sourcebooks Shakespeare in 2003. She also contributes the "Cast Speaks" essays and is the producer of the accompanying audio.

Dominique Raccah is the founder, president, and publisher of Sourcebooks. Born in Paris, France, she has a bachelor's degree in psychology and a master's in quantitative psychology from the University of Illinois. She also serves as series editor of *Poetry Speaks* and *Poetry Speaks to Children*.

ADVISORY BOARD
David Bevington is the Phyllis Fay Horton Distinguished Service Professor in the Humanities at the University of Chicago. A renowned text scholar, he has edited several Shakespeare editions including the *Bantam Shakespeare* in individual paperback volumes, *The Complete Works of Shakespeare* (Longman, 2003), and *Troilus and Cressida* (Arden, 1998). He teaches courses in Shakespeare, renaissance drama, and medieval drama.

Peter Holland is the McMeel Family Chair in Shakespeare Studies at the University of Notre Dame. A central figure in performance-oriented Shakespeare criticism, he has edited many Shakespeare plays, including *A Midsummer Night's Dream* for the Oxford Shakespeare series. He is also general editor of Shakespeare Survey and co-general editor (with Stanley Wells) of Oxford Shakespeare Topics. Currently he is completing a book, *Shakespeare on Film*, and editing *Coriolanus* for the Arden 3rd series.

ESSAYISTS

Thomas Garvey has been acting, directing, or writing about Shakespeare for over two decades. A graduate of the Massachusetts Institute of Technology, he studied acting and directing with the MIT Shakespeare Ensemble, where he played Hamlet, Jacques, Iago, and other roles, and directed *All's Well That Ends Well* and *Twelfth Night*. He has since directed and designed several other Shakespearean productions, as well as works by Chekhov, Ibsen, Sophocles, Beckett, Molière, and Shaw. Mr. Garvey has written on theatre for the *Boston Globe* and other publications.

Douglas Lanier is an associate professor of English at the University of New Hampshire. He has written many essays on Shakespeare in popular culture, including "Shakescorp Noir" in *Shakespeare Quarterly* 53.2 (Summer 2002) and "Shakespeare on the Record" in *The Blackwell Companion to Shakespeare in Performance* (edited by Barbara Hodgdon and William Worthen, Blackwell, 2005). His book *Shakespeare and Modern Popular Culture* (Oxford University Press) was published in 2002. He is currently working on a book-length study of cultural stratification in early modern British theater.

Lois Potter is Ned B. Allen Professor of English at the University of Delaware. She has also taught in England, France, and Japan, attending and reviewing as many plays as possible. Her publications include the Arden edition of *The Two Noble Kinsmen* and *Othello* for the Manchester University Press's series *Shakespeare in Performance*.

Antony Sher is a novelist, playwright, and one of the most acclaimed British classical actors of his generation. He joined the Royal Shakespeare Company (RSC) in 1982, and his big breakthrough came when he played the title role in *Richard III*, for which he won the prestigious Laurence Olivier Award. Since then, he has performed in numerous stage productions, including *The Merchant of Venice*, *Tamburlaine* and *Macbeth*, in addition to recent films such as *Shakespeare in Love* (1995) and *Mrs. Brown* (1997). *Primo*, his adaptation of Primo Levi's *If This Is a Man*, opened to critical acclaim at London's National Theatre in 2004. He made his directorial debut with Fraser Grace's play, *Breakfast With Mugabe*, in 2005 in Stratford-upon-Avon. A multi-talented artist, Antony Sher was knighted in 2000 for his service in the arts.

Andrew Wade was head of voice for the Royal Shakespeare Company from 1990 to 2003 and voice assistant director from 1987 to 1990. During this time he worked on 170 productions and with more than 80 directors. Along with Cicely Berry, Andrew recorded *Working Shakespeare* and the DVD series on *Voice and Shakespeare*, and he was the verse consultant for the movie *Shakespeare In Love*. In 2000, he won a Bronze Award from the New York International Radio Festival for the series *Lifespan*, which he co-directed and devised. He works widely teaching, lecturing, and coaching throughout the world.

AUDIO CONTRIBUTORS

Sir Derek Jacobi is one of Britain's foremost actors of stage and screen. One of his earliest roles was Cassio to Sir Laurence Olivier's Othello in Stuart Burge's 1965 movie production. More recent roles include Hamlet in the acclaimed BBC Television Shakespeare production in 1980, the Chorus in Kenneth Branagh's 1989 film of Henry V, and Claudius in Branagh's 1996 movie Hamlet. He has been accorded numerous honors in his distinguished career, including a Tony award for Best Actor in Much Ado About Nothing and a BAFTA (British Academy of Film and Television) for his landmark portrayal of Emperor Claudius in the blockbuster television series I, Claudius. He was made a Knight of the British Empire in 1994 for his services to the theatre.

John Tydeman was the Head of Drama for BBC Radio for many years and is the director of countless productions, with 15 Shakespeare plays to his credit. Among his numerous awards are the Prix Italia, Prix Europa, UK Broadcasting Guild Best Radio Programme (When The Wind Blows by Raymond Briggs), and the Sony Personal Award for services to radio. He has worked with most of Britain's leading actors and dramatists and has directed for the theatre, television, and commercial recordings. He holds an M.A. from Cambridge University.

Joe Plummer is the Director of Education for the Williamstown Theatre Festival and Assistant Professor of Shakespearean Performance (with Roger Rees) at the Lincoln Center Campus of Fordham University. He has taught Master classes on Shakespeare and Performance at Williams College, the National Shakespeare Company and Brandeis University, and also teaches privately. Joe serves as the Artist-In-Residence and Director of Educational Outreach for The Shakespeare Society in New York City and is the founder and Producing Artistic Director of poortom productions, the only all-male Shakespeare Company in the US. He has performed extensively in New York and in regional theaters.